A112

The Open University

Cultures: Book 1

Block 1: *Placing ancient cultures* edited by Joanna Paul
Block 2: *Art and power* edited by Clare Taylor

This publication forms part of the Open University module A112 *Cultures*. Details of this and other Open University modules can be obtained from Student Recruitment, The Open University, PO Box 197, Milton Keynes MK7 6BJ, United Kingdom (tel. +44 (0)300 303 5303; email general-enquiries@open.ac.uk).

Alternatively, you may visit the Open University website at www.open.ac.uk where you can learn more about the wide range of modules and packs offered at all levels by The Open University.

The Open University, Walton Hall, Milton Keynes MK7 6AA

First published 2020

Edited and designed by The Open University.

Printed and bound in the United Kingdom by Stephens and George Ltd. Dowlais, Merthyr Tydfil CF48 3TD

ISBN 978 1 4730 2873 9

1.1

Contents

Block 1:

Placing ancient cultures

Edited by Joanna Paul

Introduction

Written by Joanna Paul

In this first block of A112, you will begin your exploration of the module's theme of 'cultures' with the study of three ancient places: Athens, Rome and Delphi. By thinking carefully about the sorts of things that happened in these places, comparing them across time and space, and considering the different kinds of evidence that we have for the distant past, your work in this block will also serve as an introduction to the discipline of Classical Studies. Before we start, though, it is worth spending a little bit of time thinking about what Classical Studies means, by way of context and to provide background for what follows.

Study note

In this block, you will see that the BCE/CE dating system is used. These abbreviations stand for 'Before Common Era' and 'Common Era', and align exactly with the BC/AD dating system. You can use whichever system you prefer in your own writing.

The abbreviation *c.* stands for the Latin word *circa*, meaning 'around'; this is conventionally used when the exact date of an event is uncertain.

1 What is Classical Studies?

In very simple terms, Classical Studies is the conventional name for the academic study of the ancient cultures of Greece and Rome. It reaches back as far as the eighth century BCE (and sometimes earlier), when Greek civilisation first began to organise itself into city-states and its population significantly increased – all the way through to the slow decline and eventual collapse of the Roman empire in the fifth century CE, and beyond. It's important to note that there are no firm start or end points for the historical period typically covered by Classical Studies (and indeed in this block's Unit 4 on the module website you'll see how the study of modern responses to the classical world can also be very relevant to this discipline.)

Moreover, the geographical boundaries of Classical Studies are more expansive and permeable than you might at first think. Although Greece and Rome are often the focal points, these place names can be used in flexible ways, meaning more than just the area of the modern Greek nation or the city of Rome in Italy. For example, the Roman empire grew and changed its territory enormously over the centuries of its existence, and Greek settlers established colonies across a wide extent of the Mediterranean (there was never an ancient country of Greece that equates to the modern nation-state). Importantly, Classical Studies can also involve looking beyond Greece and Rome to neighbouring cultures, such as those of the Persians or Egypt. Although these don't play much of a role in this module, you may well encounter them if you pursue this discipline beyond A112.

The potential reach of Classical Studies, and the huge variety of ground that it covers, is just one reason why it is such a fascinating and rewarding pursuit; as your studies range through time and space, you have the opportunity to explore the development and evolution of cultures that are at once both distant from and deeply relevant to your own. While exploring these ancient cultures, we can ask an exciting range of questions that not only aim to help us better understand the people who lived many centuries ago but can also contribute to our understanding of the fundamental issues that still concern us today: everything from how cultures interact with one another, to the ways in which societies organise themselves politically, to the very question of what it is to be human.

Referencing ancient sources

Whatever discipline you're studying, learning the correct methods to reference sources is an important academic skill, especially when you're writing about them yourself. But with so many different kinds of evidence playing a role in Classical Studies, it can sometimes seem as though there is a bewildering array of different conventions to get to grips with. Rest assured, though, that you don't need to worry about them too much in this module. If you continue with your study of the ancient world beyond this module, you'll learn about how to reference ancient texts and other sources in more detail.

For now, it's enough to gain some familiarity with recognising the conventions present in this block, and to do your best to implement them in your own assessed work. In this module, references to ancient texts come in a dual format. For example, when you read a short extract by the Roman writer Pliny, you'll see it followed by the following information:

(*Natural History* 33.54; Pliny, 1952, p. 45)

The first half of the reference tells us that the quotation comes from a work that Pliny wrote called the *Natural History*. '33.54' refers to the location in the ancient text – here, Book 33, Chapter 54. Most ancient texts are divided up in some way (often right down to the level of line numbers for poetry), and these sorts of references are important to allow us to locate key passages regardless of which modern translation or edition is being used. However, we may also want to be able to pinpoint the location in the modern edition, so the second half of the reference enables you to look up Pliny in the references list that appears at the end of the chapter. There, you'll be able to find the translation of this text that was produced in 1952 and know that the quotation comes from p. 45 of that book.

In this block, you'll be introduced to a broad range of questions that can emerge in our studies of ancient places, touching on, for example, the gods that the Greeks and Romans worshipped, the kinds of entertainment these people enjoyed, and the ways in which they organised their households. You'll see how Classical Studies is, in fact, not so much a single discipline but a multidisciplinary collection that embraces the full extent of the arts and humanities, including language and literature, politics and philosophy, history and religion, art and archaeology – and much more.

As we pursue these different questions, Classical Studies requires us to engage with many different evidence types, such as coins, statues, legal speeches and poems. In this block, you'll have the chance to develop and practise the basic skills required to work confidently with a range of such sources. Much of this evidence falls into two broad groups:

- **Textual sources:** these preserve the written (or sometimes spoken) material from antiquity, and can include anything from revered works of epic literature through to snippets of a shopping list preserved on an ancient papyrus (a commonly used ancient writing material). In this module, all of the sources that you meet are translated from the original Greek and Latin, although you will also be given the opportunity to see what those original languages looked like. If you continue with your study of the classical world, you'll soon be encouraged to reflect much more deeply on what it means to translate ancient texts, and even have the choice to begin learning an ancient language yourself.

- **Archaeological sources:** archaeology is the process by which we recover the material remains of the past – from tiny fragments of pottery and bone through to the ruins of huge monuments. Analysis of these sources is very useful to the study of human cultures, revealing a great deal of information about the lived experience of ancient daily life, as well as the cultural characteristics of ancient art and architecture.

One important point that we'll keep emphasising throughout this block is the need to consider these pieces of evidence alongside each other. As you might expect from working with ancient material, there are often gaps in our evidence, and learning how to work with multiple pieces of evidence is a key skill in Classical Studies. Unsurprisingly, much of what existed in the ancient world is now lost to us, and so we have to make the most of the evidence we do have. Using these different types of evidence together can be a bit like trying to solve a mystery – and in this block you'll find out that you can't always take a piece of evidence at face value, even if it at first appears to be objective.

Classical Studies, then, is a stimulating and varied discipline through which we can attempt to untangle some of the mysteries of the ancient world. But it is also highly relevant to the modern world, as a better understanding of antiquity can provide a powerful lens through which we can better understand the present, and indeed more recent periods of history. For example, as this block explores the ways in which ancient places helped different groups of people form a sense of a shared cultural identity in antiquity, so you might reflect on how cultural identities in particular places are formed today. Or, as you study the way in which a Roman emperor exerted power over his people, so you might use this knowledge to gain a different perspective on how modern politicians operate. Examining the similarities and differences between past and present can also lead us to reflect more critically on our relationship to the ancient world, and the relevance and status that we think it holds today.

In the long tradition of studying and using antiquity as a model for art, literature, philosophy and politics, Greece and Rome were very often placed on a pedestal and regarded as a kind of 'high point' of Western civilisation. (This was one of the key motivations for a modern practice like the Grand Tour, which you'll study in Unit 4 on the module website). Antiquity was deemed worth studying precisely because it was seen as the foundational point of Western culture, with its own intrinsic value, and this is why it attracted the label 'Classical'; as you will see in Block 3 when you come to study English Literature, labelling something as a 'classic' has long been a way of signalling 'the best' of cultural achievements.

But as you will also see in Block 3, the idea of the 'classic' is also subject to debate and disagreement, and in more recent years, Classical Studies too has been open to a more critical and flexible idea of what studying antiquity means. Pursuing this discipline in the twenty-first century means recognising that ancient Greece and Rome are just part of a much wider set of influences that shaped the modern world. It means paying attention to the full diversity of people that lived in ancient societies, as well as understanding the impact of antiquity and its legacy on all modern cultures today, not just in the West. It also means recognising that its legacy has not always been a positive one, given that examples from antiquity have been (and indeed sometimes still are) used to lend support to oppressive regimes and other problematic ideologies.

2 What will you study in this block?

It's important to emphasise that you are not expected to grasp the entirety of what happened in the historical periods covered by this block! In a sense, each chapter is a snapshot of a particular place and time. In Chapter 1, you'll be focusing on Athens in the fifth and fourth centuries BCE, before jumping ahead many centuries to Rome in the first century CE in Chapter 2. In Chapter 3, you'll be back in Greece for your study of Delphi, and will also go back in time to explore the religious sanctuary in the sixth and fifth centuries BCE. Throughout each chapter, though, we'll try to point out where there are similarities, or perhaps interesting contrasts, between the approaches to ancient cultures. You might also find it helpful to refer to the Resources section at the end of the block, where you will find a map of the ancient Mediterranean (Resource 1.1) and a Classical Studies timeline (Resource 1.2) to help you keep track of where you are, both geographically and chronologically.

The big cultural questions I have mentioned in this Introduction will certainly be important if you decide to study Classical Studies in more depth, but I hope that this block will also give you a flavour of some of them. The topics of the three chapters have been chosen to give you a cross section of the variety of materials and approaches that are important to this discipline, at the same time as showing you how the study of specific ancient places is a consistently important way of better understanding ancient cultures. The activities and events that happen in each place that you will study both create and reflect ancient cultures. Any number of towns or cities could have been chosen, but by focusing on two 'capitals' of the ancient world – Athens and Rome – you will be introduced to some of the most important characteristics of the cultures that occupied them. The third location, Delphi, is perhaps less well-known, but as it is a fascinating religious site whose cultural significance spans both the Greek and Roman worlds, it's a fitting destination for this block's tour of antiquity. Finally, as previously mentioned, in Unit 4 (on the module website) you'll consider how later periods and cultures viewed the importance of some of these ancient places by studying the eighteenth and nineteenth century practice of the Grand Tour.

Chapter 1
Athens: places and people

Written by Christine Plastow

Contents

1 Introduction

Over the next three chapters on Classical Studies, the study of places is used as a way of learning about ancient cultures. We might understand a 'culture' as a way of identifying a group of people who all have some things in common. This often includes occupying a shared place, such as a country or, in the ancient Greek context, a city-state or **polis**. A particular culture might also express its ideology and values through the way it constructs its concept of place: for example, how its public and private spaces are organised. In this chapter, you'll explore the Athenian agora (often translated as 'marketplace') as a public space with numerous functions and purposes in Athenian life, before turning to examine the more private spaces of Athenian homes. In looking at both of these places, you will not only uncover important information about the physical space of Athens but also the people who occupied it in ancient times. The concept of place cannot exist without people; it is people who give undifferentiated locations meaning by attaching concepts to them (such as work and home, public and private, male-dominated and female-dominated). Through an exploration of these particular places, the people that occupied them and the things they did there, you'll begin to gain a deeper understanding of ancient Athenian culture.

Although Athens has been occupied continuously for thousands of years, this chapter will focus primarily on the period usually called the Classical period, which was when Athens was generally considered to have been at its cultural height. This ranges from about 479 BCE – when the Greeks finally defeated the Persians after years of war – to the death of Alexander the Great in 323 BCE. In the fifth century BCE, Athens was perhaps the most powerful city in the Greek world, and even after its defeat by Sparta in the Peloponnesian War (431–404 BCE), it was still very influential. It is also useful to focus on a specific time period because both the agora and Athenian homes changed considerably over the centuries – what you're going to look at here is a snapshot of the Classical period, rather than a complete, **diachronic** picture of Greek history. So, it's important to keep in mind that you are studying a particular period in Athenian culture, which also changed dramatically both before and after this era. This cultural high point is also studied more often than other periods because of the quantity and richness of evidence that survives from the time. From a historical perspective, Classical Athens is more accessible than other periods. If you ever want to remind yourself of how the Classical period related to other events that you're going to study in the next three chapters, you can refer back to the Classical Studies timeline in the Resources section at the end of the block (Resource 1.2).

1.1 Public spaces

For many people, the first location that comes to mind when they think of Athens is the Acropolis. As Figure 1 shows, the Acropolis (a complex of buildings on a hill near the centre of Athens) is impressive and imposing, and still dominates the Athenian skyline today. The surviving buildings were constructed nearly 2500 years ago in the fifth century BCE (after the previous complex was destroyed during the war between the Greeks and the Persians). For the Athenians, this was certainly an important place, especially in religious, ceremonial, and ideological terms.

But the Acropolis was primarily used for special occasions, such as religious celebrations. The more everyday business of living in Athens, in a public sense, took place in the agora, to the north-west of the Acropolis, and for this reason it will be the focus of your study of Athenian public space in this chapter. This 'marketplace' was in fact much more than just that: it was certainly a site for commerce, but also for politics, law, religion, socialising and much more. As you will learn over the course of this chapter, it had specific resonance for Athenian citizens, but they were far from the only people present in the agora and taking part in the everyday operation of the city. The way a society lives in public is an important indicator of cultural identity and values. The things that a member of a specific cultural group is expected to do by their peers suggest something about what that culture considers to be important. In the Athenian case, you will learn that this is a blend between the more well-known elements of Athenian culture (such as philosophy and politics – the themes of many famous depictions of the city and its inhabitants) and other aspects that are discussed less often (such as commerce and infrastructure).

Figure 1 The Athenian Acropolis. Photo: George E. Koronaios. Used under this licence: https://creativecommons.org/licenses/by-sa/4.0/deed.en.

1.2 The Athenian home

Although life in public spaces is an important indicator of culture, not all aspects of everyday life are public. This is why, after examining the agora, this chapter explores the ***oikos***: the Athenian home and the people who occupied it. This more private space was, ideologically at least, the domain of women. Here, while the male citizens were out engaging in public life, the wives (and other female relatives) ran their homes. But these homes are also a prime site for uncovering some of the distinctions between the ideal and reality in Athens. This is another important way to learn about a culture: the difference between how a group of people would *like* to be perceived and how they actually *act in practice* can be very informative. This is where it becomes particularly useful to compare and contrast the different types of evidence that survive from the ancient world.

2 The agora in depth

Figure 2 Plan of the Athenian agora at the end of the fifth century BCE.

You're now going to explore some of the buildings that were present in the agora in order to understand how they reflected aspects of Athenian culture and daily life. The buildings and structures are divided by their purposes:

* government

* law

* commerce

* religion.

As you will see, these four areas were some of the most important aspects of Athenian public life. I've included a plan of the agora (Figure 2) to help you get a sense of how the agora was laid out as you read about it.

2.1 Government

Athens is generally considered to have been one of the first **democracies**. This form of government was a defining feature of the way the city operated, and a range of activities associated with it happened in buildings around the agora. Athens's political system was a **direct democracy**, meaning that the majority of important decisions in the running of the city were voted on by the citizens themselves in the Assembly (which met on a hill called the Pnyx, a short distance south-west of the agora). Athens did not use elected representatives as in most modern democracies. Citizens were free men over the age of 18 born to two Athenian parents. Free women born to two Athenian parents held a kind of citizenship, but only insofar as it allowed them to give birth to legitimate citizen children. Athenian citizen men are the most visible people in our sources, and in particular they tend to be the authors and subjects of a majority of literary texts from Classical Athens. They also had a distinctive experience in Athens due to the rights and responsibilities that came with Athenian citizenship: they were the only ones who could own land in Attica (the area comprising the city itself and the farmland surrounding it), take part in the democracy and sit on juries in the law courts. They also had tax and military obligations towards the city. Out of all the people who lived in Athens, most of the surviving testimonies we have are about the experiences of its citizens, and so in many ways citizenship is a defining feature in understanding Athenian culture. Later in this chapter, you'll also find out more about what it meant to live in Athens as a non-citizen.

On average, there were probably between 30,000 and 60,000 citizen men in Athens at any one time during the Classical period. This meant that direct democracy was not feasible for the many everyday tasks that had to be undertaken to administer the city effectively. So, every year, 500 councillors were selected randomly by the drawing of lots to deal with these administrative matters, as well as nine **archons** ('magistrates') who had jurisdiction over various legal and religious matters. Other everyday matters were the province of the Council, whose term of office was split into ten **prytanies** (periods of time in which the administration of the Council was overseen by the members from each of the ten Athenian tribes). More can be learned about the Council by looking at an ancient text called *Athenaion Politeia*, also known as the *Constitution of the Athenians*. This text has historically been ascribed to the Classical Greek philosopher Aristotle, though academics now think that it was not written by Aristotle himself but perhaps by one of his students. For this reason, you'll usually see this text referred to by its title rather than its author. The text is believed to have been written in the 320s BCE, so at the very end of the Classical period.

Activity 1

(Allow around 20 minutes to complete this activity.)

Read the following extract from *Athenaion Politeia*, then answer the questions that follow.

> The Council is elected by lot, and has five hundred members, fifty from each tribe. The Presidency [prytany] is filled by each tribe in turn, in an order settled by lot, each of the first four selected holding the office for thirty-six days and each of the latter six for thirty-five days; for their year is divided into lunar months. Those of them serving as Presidents [prytaneis] first dine together in the Round-house [Tholos], receiving a sum of money from the state, and then convene meetings of the Council and the People, the Council indeed meeting on every day excepting holidays, but the People four times in each

presidency [prytany]. And the Presidents [prytaneis] put up written notice of the business to be dealt with by the Council, and of each day's agenda, and of the place of meeting. They also put up written notice of the meetings of the Assembly [...] The Presidents [prytaneis] have a single Head elected by lot; he holds office for a day and a night, and may not hold office longer, nor serve a second time. He is keeper of the keys of the temples in which the money and documents of the state are lodged, and of the state seal, and he is required to stay in the Round-house [Tholos], and so is whichever Third of the Presidential Boards [prytaneis] he orders.

(Aristotle, *Athenaion Politeia* 43–44; Aristotle, 1935, pp. 123–125)

1 How long did each prytany last?
2 How often did a) the Council and b) the Assembly (called 'the People' in this extract) meet?
3 What were the duties of the **prytaneis** (the 'Presidents' serving in each prytany)?
4 How was the **Tholos**, the round building that sits just to the south of the Old Bouleuterion (on the left side of Figure 2), used?

Discussion

1 Each of the first four prytanies lasted 36 days, and the final six lasted 35 days each.
2 The Council met every day except holidays. The Assembly met four times in each prytany; roughly every nine days.
3 The prytaneis set the agenda for and announced each meeting of the Council and the Assembly.
4 The Tholos was where the prytaneis dined together, and where the head prytanis and one third of the prytaneis stayed every night.

When the prytaneis dined together in the Tholos, they would have used publicly owned dinnerware such as that seen in Figure 3, which would have been simply decorated as it was used so often.

Figure 3 Public dinnerware, fifth century BCE. Photo: 'American School of Classical Studies at Athens: Agora Excavations'. A two-handled drinking cup and a small bottle, possibly for serving water or wine, found near the Tholos and marked with ΔE ('DE'), an abbreviation of *demosion* ('public').

If you look at the left of Figure 2, you will note that the Old Bouleuterion, New Bouleuterion and Tholos seem to form a small complex of their own. This is where much of the everyday administration of the city would have occurred, with the Council meeting every day that was not a public holiday. Once the New Bouleuterion was built (probably in the late fifth century BCE), the Old Bouleuterion was used for storage of the city's archives, meaning that the Council would have had a large amount of potentially relevant information to hand for their meetings. Sitting apart from this complex of buildings in the north-west corner of the agora was the Royal Stoa, known properly as the Stoa Basileios, the seat of the **Archon Basileus**, or King Archon, one of the archons who had specific jurisdiction over religious matters. In this building, a number of the city's religious laws were inscribed on stone. There was also an oath stone (Figure 4) in front of the building, upon which all archons stood each year to take their oath of office.

Figure 4 The oath stone that was set up on the steps of the Stoa Basileios. Photo: 'American School of Classical Studies at Athens: Agora Excavations'.

2.2 Law

A city the size of Athens required laws to maintain order, and Athens's legal system was quite well developed and complex. Towards the northeast corner of the agora, there is a structure that has been labelled 'BLDG A' (Building A) on Figure 2. The remains of the building are unremarkable; not much can be restored of the construction, as several other buildings were built on top of it in later periods. One find does identify the building, though: at the eastern end, excavators found a container made out of two U-shaped drainage tiles standing on their ends (Figure 5). Inside the container were seven metal ballots (Figure 6), which were used by jury members in the Athenian law courts for voting on legal matters, suggesting that the container was used as a ballot box. The location of the find is labelled 'Dikasts ballots' on Figure 2, '*dikast*' being the Greek word for a juror.

Figure 5 (left) A possible ballot box made of drainage tiles found at the eastern end of Building A, discovered containing seven metal ballots. Photo: 'American School of Classical Studies at Athens: Agora Excavations'. **Figure 6 (right)** Metal ballots of the kind found in the ballot box in Building A, inscribed with the phrase '*psephos demosia*' ('public ballot'). Photo: © akg-images/jh-Lightbox_Ltd./ John Hios.

Law played a central role in Athenian life. As there was no police force or state-run prosecution system, it was the right and duty of individual Athenians to pursue prosecution for crimes that they were aware of. There also weren't any lawyers in the Athenian legal system, so the individual litigants had to defend themselves by way of persuasive speeches. Many of these speeches survive, and you'll look at some of them later in this chapter. The jury was manned by Athenian citizens, with usually around 201 serving on each panel, but sometimes as many as 501. An odd number of jurors always served so that there would never be a tied vote, only innocent or guilty.

The Athenian comic poet Eubulus, writing in the mid 300s BCE, gives us an interesting quotation about law at Athens. Most of Eubulus' work is lost, and only fragments survive. This fragment is taken from one of his comic plays and is clearly intended to be humorous:

> You will find everything sold together in the same place at Athens: figs, witnesses to summonses, bunches of grapes, turnips, pears, apples, givers of evidence, roses, medlars, porridge,

> honeycombs, chickpeas, lawsuits, first milk, puddings, myrtle,
> allotment machines, irises, lambs, water-clocks, laws, indictments.
>
> (Eubulus quoted in Athenaeus 14.460b-c; translation quoted in McK. Camp,
> 2010, p. 11)

Eubulus lists items that could be bought in Athens. Some of the items listed may be unfamiliar to you: for example, 'allotment machines' were devices used to assign potential jurors to cases, and 'water-clocks' were used to measure the amount of time that litigants had to speak in the courtroom. Among the more usual food and flowers, then, the author satirically juxtaposes items associated with the law courts: 'witnesses to summonses', 'givers of evidence', 'lawsuits', 'allotment machines', 'water-clocks', 'laws' and 'indictments'. The listing of these items together suggests that the author considers the legal system to be commercial in Athens – and perhaps that the right kind of outcome in a court case could be bought and sold as easily as anything else. Of course, this is a comic source, designed to entertain an audience rather than present historical fact, so it can't necessarily be taken at face value – its satirical nature means that it may be exaggerating the situation, although some of the humour will have come from the grains of truth within that exaggeration.

This passage is also interesting because it gives a sense that legal (and political) procedures happened in Athens right next to commercial activity, with both occurring in the central part of the city. The impression is that both law and shopping for produce were part of everyday life in Athens, which is rather different from most people's everyday experience today.

2.3 Commerce

As in any major city, trade and commerce were necessary to keep goods and money flowing into and out of Athens. In the Classical period, the majority of the commercial activity that took place in the agora would not have been housed in stone buildings but instead in smaller stalls made of perishable materials, such as wood and textiles, and so little evidence of these has been left in the archaeological record. These moveable stalls would have been erected in the open area in the centre of the agora marked on the plan (Figure 2) as 'Orchestra', an ancient Greek term signifying an open space. Later in the agora's life, more permanent buildings were erected within it for this purpose. The most prominent of these was the large Stoa of Attalus, built in the mid second century BCE by King Attalus II of Pergamon in Asia Minor (part of modern-day Turkey) as a gift to the city (and so it does not appear on Figure 2, which illustrates the city about 250 years before the stoa was built). A reconstructed version of this building can be seen in Athens today (Figure 7). This would have housed many small but permanent shops in one building, like a kind of early shopping centre.

Figure 7 The reconstructed Stoa of Attalos viewed from the north-west, with the Acropolis in the background. Photo: 'American School of Classical Studies at Athens: Agora Excavations'.

In the Classical period, the moveable stalls would have been supplemented by smaller complexes of permanent shop buildings or even single shops, which could be found around the edge of the agora rather than in the agora proper. Vendors selling particular items would have clustered together. A fragmentary line written by another comic poet, Menander, reads: 'Wait for me at the olive oil' (Rotroff, 2009, p. 39). This demonstrates that olive oil was sold in a certain place, and that this location would have been familiar to most Athenians. A modern equivalent would be arranging to meet a friend in town outside a well-known shop. Menander's line is the Athenian equivalent of: 'I'll meet you at the bakery!'.

Although many stalls and shops would have sold perishable items such as food, which makes identifying their locations and uses difficult, some have left more long-lasting evidence that can be examined by archaeologists in order to learn more about commercial buildings.

Activity 2

(Allow around 30 minutes to complete this activity.)

Turn to the end of this chapter and read Reading 1.1, which is an extract on identifying commercial buildings from archaeologist Susan I. Rotroff's chapter, 'Commerce and crafts around the Athenian agora'. As you read, make some brief notes on the following points:

1   What objects does Rotroff note that assist archaeologists in identifying the use of buildings or the presence of commercial activity? What specific types of vendors does she identify?

2   How do the shops and private residences relate to each other?

3   Why might vendors have wished to set up shop as close to the agora as possible?

Study note

This is a good opportunity to practise taking notes. The questions are there to help guide you towards the key information in the reading. You can take notes in any form you choose – in full sentences, bullet points with key ideas, or another method that works for you.

Discussion

1   The presence of many amphorae (large jars used to store wine or oil) is used to identify wine importers in a certain area, and perfume bottles identify a perfume district. Marble and metal waste are found elsewhere, indicating the work of craftsmen. The presence of large containers set into the floor cannot be linked to a specific trade, but would have been connected to an activity requiring large quantities of liquid close to hand. The discovery of coins can also indicate commercial activity.

2   Homes and shops appear very close to each other, rather than large swathes of buildings being given over to one or the other purpose. Indeed, the layout of some buildings seems to suggest that people lived and worked in the same building, with one or more rooms acting as a shop and/or workshop, and the rest of the building reserved for private living.

3   It is likely that proximity to the agora would have served shopkeepers well in gaining more trade, as the area was so commonly frequented by a large number of the city's inhabitants.

In the Classical period, a law stated that only Athenian citizens were allowed to trade in the agora, and another stated that telling lies in the agora – for example, when making a sale or compiling a contract – was illegal. As such, commerce in the agora did not escape the association with citizenship that was also found in aspects of government and law performed there. Non-Athenians would have had to trade outside of the boundary of the agora in nearby buildings.

2.4 Religion

The ancient Greeks followed a polytheistic religion, meaning that they believed in many gods. This was not an organised religion with specific churches and rules like many modern religions, but a more fluid set of practices and rituals that could be carried out both in specifically religious places and elsewhere. Religious activity permeated almost every aspect of Athenian life. Most large civic celebrations were also religious festivals – for example, the annual City Dionysia, a theatrical festival that was sacred to the god Dionysus. Smaller, more everyday civic activities (such as trials and assemblies) would have involved the swearing of oaths to the gods; and households would have had their own shrines, household gods (deities that guarded the home) and ritual practices. You'll learn a bit more about Greek religion in Chapter 3, 'Delphi: centre of the Greek world', but one important aspect to remember here is that, both within Athens and in Greece more widely, the gods were worshipped for their different characteristics at different locations. For example, the famous Parthenon temple on top of the Acropolis was dedicated to Athena (the goddess of wisdom and justice, and the patron goddess of Athens), but particularly to Athena Parthenos, meaning Athena in her specific role as a goddess devoted to young, unmarried women. Many of the religious sites in the agora also reflect this interest in worshipping specific aspects of the different gods.

The largest and best-preserved religious building in the area of the agora is the Hephaisteion, a temple to Hephaestus (the god of the forge), which was located on the agora hill to the west of the agora. The goddess Athena was also associated with the temple, and large bronze statues of both gods would have been housed within it. The temple was large (as can be seen in Figure 8) and its exterior was decorated with sculptures depicting the labours of the mythical heroes Heracles and Theseus; stories about these would have been well known by the Athenians.

Figure 8 The Hephaisteion, or Temple of Hephaestus, to the west of the Athenian agora. Photo: Ivan Vdovin/Alamy.

In the north-west corner of the agora, just south of the Royal Stoa, sat three temples of varying sizes (not all can be seen on the simplified plan in Figure 2). Each of these showcased a particular aspect of the gods that they honoured that was especially relevant to Athenian identity and culture. The furthest south was the Temple of Apollo Patroos ('Fatherly Apollo'). Apollo was usually considered to be the god of the sun, music and prophecy, among other characteristics, but this particular temple represented his legendary role as the father of Ion from whom the Ionian race (including the Athenians) were said to be descended. North of this was the even smaller Temple of Zeus Phratrios and Athena Phratria, who were the patron gods of the Athenian **phratries** (social groups within the ten Athenian tribes). The location of these two temples in the agora represents the significance of the citizen experience to life in Athens, at least in terms of the image that Athens wished to project both to itself and to outsiders.

The northernmost religious building of this group is the much larger Stoa of Zeus Eleutherios ('Zeus of Freedom'; labelled as 'Stoa of Zeus' towards the top left in Figure 2). Besides a statue of Zeus (the god of the sky and the king of the gods), the Stoa contained a number of **dedications** that indicated the connection with victory and freedom, including statues of the goddess Nike (or 'Victory') and the shields of soldiers who had died fighting to defend Athens. The placement of a temple signifying Athenian military victory and freedom in the central space of the agora showed the importance of these values in Athenian culture, and helped to project this idea to both inhabitants and visitors of the city.

As previously mentioned in the online unit, the Panathenaic Way ran across the agora from north-west to south-east. This was a major thoroughfare that served as the route of the procession that formed an important part of the annual Panathenaia festival, a key religious event that culminated on the Acropolis with a large animal sacrifice and was famously depicted on the **friezes** of the Parthenon. The procession would have been an impressive display of Athenian prosperity and piety. The Panathenaic Way also served as the site for chariot and foot races that took place during the festival, such as those depicted on Panathenaic amphorae, which were decorated vases awarded as prizes in these contests (Figure 9).

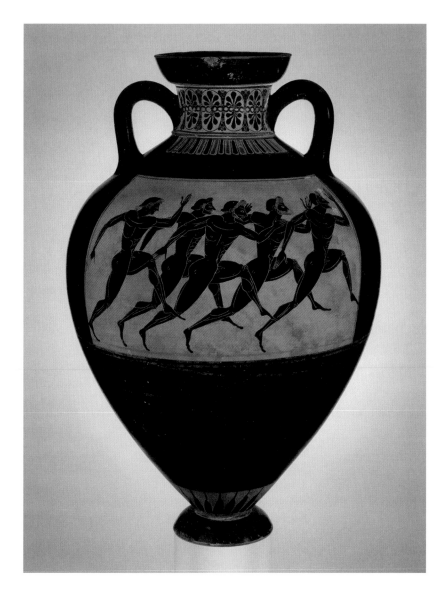

Figure 9 Attributed to the Euphiletos painter. An amphora (a container used for wine or oil) decorated in the black-figure style and depicting a foot race, which would have been awarded as part of the Panathenaia festival, *c*.530 BCE, terracotta, height 62 cm. Metropolitan Museum of Art, New York. Photo: © Metropolitan Museum of Art/Bridgeman Images.

2.5 Performing citizenship, performing culture

By now you should have a good sense of the many types of structures and evidence of activities that can be identified with the agora. What does this mean for understanding Athenian culture? An important point to note is that the Athenian people created the space of the agora over time to fit their needs. As you have seen, the agora was a central space in Athens with a specific connection to Athenian citizens, although it could also be accessed by other groups. The centrality of the 'marketplace', both within the city and in everyday Athenian activity, suggests that the buildings and structures within it (and therefore the institutions they represented) were some of the most important aspects of Athenian life. As a summary, these included:

- **Aspects of government**: essential for keeping the city running smoothly on a day-to-day basis and upholding democratic ideals; only citizens of Athens could take part.

- **Law courts**: necessary to maintain order in line with the laws of the city, thus promoting the city's values; although open to everyone (including foreigners, slaves and women), citizens played a prominent role.

- **Commerce**: contributing to the city's economy and the livelihoods of citizens and residents; the agora enforced a boundary within which only citizens could trade.

- **Religion**: practised both at dedicated religious sites and in other locations, and especially used to promote specific values in the public space, such as freedom and citizenship.

In this way, the agora was a public reflection of Athenian cultural values: the importance of citizenship and democracy, the enforcement of law and order, the freedom of the city, a thriving economy and observance of religious tradition. The Athenian agora was a site where values were displayed and daily life was lived, and studying it offers an insight on these aspects, which can be said to be the components of a society's culture. It should also be clear that whether you were a citizen mattered greatly in Athenian public life, and dictated which aspects of the culture you could or could not create and take part in.

But public life did not begin and end with taking part in the Assembly, or even with sitting on juries in the law courts. Another important factor was simply being seen in public. The agora was the natural place for this: as well as being a civic and commercial centre, it was also a key meeting place and an open public space in which to 'perform' one's Athenian citizenship. This performance meant simply doing the things that Athenian citizens do – perhaps attending the law courts, holding public office, engaging in religious activity or just strolling around being seen and acknowledged by other citizens, whose approval acted as a kind of endorsement of one's citizenship. As you read in Section 2.1 of this chapter, Athenian citizens were free men over the age of 18 born to two Athenian parents. This meant that there was often no other way to tell citizens apart from other adult male members of the Athenian population, such as foreigners and slaves, and so this kind of performance was important. The effect was perhaps most obvious when it worked the other way: citizens seen behaving badly in public would be perceived negatively by other citizens. Some types of bad behaviour (such as mistreating one's parents or stealing someone's cloak) actually broke Athenian laws, and certain crimes, which were perhaps perceived as being 'anti-citizen' (such as owing a debt to the state or prostituting oneself), could be punished by *atimia*, the removal of certain citizen rights. This often included being barred from the agora as well as other places important to citizenship, such as the Assembly and courts. It should be clear, then, that being seen in the agora was important for an Athenian citizen, and thus an important aspect of Athenian culture.

3 Who else was in the agora?

Although, as we have now established, the agora was an important citizen space in Athens, citizens were far from the only people present there, or in public in Athens more generally. The Athenians would have us believe that women (and children) were confined to the home, and you'll look at that particular issue more closely when you examine the Athenian household later in this chapter. For now, there are two other important categories of people in Athens who composed the rest of the population besides citizens: **metics** (resident foreigners) and enslaved people.

Slaves or enslaved people?

In this chapter, I've chosen to use the term 'enslaved people' (rather than 'slaves'), but you'll see that other scholars in the readings and translators of the ancient texts in this chapter use the term 'slaves'. Some people prefer this term as they feel that it conveys the removal of personhood that came with being sold and owned as property. Here, I'm using 'enslaved people' because I want to draw attention to the fact that slaves were just that – people who were present throughout Athenian everyday life in the same way as everyone else. They would often have been indistinguishable from citizens and metics in terms of appearance. You can use whatever term you prefer in your own work.

Metics had many of the same freedoms as citizens, though without certain rights. They could not vote in the Assembly, serve on juries in the law courts or own property in Attica (the land encompassing Athens), for example. However, they were free people who held a variety of jobs and could become very well known: the philosopher Aristotle, for example, was a metic, as was the well-known orator Lysias, who you will learn more about in Section 5. Metics could also range across social classes, from low-level craftsmen and those freed from slavery to the very richest members of Athenian society. Just like Athenian citizens, metics had a duty to fight for Athens and were subject to taxes (if they qualified in terms of wealth), while also being liable to pay a separate metic tax.

Enslaved people, on the other hand, occupied quite a different status. Despite the fact that some of them could earn their own money from their work, they were ultimately the property of another person and at least a proportion of the money they made always went to their masters. Enslaved people did varied work in Athens, from working in the home, to occupying public roles such as scribes, to being craftspeople of all kinds. The existence of slavery in Athens had certain implications for other members of the population, which the historian T.E. Rihll writes about in the reading you'll now explore.

Activity 3

(Allow around 1 hour to complete this activity.)

Turn to Reading 1.2, which is an extract from Rihll's chapter, 'Classical Athens'. Then answer the following questions, writing a few sentences for each:

1   According to Rihll, what effects did the existence of slavery have on citizenship in Athens?

2   What does the author think the relationship between metic and enslaved status was?

3   What does the reading say were the jobs that enslaved people could hold that would have made them visible in everyday life?

> **Study note**
>
> This activity gives you the chance to practise picking out the argument in a piece of secondary scholarship. You might find it useful to read the extract once for sense and then again more closely, making some notes or jotting down some of the key points that you think relate to each of the questions before you formulate your answers.

Discussion

1   Rihll argues that the existence of slavery preserved 'citizen equality', as it meant that citizens generally did not have to perform menial or dangerous tasks, such as domestic labour or arresting criminals. But she also suggests that it was not the labour of enslaved people that allowed poorer citizens to engage in democratic activity, but the fact that they would be paid to do so.

2 Rihll notes that those freed from slavery would become metics, and that this could be a stepping stone on the way to gaining citizen status. She also argues that the institution of metic status could have reinforced the dominance of citizens over enslaved people even after they were freed. This was because it was necessary for metics to have a citizen patron who, in the case of a freed person, had to be their ex-master. She also notes that metics were liable to the punishment of being sold into slavery for certain crimes, and identifies being a metic as a kind of middle ground between being enslaved and being a citizen.

3 Reading 1.2 mentions numerous jobs that enslaved people would have performed. Domestic tasks included grinding grain, farming, fishing, herding, marketing, performing religious rites and assisting the master if he was called up to fight in a war. These tasks would have meant that enslaved people had a major role in private homes. But other tasks also made them visible in public, including sewage removal, assaying silver, record keeping, measuring the grain allowance for individuals, running gambling dens, working as enforcers in the Assembly or as state executioner, and various other manufacturing and service roles.

Much of the labour performed by enslaved people (particularly those owned by the state rather than private individuals) meant that citizens and other members of the population would likely encounter enslaved people in public on a day-to-day basis. Very little record of this presence is preserved in the surviving sources, particularly textual ones, which were almost exclusively written by elite members of society and tended to be more concerned with the activities of Athenian citizens, and occasionally metics. It's important to remember that these writers don't necessarily represent what everyday life in Athens was *actually* like in terms of the people present in public spaces (and indeed, in private spaces, as you will discover in the next section).

What this means for the study of the Athenian agora is that, although the agora was an extremely important space for citizens (and one especially associated with citizen activity), it was also occupied by people who, while marginalised in Athenian society and in our sources, made essential contributions to the everyday running of the city. Athens was one of few Greek cities to allow foreigners to hold metic status, and this contributed to the cosmopolitanism of the city and its status as a centre of culture. Athens was enriched both financially and culturally by metics, who in the fifth century BCE were attracted to the city's prosperity and brought with them expertise in art, literature, philosophy and other fields from across the Greek world. Metics were expected to conform to the norms of Athenian life and could never be the equals of Athenian citizens in a legal sense, but they were still a key component of Athenian culture during the Classical period.

Nevertheless, while the most prominent aspects of Athenian culture were centred on citizens and enriched by metics, they were also built on the back of enslavement. The large enslaved population performed most of the more menial everyday tasks that citizens preferred not to do; it seems that very few Athenian citizens had any moral objection to this. Without this labour, which is largely invisible in the surviving sources, Athens would have been unable to operate as effectively as it did and become such a vibrant cultural centre of the Greek world in the Classical period. When we imagine the ancient Athenian agora then, we should populate it not only with citizens performing their democratic duties but also metics and enslaved people all going about their daily business, be it commercial, religious, social or more menial work. For our study of Athens, this is a reminder that the outward appearance of a culture may be deceptive, particularly if it is constructed by elite members of society. Those who are marginalised in a society still contribute to producing its culture – in this case, by facilitating citizens' engagement with the more prominent aspects of Athenian culture through undertaking their everyday labour.

4 Introducing the *oikos*

Now that you've looked at the agora, a public space in Athens, and what it can tell us about 'public life' in the city, it's time to turn to a more private location: the Athenian home, or *oikos*. The ancient Greek word *oikos* has two meanings: it can indicate the house itself, but also the people who live there and who comprise what is usually called the household. Both of these definitions are useful to consider when examining private life in Athens. The word is the root of the modern word 'economy'; in fact, for the Greeks, *oikonomia* meant the way a household was managed.

Activity 4

(Allow around 30 minutes to complete this activity.)

In order to learn more about the Athenian conceptions of the house and household, turn to Reading 1.3, which is a short extract from archaeologist Monika Trümper's chapter, 'Space and social relationships in the Greek oikos of the Classical and Hellenistic periods'.

Note down one or two sentences in response to each of the following questions:

1   Who was part of the *oikos* and where did they live?
2   What activities took place in the home?
3   What kinds of households do we have less information about?

Study note

Trümper refers to the work of other scholars in this passage using in-text references. Although you don't need to refer to these other works at this stage, it's important to notice how she uses the work of others to support her own arguments, and that she makes sure to acknowledge this with clear references. This allows the reader to know where Trümper is presenting her own ideas and where she is referring to someone else's work. You should make sure to include references in your own work when you refer to someone else's ideas.

Discussion

1   Trümper notes that Greek households consisted of core family members (such as parents and children), but that they may also have contained other extended family members (such as grandparents and aunts), as well as non-family members such as enslaved people and friends. They may all have lived together in one house or across multiple properties.

2   The home was a location for entertaining guests and hosting parties, and also a place of preparing, eating and storing food as well as washing, producing textiles, raising children and carrying out religious activities.

3   We know more about elite citizen households than other types, particularly those that Trümper identifies as being on the 'margins' of society: the poor, non-citizens and people who lived on the geographical borders of the Greek world.

Although Trümper is writing generally about Greek ways of living, these would have specifically applied in Athens too. Trümper notes the ideals that dictated certain parts of Athenian home life, which you'll look at more closely in the next section. As you have seen from Reading 1.3, she also draws attention to the way that the sources are skewed towards the lives of elite people. These would have been the ones who could afford to conform to the social expectations of Athenian culture, whereas poorer people had to prioritise the needs of everyday life; for example, in non-slave-owning households, Athenian women would have had to do their share of the labour, particularly tasks necessary for the home, such as fetching water. The nature of the evidence that survives means that we know far less about these non-elite households.

Trümper also gives us a good overview of the kinds of activities that would have taken place in the Athenian home. These were the activities of everyday life just as much as those public activities that took place in the agora and other public places. And, like those public activities, they shaped the place in which they happened; houses would need to be laid out in a way that made it easier to do these things. For example, natural light would be needed for the production of textiles, enough space would have to be available to store supplies for the household, and a more impressively decorated room might be reserved for entertaining guests.

For now, it's important to remember that, as a concept, the Athenian home combined the practicalities of everyday life and the expectations of citizen society. In this way, although the home was ostensibly a private space, it could have strong public resonances in the Athenian imagination. In the next section, you'll look at what these qualities were and how they were conveyed.

5 The ideal home

As you learned in the previous section, the Athenians had an idealised view of what life at home should be like for citizens. An Athenian man was the master of his home, and his household might contain both immediate and extended family members, free people employed by him, and enslaved people. This man would ultimately be in charge of and responsible for all of these people, particularly the women of the household. Idealised expectations of women suggested that they should remain indoors most of the time and not be seen by any male visitors to the house. In the Athenian ideal, the only time a respectable woman should be seen in public was at religious festivals, for which women had special responsibility. But the ideal also suggested that a wife should be able to manage the household well, to lessen the burden on her husband, and a desirable wife would be one who had a good sense of *oikonomia* (the running of the household). The home was so important to the Greeks that there was even a goddess of the hearth called Hestia, and the hearth itself was believed to be a sacred place.

Activity 5

(Allow around 20 minutes to complete this activity.)

Examine Figure 10, which is an image of a Greek clay jar showing a domestic scene. Think about what this scene, as well as the jar itself, might suggest about the ideals of Athenian home life. (This image can be seen in more detail in the online gallery on the module website.) The information given in the bullet points below will help you to interpret the figures on the jar:

- The standing figure on the right is male and dressed as a citizen.

- The seated figure in the centre-right is female.

- The standing figure on the left is female and dressed as a servant.

- The object on the left is a loom for weaving textiles.

- This shape of pot, called a *hydria*, was used for storing water.

Figure 10 A clay water jar (*hydria*) decorated in the red-figure style and depicting a domestic scene, 440–430 BCE, height 35 cm. Harvard Art Museums/Arthur M. Sackler Museum, Bequest of David M. Robinson, Obj. No.: 1960.342. Photo: © President and Fellows of Harvard College.

Study note

In Block 2, which focuses on Art History, you will learn more about how to visually analyse images such as this one. For now, just focus on what you can see in the image. You might think about the positioning, poses and dress of the figures; the objects included in the scene; and the function of the jar on which the illustration appears.

Discussion

The male figure on the right is dressed as a citizen, and so might represent the head of this household. The female figure seated in front of him is probably his wife. She wears a head covering, which may suggest modesty. She hands a small child, which appears to be male, to another standing female figure dressed as a servant, who is probably a maid involved in looking after the child. The presence of the loom to the left may indicate the value of domestic textile production to this kind of family.

The scene as a whole suggests an idealised family lifestyle, with a citizen father, a modest mother who is assisted in the home by one or more servants, and a male heir; the household is industrious and well managed, as the loom suggests.

A water jar was a necessary item in every household, used to store drinking water for use throughout the day without needing to return to the well. This item may have been designed to be used often and occupy a prominent place in the home, projecting the ideal displayed in its decoration.

A family like the one depicted on this water jar would have been aspirational for Athenian citizens and represented an ideal about the roles of men and women based on Athenian cultural values. It's quite difficult to see on this image but the male figure is holding a staff, which signifies his place in the outside world. The seated position of his wife would have indicated to the Athenian viewer that she did not have to work. A male child, like this one, would also have been the ideal, as he would act as an heir to his father's *oikos* and property. Female children, by contrast, would have been married into other families, and could only inherit an estate if no male heirs existed and in order to pass the property on to their husbands.

5.1 Ideal homes in textual sources

The layout of the home itself was also idealised. Several Athenian sources suggest that there were parts of the house to which women were confined, out of the way of prying eyes. Similarly, rooms existed that were designed solely for men to entertain their male guests. Their property was also a mark of an Athenian man's status, as only citizens were allowed to own property in Attica, and in many ways a man's home was his castle. In order to find out more about these ideals, you're now going to look at two extracts from Athenian **forensic oratory**. This is a term that describes law court speeches delivered by the prosecutor and the defendant in trials in Athens. In the Classical Athenian legal system there were no lawyers and no evidence beyond sworn witness testimony, and so people embroiled in legal matters had to deliver their own arguments in court in order to persuade the jurors that their side was the right one. As not everyone naturally had the skills to do this well, professional speech-writers arose who could be hired to write persuasive speeches. These law court speeches are particularly interesting because their narratives often include more commonplace details about everyday life (albeit usually that of the Athenian elite) that we do not hear much about in other sources.

Let's start by reading through an extract together. This speech is by the speech-writer and orator Lysias (who was mentioned briefly as a metic in Section 3). He was born in the mid fifth century BCE and was reputed to have lived to about 80 years old. We have 34 surviving speeches and numerous fragments by Lysias, not all of which are law court speeches. This extract is from the first speech in the **corpus** of Lysias and is sometimes called 'On the death of Eratosthenes'. It comes from a trial for lawful homicide – that is, a case where a person has been killed, and the person who killed them does not deny the killing but argues that they were legally permitted to carry it out. In Athens, it was lawful for a person to kill someone violently attempting to rob them, or for a man to kill another man who he discovered having sex with his wife, mother, daughter or another woman belonging to his household, as long as he caught the seducer in the act and killed him immediately. The case in question is an instance of the latter situation: the speaker and defendant (a man named Euphiletus) killed a man named Eratosthenes who, Euphiletus says, he discovered in bed with his wife. Despite the fact that such a killing was legally allowable, Euphiletus still had to face trial because Eratosthenes' family accused him of having plotted to kill Eratosthenes in advance, rather than catching him in the act.

As he explains his side of the story (or at least the version that Lysias has written for him), Euphiletus tells the jury about his relationship with his wife, and in doing so provides some quite detailed information about the layout of his house:

> After I decided to get married, men of Athens, and brought my bride home, for a while my attitude was not to trouble her too much but not to let her do whatever she wanted either. I watched her as best I could and gave her the proper amount of attention. But from the moment my son was born, I began to have full confidence in her and placed everything in her hands, reckoning that this was the best relationship. In those early days, men of Athens, she was the best of women: a good housekeeper, thrifty, with a sharp eye on every detail. But my mother's death was the cause of all my troubles. For it was while attending her funeral that my wife was seen by this fellow and eventually corrupted by him: he kept an eye out for the slave girl who did the shopping, put forward proposals, and seduced her.
>
> Now before continuing, gentlemen, I need to explain something. My house has two stories, and in the part with the women's rooms and the men's rooms, the upper floor is the same size as the floor below. When our baby was born, his mother nursed him. To avoid her risking an accident coming down the stairs whenever he needed washing, I took over the upstairs rooms, and the women moved downstairs. Eventually we became so used to this arrangement that my wife would often leave me to go down and sleep with the baby, so that she could nurse it and stop it crying. Things went on in this way for a long time, and I never had the slightest suspicion; indeed, I was so naive that I thought my wife was the most respectable woman in Athens.
>
> (Lysias 1.6–10; Lysias, 2000, p. 17 [footnotes removed])

Euphiletus is describing an ideal relationship from the Athenian perspective. His relationship with his wife was successful, at least in the beginning, because she proved trustworthy and they were able to compromise. She also produced a male heir, which made him trust her all the more. In fact, he trusted her enough to allow her to live in the downstairs quarters, which were the same size as those upstairs and must have included either a room for washing or a source of water, as he says his wife needed to carry the baby downstairs in order to bathe him. The downstairs rooms were also accessed more easily from outside of the house than the secluded upstairs area, and in this way implicitly made it easier for Eratosthenes to commit adultery with Euphiletus' wife. It sounds like this arrangement of living quarters, with the women downstairs and the men upstairs, was unusual: Euphiletus doesn't bother to explain why the women's quarters were originally upstairs, which suggests that this would be the normal place for them to be. Lysias probably hoped that the Athenian jurors would have seen their own (ideal) lives reflected in Euphiletus' narrative, and thus sympathised with his plight when his apparently idyllic life was upheaved by adultery. It's also interesting that Euphiletus' wife is never named. Often, when a woman was widely known by name it was because she had a bad reputation, so the lack of a name would have reinforced the idea that Euphiletus' wife was a good woman and that they had an ideal relationship.

You're now going to try extracting this kind of information about an Athenian home from a forensic speech by yourself. This second extract is by Demosthenes, perhaps the most famous of the Athenian orators, who lived from 384 to 322 BCE and had a high-profile political career as well as working as a speech-writer. Over 60 of his speeches have been preserved, including forensic and political oratory. This extract is from the forty-seventh speech in his corpus and is called 'Against Evergus and Mnesibulus'. The case itself is quite complicated, and though he is not named in the title of the speech, the speaker's primary opponent appears to be a man named Theophemus. The speaker tells of their extended quarrel over some naval equipment and claims that at some point in their enmity Theophemus conspired with Evergus and Mnesibulus to bring a wrongful legal suit against him, resulting in the speaker having to pay a fine directly to Theophemus. This extract deals with the portion of the narrative where Theophemus, impatient to receive the money, allegedly came to the speaker's property to seize goods equal to the amount of the fine.

Activity 6

(Allow around 40 minutes to complete this activity.)

Turn to Reading 1.4, which is an extract from Demosthenes 47 'Against Evergus and Mnesibulus'. Then jot down some notes in response to the following questions:

1   What information can be learned about the speaker's property?

2   What do Theophemus and his companions do that is particularly shocking?

3   How does the passer-by, Hagnophilus, react to the scene?

Discussion

1   The speaker's property is on farmland, near the Hippodrome (a stadium for horse racing and chariot racing). It has a garden and a courtyard as well as a 'tower', the latter of which formed the residence for a number of enslaved women.

2   Theophemus and his companions begin carrying off the speaker's furniture, despite having already taken a large quantity of sheep. More shockingly, they enter into the presence of the women and children of the household, and, worst of all, they attack the old freedwoman (a woman who had been freed from enslavement) in order to take away a cup that she is holding.

3   Hagnophilus, when he comes upon the scene, decides not to enter the house, because he thinks that this would not be proper with the master of the house absent.

We learn a lot about Athenian household ideals from this passage. Theophemus and his companions are clearly meant to appear to be violent and ruthless, ready to break any norm in order to steal from the speaker. Their treatment of the women in the household is particularly shocking in a society where women are supposed to be safe if they are kept at home. Their disrespect of the wife and her property would have been seen as entirely unacceptable by the Athenian audience, as well as their physical aggression towards the old freedwoman, a respected member of the household even though she was not related by blood. The passage contrasts this aberrant and trespassing behaviour with that of Hagnophilus, a passer-by who, despite witnessing the terrible things happening to the speaker's household, still feels that it would be disrespectful to enter the property with the master away.

Although the two pieces of forensic oratory we have looked at are only short extracts, they have a lot to say about the cultural ideals of Athenian home life. From this ideal perspective, the home was a place where women were sequestered, even being confined to certain rooms within the building itself. They may venture out to dine in the courtyard, but here they risked being exposed to unexpected male visitors to the house. Children and enslaved people are hardly mentioned and may have been expected to be seen and not heard. A man's home was representative of his citizenship, wealth and prosperity, and a household that operated efficiently and produced revenue was to be prized. Respectable citizens knew not to enter a man's home when he was absent, and absent he often was. A man's public reputation depended on being out in public more often than he was at home, just as much as a woman's depended on her being concealed from public view except during particular religious events.

6 Summary

In this chapter, you've undertaken an in-depth study of the Athenian agora as a public space and as somewhere where Athenian public life was enacted. In doing so, you've learned about one of the ways in which Athenians both created and expressed their culture. The agora was a central space in the city inhabited prominently by Athenian citizens, though metics and enslaved people would also have been present there. By performing different tasks in the agora – for example, governing the city, taking part in trials, buying and selling goods or performing religious rites – Athenians gave that place meaning and associated it with the key cultural values associated with these actions. By ascribing this meaning to the buildings in the agora and the agora itself, Athens turned its central space into a display of its culture: upon entering the agora, visitors to the city and the inhabitants themselves would immediately be reminded that this was a city that prized democracy, freedom, citizenship, piety, trade and orderly living.

You've also begun your study of the Athenian home by looking at the ideals of home life projected by some forensic speeches from Athenian orators. Here, you've begun to see the idealised cultural values that extended into the private lives of Athenians: that women should be secluded within the home and that trespassing within this private space would have been deeply disrespectful. Now, you will return online to examine the archaeological evidence for Athenian homes in order to see whether the reality of the way Athenians lived aligns with this ideal, as well as to explore the shared expressions of culture that occurred when public life extended into private space.

You should now return to the module website to continue your study of this unit.

References

Aristotle (1935) *Athenian constitution. Eudemian ethics. Virtues and vices.* Translated by H. Rackham. Loeb Classical Library 285. Cambridge, MA: Harvard University Press.

Demosthenes (2011) *Speeches 39–49.* Translated by A.C. Scafuro. Austin, TX: University of Texas Press.

Lysias (2000) *Lysias.* Translated by S.C. Todd. Austin, TX: University of Texas Press.

McK. Camp II, J. (2010) *The Athenian agora: site guide.* 5th edn. Princeton, NJ: American School of Classical Studies at Athens.

Rihll, T.E. (2011) 'Classical Athens', in Bradley, K. and Cartledge, P. (eds) *The Cambridge world history of slavery, volume 1: the ancient Mediterranean world.* Cambridge: Cambridge University Press, pp. 48–73.

Rotroff, S.I. (2009) 'Commerce and crafts around the Athenian agora', in McK. Camp II, J. and Mauzy, C.A. (eds) *The Athenian agora: new perspectives on an ancient site.* Mainz am Rhain: Philipp von Zabern, pp. 39–46.

Trümper, M. (2011) 'Space and social relationships in the Greek oikos of the Classical and Hellenistic periods', in Rawson, B. (ed.) *A companion to families in the Greek and Roman worlds.* Chichester: Wiley-Blackwell, pp. 32–52.

Readings

Reading 1.1 Commerce and crafts around the Athenian agora

Source: Rotroff, S.I. (2009) 'Commerce and crafts around the Athenian agora', in McK. Camp II, J. and Mauzy, C.A. (eds) *The Athenian agora: new perspectives on an ancient site*. Mainz am Rhain: Philipp von Zabern, p. 40.

Sometimes we can pinpoint the location of particular merchants by studying the broken and discarded objects they left behind. Thus, a heavy concentration of large clay amphoras (vessels designed for the long-distance shipping of liquids [...]) spread over a large area just outside the south-east corner of the square tells us that wine importers did business there in the 5th century B.C. Nearby, a similar collection of perfume bottles, thrown into wells and cisterns of the 5th to the 2nd century B.C., reveals that here was the perfume market, described by the 5th-century comic poet Aristophanes as the haunt of gossips and feckless young men.

A more concrete picture emerges from the remains of Classical buildings that clearly served commercial purposes: places not only where objects were sold but also where they were manufactured. Without exception, and as we would expect, these lay outside the Agora proper, but often as close to it as the builders could manage. They are nestled among dwellings, and some are indistinguishable from private houses in their plans. In these cases, the owner or tenant simply devoted part of his living space to his profession. For example, a hearth and deposits of marble and metal waste show that craftsmen worked in house D, a dwelling located along a road running south from the southwest corner of the square [...]. In the larger house C, next door and to the south and, in one phase of its history, connected by a door to house D, an isolated room opens directly onto the street and probably served as a shop, where items manufactured inside were offered to the public. In another house, part of a block of dwellings just to the south of the public square [...], large containers (pithoi) set into a plastered floor bear witness to industrial or commercial activity (dyeing? felting? laundering?), while the profits are attested by the many lost coins – including two rare silver ones – discovered in the successive floor levels of one of the house's rooms. The same cheek-by-jowl arrangement of living and working space is evoked in a 4th-century B.C. Athenian inscription found at the Agora (I 1749 [reference to the inscription]), describing property confiscated from Philokrates of Hagnous, a prominent citizen who, indicted for treason by his political enemies, had left town rather than stand trial. The accused has owned two workshops (ergostasia), bounded on the north and east by two houses (also his property), on the west by a workshop owned by someone else, and on the south by a road leading to the square.

Reading 1.2 Classical Athens

Source: Rihll, T.E. (2011) 'Classical Athens', in Bradley, K. and Cartledge, P. (eds.) *The Cambridge world history of slavery, volume 1: the ancient Mediterranean world*. Cambridge: Cambridge University Press, pp. 58–62 [footnotes removed].

In the Athenian democracy, citizen equality was preserved by the actions of slaves, from cleaning floors to arresting traitors. Educated Greeks thought that domestic chores such as grinding grain and other laborious tasks were to be done by someone else. Working the mill was considered so unpleasant it was regularly used to threaten recalcitrant slaves. By contrast, 'a life ready-ground' was proverbial for a life of ease (Amphis Fr. 9). Throughout Greek literature it is assumed that anyone, including a slave, would want a slave if possible for domestic chores. The poor man who could not afford a slave used his wife and children instead (Aristotle, *Pol.* 1323a5–6). Aristotle (*Pol.* 1293a1–9) explains that the poor can participate in politics not because they have slaves to work for them, but because they are paid by the state when they participate. Thus political participation in extreme democracy has nothing intrinsically to do with slavery; it depends instead on public finance, paying day or wage labour on a regular piece-rate model for political meetings or court cases attended. The Athenian poor could make a living as the foot-soldiers of the political system. This is presumably what Aristotle (*Pol.* 1296b29) was referring to when he said that if the masses were predominantly artisans (*banausoi*) and wage labourers (*mistharnai*), the democracy would be radical, as Athens was. He assumes that adequate food, shelter and other necessities were available for purchase.

In some states with relatively vigorous craft sectors, artisans were denied citizenship; Aristotle cites Corinth as an example. Corinth's oligarchical constitution confined citizenship to landholders, and free people working in trade and service had a lower status. There were also reputedly very large numbers of slaves in Corinth – 460,000 to be precise, a figure that most scholars find impossibly large. In view of how the term 'slave' could be used by people like Aristotle to mean (free) artisans and service providers who sold their skills, wares or labour to the general public, this figure, if it has any basis in fact at all, may represent the total number of slaves and free non-citizens. (The other microstate with reputedly huge slave numbers, Aegina, was an oligarchy too.)

The creation of the concept of the metic, the resident alien, the immigrant who was not allowed to participate fully in society but who was free and not a slave, was a key development in the history of slavery in ancient Athens. A slave manumitted [freed] in Homeric Greece joined the master class. A slave manumitted in classical Athens became a metic. Whitehead (1977: 140–7) dates this development to Cleisthenes' reforms at the end of the sixth century BC, which laid the basis of the Athenian democracy.

The metic was prohibited from participation in the political, religious and legal life of Athens. The metic was also liable to some burdens from which the citizen was free, such as sale into slavery as a judicial punishment, examination under torture for evidence, and direct head tax. It was in many ways a middle status between slave and free, foreigner and citizen, and its creation may have had as much to do with the manumission of slaves as it did with the voluntary immigration of free foreigners into Athens. The fact that the penalty of slavery was imposed automatically on a metic convicted of certain crimes that involved impersonating a citizen suggests the same. Metic status also institutionalised the master's continuing dominance over the slave, even after manumission. For metics were required to have a *prostates*, a citizen patron to represent them in any dealings with the state. For ex-slaves, the patron had to be the ex-master, or the ex-master's patron if the master was himself a metic.

A slave could become a citizen through the status of metic. Pasion is the most famous case, who started his life in Athens as a slave banker, was set free and became a metic. Continued success and generous donations to the Athenian state resulted in his being awarded *enktesis*, the right to own land and a house in Attica. After more years of outstanding civic generosity, he was awarded citizenship by the sovereign assembly of citizens. His slave Phormio followed his example, from slave to citizen, working in the same bank. His story is told in Demosthenes 36 (*For Phormion*). Phormio's route to citizenship included guardianship of his ex-master's youngest son and estate until the boy came of age, and marriage to his ex-master's widow (both specified in Pasion's will). Marriage to the widow was a common adjunct to guardianship of that woman's son – it happened to Demosthenes himself (see 27.4–5). The logic of this action – even when it involved making a newly manumitted slave the step-father of one's own citizen son – is explained by Demosthenes (36.28–30).

In Athens, though not everywhere, there were slaves owned by the state. The convention seems to have begun with the sixth-century tyrant Peisistratos' mercenary bodyguard of foreign archers, which developed into the Scythian 'police' force of Pericles' time. The Scythian archers outlasted the tyranny to become the sole state-sponsored source of physical power available to magistrates. They wore characteristic Scythian clothing and carried bows and quivers, which served as insignia rather than weapons. Their principal roles were to eject disruptive citizens from the Athenian Assembly when ordered by the Presidents, and to arrest people in the presence of and on the orders of a magistrate. They also guarded the prison. Classical Athens employed more slaves to undertake tasks that people regarded as unsuitable for either citizens or metics: tasks such as sewage removal ([Arist.] *Ath. Pol.* 54.1), assaying silver for new coin, keeping the records of state debtors and measuring out the grain allowance (Dinarchus 7.2).

We rationalise their employment in such responsible roles with the argument that the public slave was perceived as less corruptible than a free man or private slave, since only the state could free him and he was independent of connections with any citizen or metic. The public slave could also be threatened with corporal punishment, though he was not supposed to be beaten by private citizens (Aeschin. 1.59–60). The state executioner was also a public slave, and the reason for this might be religious: whatever divine wrath might be visited on the executioner as killer would not extend to the citizen community since the slave was an outsider. Another reason was because citizens were the only other 'civil servants' in classical Athenian society. Citizens were allotted to almost all of the 1,200 public posts to be filled annually by random selection. Some were selected for council duty, others for priesthoods, others for trading standards, and so on. It is not obvious how a citizen picked at random could be made to serve as executioner against his will, and easy to imagine how the citizens would vote against any motion that they should take turns performing this role.

Some public slaves had more unexpected jobs. Pittalakos, who is known to have lived independently, ran a gambling and cock-fighting den (Aeschin. 1.59, 68). According to *IG* II^2 1672.4–5 (329/8 BC), they received a daily allowance of three obols, implying that they fended for themselves with respect to food and lodging. But this is all that is known of how Athens supported public slaves. The only publicly funded meals available were those served in the Prytaneion. There is also some evidence of public slaves being freed (*IG* II ^{2} 1570 line 79).

[…]

Most Athenians were farmers, but Athens unusually had a relatively large manufacturing and service sector in which slaves were heavily involved. This allowed owners to engage in education, politics and sport. As Aristotle observed (*Metaphysics* I.I), the necessities of life have to be secured before there is time for luxuries like philosophy. However, not all Athenians lived parasitically off slaves, nor did slaves alone produce the material base of Athenian culture. Not all Athenians owned slaves. The oft-cited case of the disabled cobbler whose case for a means-tested state pension of an obol per day included the point that he could not yet afford someone to help him in his work is not evidence that people 'well down the social scale' owned slaves, but that such a person aspired to owning a slave. In this case aspiration was probably unfulfilled. Note especially that the slave was sought to help, not replace, the master.

Where the household had only one slave, the slave lived and worked alongside the master as a partner, as Aristotle put it (*Pol.* 1260a39–40), drawing a contrast between the slave and the free artisan whose 'slavery' was 'limited' to his artisanal function. In such circumstances, the slave's principal economic function might be farming, fishing, herding or making objects for sale, but he would also help with everything else – marketing, performing religious rites, acting as a batman in war if the master were summoned to fight. On the verge of defeat in the Peloponnesian War, the citizens in the Assembly voted to override their own property rights, as private individuals, by offering freedom to any slave who volunteered for service in a forthcoming battle and survived it (the battle of Arginusae in 406 BC; Ar., *Frogs* 694). A later parallel is Hyperides' proposal to free slaves who came forward to defend the city against an attack by Philip II, which Hyperides anticipated (wrongly) after the Athenians were defeated at the battle of Chaeronea in 338 BC.

Reading 1.3 Space and social relationships in the Greek oikos of the Classical and Hellenistic periods

Source: Trümper, M. (2011) 'Space and social relationships in the Greek oikos of the Classical and Hellenistic periods', in Rawson, B. (ed.) *A companion to families in the Greek and Roman worlds.* Chicester: Wiley-Blackwell, pp. 33–34.

The Greek term *oikos* designates both the property and the members of a citizen household. Conceptually the *oikos* of the Classical period is often equated with the nuclear family that consisted of a couple and their children (and possibly slaves), inhabited a single-family home, and was organized along clear hierarchies and dichotomies: male-female, free-slave, and insider-outsider. It has recently been emphasized, however, that the (Athenian) *oikos* was not a static unit, but often a complex entity, which included various types of kinsmen (grandparents, aunts, etc.) and also non-kinsmen (slaves, friends, concubines, etc.) and owned more than one house. Consequently, houses could have accommodated various groups other than nuclear or extended families, and average household sizes cannot be safely calculated (Cox (1998) 130–208) [...] The contrast between male/outside/public and female/inside/private is thought to have significantly shaped Greek society and consequently men were often not at home. Houses were nevertheless the setting for important male activities such as the reception and entertainment of guests, notably during the *symposion* [symposium] (drinking party). Other typical daily activities of households mentioned in texts include storage, processing, preparation, and consumption of food; washing; textile production; upbringing of children; and the performance of domestic cult. Thus, literary sources evoke the ideal of an agrarian-based self-sufficiency and stigmatize an involvement of citizen households in non-agrarian [...] and mercantile activities (Ault (2007)). Households at the margins of Greek *polis*-societies – including, for example, the poor, non-citizens and communities at the boundaries of the Greek world – are little known and discussed, both in their socio-cultural significance and with a view to the traces that they might have left in the archaeological record (see, however, Ault and Nevett (2005)).

Reading 1.4 Demosthenes Speech 47

Source: Demosthenes (2011) *Speeches 39–49*. Translated by A.C. Scafuro. Austin, TX: University of Texas Press, pp. 317–319.

[…] Theophemus went and seized fifty soft-fleeced sheep of mine as they were grazing the pastures, and along with them, the shepherd and all accessories of the flock, and then a slave boy who was carrying a bronze pitcher, not ours but a borrowed one of great value. Even this was not enough for them; no, they rushed onto my property (I farm near the Hippodrome and have lived there ever since I was a boy). First, they darted after the household servants, but when these escaped them, fleeing in different directions, they went to the house and broke in the door leading to the garden. […] these men entered into the presence of my wife and children and carried off as much furniture as remained in the house. […]

In addition, judges, my wife chanced to be having lunch with the children in the courtyard and with her was an elderly woman who had been my nurse, a loyal and faithful creature whom my father had set free. […] They were having lunch in the courtyard when these men leapt in and found them and began to seize the furniture. When they heard the screaming, the rest of the female slaves (they were in the tower where they live) blocked off the tower, and although the men didn't enter there, they did carry off the furnishings from the rest of the house.

They did this in spite of the fact that my wife forbade them to touch anything and told them that the items were hers since they had been assessed in her dowry […] In spite of my wife's words, not only did they not stop their rampage but when the nurse took hold of the small cup that was set before her from which she had been drinking and when she put it in her bosom to prevent the men from seizing it since she saw they were inside the house, then the men—Theophemus and Evergus his brother—caught sight of her and treated her so brutally as they were wrenching the small cup away from her that her arms and wrists were all bloodied from having her hands twisted and pulled this way and that by them as they wrenched the cup away, and she had bruises on her throat from being strangled by them, and her chest was black and blue. Indeed, their meanness was such that they didn't stop throttling and striking the old woman until they had yanked the cup free from her bosom.

When my neighbours' servants heard the shrieking and saw my house being plundered, some from their own rooftops were calling out to passersby while others, going into another street and, seeing Hagnophilus passing by, urged him to come. And when Hagnophilus approached, summoned by the servant of Anthemion who is my neighbour, he didn't enter my house (for he thought it wasn't right to do so, at least not while its master was absent), but from his vantage point on Anthemion's property he saw the furniture being carried off and Evergus and Theophemus leaving my house.

Chapter 2
Rome: a world in one city

Written by Joanna Paul

Contents

1 Introduction

By the time Nero became emperor in 54 CE, Rome and its empire had been ruled by a ***princeps*** (a Latin word that we roughly translate as 'emperor') for well over half a century. Augustus, the first emperor, gained this title in 27 BCE, and successfully established the Julio-Claudian dynasty, succeeded in turn by the emperors Tiberius, Caligula, Claudius, and finally Nero himself. The *princeps* ruled over a vast (and still expanding) empire and benefited from its huge wealth, in both economic and cultural terms. The physical structures of the city of Rome were the most visible manifestations of this imperial power. Studying ancient cities can reveal a good deal about how the ancients defined their own identity and culture and about how they lived their lives on a day-to-day basis. In this chapter, though, we shift our focus from the more domestic, everyday structures of Classical Athens (which you studied in Chapter 1) towards one of the most grandiose palatial residences that the world has ever known.

Figure 1 Fragment of fresco from the ceiling of the Domus Transitoria. Photo: Scala, Florence – courtesy of the Ministero Beni e Att. Culturali e del Turismo.

Each of the Julio-Claudian emperors had been somewhat preoccupied with living in a private house or palace appropriate to the new office. Augustus was the first to set up a residence on the Palatine Hill (a part of the city that had always been an exclusive location for elite residences; it's where the English word 'palace' comes from), and this remained the preferred spot for official imperial palaces until Nero's time – although it did not always allow the space or seclusion that some emperors felt necessary. Tiberius, for example, spent much of his time in two large coastal **villas**, one at Sperlonga (midway along the coast between Naples and Rome), and one perched high on the cliffs on the island of Capri (in the Bay of Naples). Nero, too, aspired towards more grandiose living quarters, and *c*.60 CE, work began on his new palace project, the Domus Transitoria (the 'House of Transit' or 'Passage'). This would have extended from the Palatine Hill towards the Oppian Hill, the southernmost spur of the Esquiline Hill, and we know (from the very limited archaeological remains that have been identified on the Palatine, an example of which can be seen in Figure 1) that it was luxuriously decorated.

2 Nero and the Domus Aurea

A few years after the building of the Domus Transitoria commenced, a catastrophic event would result in a major change of direction for Nero's grand design.

2.1 The Great Fire of Rome

One night in July in the year 64 CE, a fire broke out in Rome, beginning in the neighbourhood of the **Circus Maximus**. It quickly spread and would burn for over a week. By the time it was fully extinguished, a huge part of the city had been destroyed. According to the ancient historian Cassius Dio, writing more than a century later, this could have been as much as two-thirds of Rome, but perhaps more likely – according to modern estimations – somewhere between a quarter and a third of the city (*History of Rome* 62.18.2; Cassius Dio, 1925). Whatever the causes of the fire (something we'll move on to consider in the next section), its consequences were fortuitous for Nero's architectural ambitions.

Although much of the Domus Transitoria was lost to the flames, Nero lost no time in ordering the construction of a new, far bigger palace complex, which would come to be known as the Domus Aurea, or 'Golden House'. Stretching from the Palatine to the slopes of the Oppian and beyond, the complex incorporated huge palatial structures in the style of luxury villas, a large artificial 'lake', extensive surrounding parkland, and probably in the *vestibulum* (vestibule) – its main ceremonial entranceway – a colossal statue of Nero himself. It was intended, no doubt, to stand as a grandiose and unavoidable statement of Nero's vision of Rome as a mighty imperial power – a city, and empire, whose culture was defined by the emperor himself at its very centre.

Activity 1

(Allow around 15 minutes to complete this activity.)

Keeping in mind the brief overview of the palace complex that you have just learned about, now read the following two short quotations from the Roman author and general, Pliny the Elder.

Pliny the Elder famously died in the eruption of the volcano Mount Vesuvius in 79 CE, but in the years before his death he was writing a great encyclopaedic work called the *Natural History*. The following quotes are two of several references to the Domus Aurea, which Pliny wrote about in this work:

> Twice have we seen the whole city girdled by imperial palaces, those of Gaius [Caligula] and Nero, the latter's palace, to crown all, being indeed a House of Gold.
>
> *(Natural History* 36.111; Pliny, 1962, p. 87)

> Yet how small was the theatre [of Pompey] in comparison with Nero's Golden Palace which goes all round the city!
>
> *(Natural History* 33.54; Pliny, 1952, p. 45)

Having read these two quotations, note down your thoughts on the following points:

1 What are the key characteristics of the Domus Aurea that Pliny highlights here?
2 Do you think that Pliny's descriptions of the palace are likely to be accurate?

Discussion

1 Pliny is clearly concerned to highlight the sheer size of the Domus Aurea by describing it as something that encircles the whole city of Rome. He emphasises its size in comparison to another building, the Theatre of Pompey. By describing the Domus Aurea as a 'House of Gold' and a 'Golden Palace', he also depicts it as a building of supreme luxury (and expense), as if it was built from this precious metal.
2 On the one hand, Pliny's observations were made relatively soon after the building of the palace (he was perhaps writing a decade or

so after its construction began) and you would probably be safe in assuming that he had seen it with his own eyes. On the other hand, the emphasis on the size surely seems to be an exaggeration. Are we really expected to imagine that the palace complex encompassed the *whole* city?

It would certainly seem reasonable to query whether Pliny's description of the Domus Aurea taking up the whole city is an accurate one, and to wonder whether any firm evidence for its size can corroborate Pliny's account. In fact, not much remains of the Domus Aurea today, but there is enough archaeological evidence to demonstrate its likely extent and appearance. The map in Figure 2 gives an indication of some of the structures of the palace complex, while Figure 3 offers an imaginative reconstruction of how it might have looked.

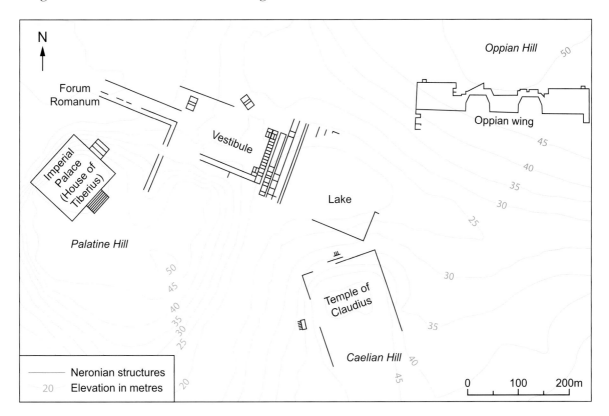

Figure 2 Map showing the likely structures of the Domus Aurea.

Figure 3 Reconstruction of the Domus Aurea. The light-coloured square structure slightly above the centre of the image is the lake, with the vestibule above it, while the Oppian Wing can be seen to the right-hand side of the image, running vertically towards the bottom of the frame. © Progetto KatatexiLux.

Certainly, it would have been a sprawling and very impressive imperial residence. The main archaeological remains are of just one part of the palace's buildings – a large structure of around 150 rooms stretching over 300 metres along the slope of the Oppian Hill. (In Figure 3, these are the buildings that occupy the bottom-right quarter of the image.) This structure is therefore sometimes referred to as the Oppian Wing or Pavilion (and sometimes as the Esquiline Wing since the Oppian is the southernmost spur of the Esquiline Hill). There would also have been a large structure on the Palatine Hill, although scarcely anything remains of this. But clearly, although huge, the Domus Aurea did not cover the whole city, suggesting that we need to take Pliny's assertions with a pinch of salt. This is a useful reminder that, as we now proceed to consider the rest of the evidence for the Domus Aurea, we should be on the lookout for the gaps and uncertainties that often exist between the sources and the likely reality of a structure such as this.

2.2 Archaeological evidence for the Domus Aurea

Let's now move on to look at the remains of the Oppian Wing in more detail. The plan in Figure 4 shows the layout of the rooms and also gives some indication of the difficulty of interpreting those archaeological remains today. Notice that the walls of the Domus Aurea are in black, but that there are also additional walls criss-crossing the structure, marked in grey. These are the walls of the Baths of Trajan, another enormous imperial building project that, in the early second century CE, was built directly on top of this part of the ruined palace. Many of the rooms in the Oppian Wing were preserved in the baths' subterranean foundations, but they remain underground and, with the baths' walls still cutting through some of the palace, it can be difficult to get a sense of the original impact of the building.

As one expert on the building notes, 'A visitor to the Esquiline wing must therefore exercise considerable imagination to get any sense of the original aesthetics' (Ball, 2003, p. 10). When the Domus Aurea was first rediscovered towards the end of the fifteenth century, visitors would descend into these underground 'grottoes' through holes dug down into the vineyards and gardens that had long since overtaken the Oppian Hill. And though the Oppian Wing can be visited today on a fascinating guided tour, the structures have been subject to regular and lengthy closures in recent years, when collapses caused by damp and the weight of the earth above them have made them unsafe.

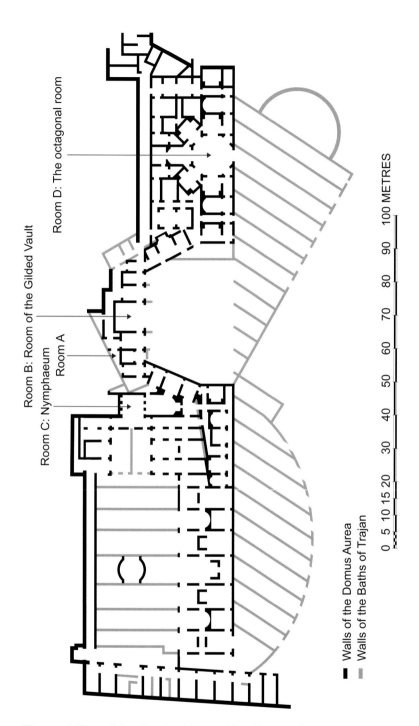

Figure 4 Plan of the Oppian Wing of the Domus Aurea.

Figure 5 Room of the Sphinx, Domus Aurea. Photo: ANSA.

Still, if you visited the Domus Aurea today, you would be able to get a sense of its grandeur through its sheer scale, and through the fragmentary remains of some of its splendid interior decorations. In the fifteenth century and beyond, famous Renaissance artists such as Raphael descended into the ruins (even leaving their names scratched into the walls in places!) and were astounded and deeply influenced by the Roman frescoes (wall paintings) that they saw on the walls. Although those paintings are now much more damaged by the passage of time, we are still able to get a sense of their impact.

The recent discovery of a previously unknown room, found in excavations at the end of 2018 and named as the 'Room of the Sphinx', is a useful example of just how inaccessible some of the palace's rooms are. (The location of this room is just to the north of where Room A is marked on the plan in Figure 4. At the time of writing, the discovery is so recent that the authoritative plan of the Domus Aurea has not yet been redrawn in order to show it.) Figure 5 shows how the space is filled with earth and rubble almost up to the height of the ceiling. But the image also reveals the finely painted and vividly coloured scenes, often incorporating characters and creatures drawn from the rich body of stories from Greek mythology (such as a **sphinx** – hence the modern labelling of the room as the 'Room of the Sphinx' – or the **centaur** shown in detail in Figure 6). These ancient Greek myths were a cultural and religious tradition that retained a great deal of significance for the Romans.

Figure 6 Detail of a centaur from a fresco in the Room of the Sphinx, Domus Aurea. Photo: ANSA.

Other frescoes depicted the architectural fantasies that were so popular with the Romans, such as the columnar structure seen on the far wall in the centre of the image in Figure 5. As well as frescoes and other such adornments to the palace structures, its rooms would also have been filled with splendid artworks, again drawing very heavily on the cultural prestige of the Greek world. Often these were acquired by the wholesale looting of the Greek sanctuaries and cities that were by now firmly under Roman control. For example, a later Greek author, Pausanias, tells us that the sanctuary at Delphi (the subject of Chapter 3, where you'll meet Pausanias again):

> was to suffer from the universal irreverence of Nero, who robbed Apollo [the god of the sanctuary] of five hundred bronze statues, some of gods, some of men.
>
> (Pausanias, *Description of Greece* 10.7.4; Pausanias, 1935, p. 403)

Greek statues were highly prized in the Roman world, and many of these 'acquisitions' would likely have ended up in the Domus Aurea as further manifestations of Nero's power and cultural aspirations.

Activity 2

(Allow around 30 minutes to complete this activity.)

Take a little time to look at the following Sources A to E. Sources A–D (Figures 7–10) all provide evidence for the decorations in the Domus Aurea's interiors and focus particularly on the Room of the Gilded **Vault** (Room B on the plan in Figure 4). You should also read the textual source (Source E), another description from Pliny's *Natural History*, which appears after the images.

While you are looking at the five sources, imagine that you were an important visitor to the palace in the 60s CE, perhaps an ambassador from another part of the Roman empire. What sort of impression of the emperor – and of Roman power more broadly – do you think you might have gained? How do the sources presented here help you in this thought experiment?

Source A

Figure 7 Painted ceiling of the room of the Gilded Vault, Domus Aurea.
Photo: ANDREAS SOLARO/AFP/Getty Images

As Figure 7 shows, the original decoration consisted of gilded **stucco** frames (now showing as white) surrounding elaborately painted panels, which consisted of figured scenes, geometrically arranged shapes and borders. The holes through which people originally descended into the room in the fifteenth and sixteenth centuries are clearly visible on the ceiling.

Source B

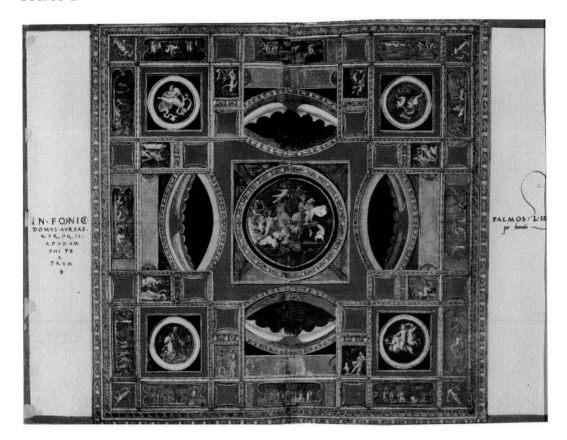

Figure 8 A sixteenth-century imaginative reconstruction of the painted ceiling in the Room of the Gilded Vault. 'Volta Dorata de la Domus Aurea', painting by Francisco de Hollanda in *Dos Desenhos das Antigualhas*, 1538.

This reconstruction (Figure 8) shows the likely content of some of the figured panels. They depicted various scenes from Greek mythology, including, perhaps, the abduction of Ganymede by Zeus and the story of Phaedra and Hippolytus.

Source C

Figure 9 A twenty-first-century digital reconstruction of the ceiling from the Room of the Gilded Vault. © Progetto KatatexiLux.

Figure 9 shows the extent of the gilded stucco as well as the glass panels that may have adjoined the vaulted ceiling. The use of glass and vaulted constructions were relatively innovative architectural features at the time.

Source D

Figure 10 Remains of a mosaic on the ceiling of the Domus Aurea's nymphaeum. Photo: Carole Raddato. Used under this licence: https://creativecommons.org/licenses/by-sa/2.0/.

A nymphaeum was a grotto-like room with water features that served as a kind of shrine to water nymphs. Its location in the Domus Aurea is marked as Room C on the plan in Figure 4. The mosaic (Figure 10) depicts a scene from Greek mythology: the hero Ulysses (Odysseus in Greek) encounters the monstrous one-eyed Cyclops, Polyphemus, an episode most famously recounted in Homer's epic poem, the *Odyssey*.

Source E

After a lengthy catalogue of sculptures by some of the Greek and Roman world's most famous artists (including the Greek artists Praxiteles, Myron, and Lysippus), Pliny remarks:

> And among the list of works I have referred to all the most celebrated have now been dedicated by the emperor Vespasian in the Temple of Peace and his other public buildings; they had been looted by Nero, who conveyed them all to Rome and arranged them in the sitting-rooms of his Golden Mansion.

(Pliny, *Natural History* 34.84; Pliny, 1952, pp. 189, 191)

Discussion

The evidence suggests that the interior decorations of Nero's palace were an important marker of his overwhelming power and status as emperor. An ambassador to the imperial court would surely have been impressed – perhaps overwhelmed – by such rich decorations as the ceiling in the Room of the Gilded Vault, and left in no doubt as to Nero's power to amass such wealth. Whether Figure 7's depiction of this room as it appears today provided much inspiration for this thought experiment is another matter entirely, though! You will no doubt have noticed how little now survives of the ceiling decorations, and perhaps relied on the two reconstructions to help fire your imagination – at the same time as wondering just how imaginative those reconstructions were themselves.

You might also have thought a little about the subject matter of some of the decor. Even without knowing the details of the stories from Greek mythology that were depicted, you might have wondered about the general effects of decorating the palace interiors with this kind of imagery. The heavy use of gilding and other precious materials always carried with it the possibility that Nero's luxurious tastes could be condemned as vulgar, or even immoral, but might the mythological subject matter have been intended to cast the emperor in a different light? By advertising his fascination with Greek culture through its mythology and its artworks, perhaps he intended to show his visitors that he was possessed of a more intellectual, refined set of cultural reference points.

At the same time, Pliny makes it clear just how much Nero exploited Greece by literally looting its famous statues and bringing them to Rome (and remember that Pausanias described his irreverence in plundering religious sanctuaries for statues that, in many cases, might actually have had an important religious function as cult images of a god or goddess). So, as a visiting ambassador, I imagine that I would have been impressed by Nero's evident wealth, and perhaps might have appreciated his learning on display through his mythological paintings and mosaics – but there's also every chance that I might have felt a little intimidated by such an obvious display of power; and, if those statues had come from my own province, perhaps even rather angry!

The previous activity has hopefully helped us to get closer to how Nero might have intended his palace to be seen in the 60s CE (at least by those visitors who were able to see inside it; we'll briefly return to the question of how publicly accessible the Domus Aurea was later in this chapter). In the process, we've gained some insight into how Roman elite culture defined itself at this point in time. As the historian Tom Holland describes it, 'The Golden House […] was to offer the Roman people nothing less than a vision of what it meant to rule the world' (2015, p. 385) – an architectural manifestation of Rome's supreme wealth. It also shows Roman imperial culture's ability to exploit and appropriate the cultural achievements of the Greek world, whether by depicting its myths on the walls and ceilings of the palace, or by forcibly transporting Greek artefacts to their own capital city – a useful reminder of how cultures are often shaped by lots of interweaving influences. And this was a city itself dominated by the power of the emperor, embodied in this unavoidable and ostentatious building complex right in the middle of the city. In fact, some historians suggest that one of the central motivations for building the Domus Aurea was to provide a ceremonial space in which to receive – and impress – the King of Armenia, Tiridates I, who visited Rome in 66 CE. As emperor, with access to extensive resources and with overwhelming power over others, Nero had the ability to manipulate this portion of Rome to his own ends, making a powerful new version of a place in order to demonstrate his own status.

A brief look at the archaeological evidence for the Domus Aurea has certainly been useful, but it only gets us so far. As we have seen, the remains are partial and difficult to interpret; and what we can access in the Oppian Wing is, as we know, only one part of a much larger project. It also gives us just one perspective on how Nero wished to present himself to the world. To gain a more complete view of the

Domus Aurea, then – what it incorporated, and what it tells us about Roman culture in the first century CE – we need to look beyond the archaeology.

2.3 Textual evidence for the Domus Aurea

Textual sources, like the brief extract from Pliny that you read in Activity 2, can provide full descriptions of the Domus Aurea. Nevertheless, just as the archaeology offers challenges to the modern historian or classicist (and is not always easy to access or interpret), so too do textual sources need to be treated carefully. In this section, we'll spend a little time looking at three key texts in some detail, considering whether the information they provide gives us a different view on the palace and its possible meanings.

Activity 3

(Allow around 30 minutes to complete this activity.)

Let's begin with the following short passage from a 'Life of Nero' written by the Roman historian Suetonius. Read the passage through quite quickly and answer the following questions:

1   What details of the Domus Aurea's physical structures does Suetonius provide? Do any of them correspond with the information that you gained from the brief look at the archaeology in Section 2.2?

2   Do you think that this is presenting a positive or negative depiction of the emperor?

> There was, however, nothing in which he was more prodigal than in construction, extending from the Palatine as far as the Esquiline the palace which he called first the House of Passage [Domus Transitoria], then, after it had been destroyed by fire and rebuilt, the Golden House [Domus Aurea]. It should suffice to relate the following concerning its extent and splendour. There was a vestibule area in which stood a colossal statue, one hundred and twenty feet tall, in the image of the emperor himself. So great was its extent that its triple colonnade was a mile in length. There was also a lake, which resembled the sea, surrounded by buildings made to look like cities. Besides this, there were grounds of all kinds, with fields and vineyards, pasture and woodland, and a multitude of all sorts of domestic and wild animals. Other

areas were all covered in gold and picked out with jewels and mother-of-pearl. The banqueting halls had coffered ceilings fitted with panels of ivory which would revolve, scattering flowers, and pipes which would spray perfume on those beneath. The principal banqueting chamber had a dome which revolved continuously both day and night, like the world itself. There were baths running with sea water and spa water. When the house was brought to completion in this style and he dedicated it, he said nothing more to indicate his approval than to declare that he had at last begun to live like a human being.

(Suetonius, *Life of Nero* 31; Suetonius, 2000, p. 211)

Discussion

1   I won't recount all of Suetonius' account here, but I'm sure you'll have been struck by the details he offers, which emphasise not only the size and grandeur of the complex (as did Pliny in the extracts you read in Activities 1 and 2) but also the rich sensory experience of the palace, with its sprays of perfume, running water and even entire rooms on the move! You hopefully also noticed that Suetonius' description of the luxurious interior decoration, with its use of gold and other precious materials, is in keeping with the evidence that you looked at in Section 2.2.

2   Suetonius does seem quite impressed with the palace; although perhaps the last line gives us pause for thought. Having just described such an opulent and excessive space, is there perhaps more than a touch of arrogance in Nero's reported statement that only now had he 'begun to live like a human being'?

Taken on its own terms, Suetonius' account would seem to provide some useful extra information about the scope and appearance of the Domus Aurea, and some scholars have attempted to match it up with the archaeological evidence; for example, it has been suggested that the large octagonal room (Room D on the plan in Figure 4) was the location of the banqueting chamber with a revolving dome. But it is important not to take the passage at face value and out of context. In order to understand how this passage might work as a source of historical evidence, we need to know a little more about its author and the kind of text he was writing. Suetonius was a scholar, writing in Rome in the late first and early second centuries CE, so some decades after Nero's reign. His most important work was a series of 'Lives' of 12 emperors of Rome stretching from Julius Caesar to Domitian (often referred to as the *Lives of the Caesars*). These texts were closer to modern biographies than conventional histories, with a focus on outlining the personality of the emperor rather than giving a blow-by-blow account of his reign. Each 'Life' focused on the virtues – or vices – of its subject, illustrated with often scandalous anecdotes. For Nero, the emphasis was quite firmly on the latter. Shortly before the passage that you have just read, Suetonius describes him like this:

> [26] At first the signs he [Nero] showed of insolence, lust, luxury, greed, and cruelty were gradual and covert and could be put down to the errors of youth, but even then it was clear to all that these vices were due not to his age but to his nature. As soon as night had fallen, he would throw on a freedman's cap [a kind of hat worn by freed slaves] or a wig and would go around the cook-shops and wander about the streets looking for amusement […] he was in the habit of setting upon people returning home from dinner and would hurt anyone who fought back […] [28] […] [a]ll were convinced that he had desired to sleep with his mother but was frightened off by her detractors […] [29] He prostituted his own body to such a degree that, when virtually every part of his person had been employed in filthy lusts, he devised a new and unprecedented practice as a kind of game, in which, disguised in the pelt of a wild animal, he would rush out of a den and attack the private parts of men and women who had been tied to stakes […] [30] He believed that the proper use for riches and wealth was extravagance and that people who kept an account of their expenses were vulgar and miserly, while those who squandered and frittered away their money were refined and truly splendid.
>
> (Suetonius, *Life of Nero* 26, 28–30; Suetonius, 2000, pp. 208–210)

Put simply, Suetonius' account of Nero needs to be seen not as an objective historical account but as a literary construction with a particular agenda, as the historian Susanna Morton Braund notes:

It will be obvious that Suetonius is in the business of passing judgements about his subjects. Analysis in terms of virtues and vices amounts to an invitation to see the *Caesars* as heroes or villains.

(2017, p. 132)

The end of Nero's reign, as you will soon see, made him – in Suetonius' eyes – very much a villain, characterised by cruelty, debauched tastes and a love of *luxuria* (a Latin concept denoting an excessive, often offensive, enjoyment of luxury).

Study note

Ancient texts are often broken down into shorter numbered sections. These numbers appear inside square brackets, like in Suetonius' extract. They are a useful way of finding your way around ancient texts, as the sections remain consistent, whatever translation or edition you are using.

Activity 4

(Allow around 15 minutes to complete this activity.)

Read Suetonius' passage from Activity 3 again:

There was, however, nothing in which he was more prodigal than in construction, extending from the Palatine as far as the Esquiline the palace which he called first the House of Passage [Domus Transitoria], then, after it had been destroyed by fire and rebuilt, the Golden House [Domus Aurea]. It should suffice to relate the following concerning its extent and splendour. There was a vestibule area in which stood a colossal statue, one hundred and twenty feet tall, in the image of the emperor himself. So great was its extent that its triple colonnade was a mile in length. There was also a lake, which resembled the sea, surrounded by buildings made to look like cities. Besides this, there were grounds of all kinds, with fields and vineyards, pasture and woodland, and a multitude of all sorts of domestic and wild animals. Other areas were all covered in gold and picked out with jewels and mother-of-pearl. The banqueting halls had coffered ceilings fitted with panels of ivory which would revolve, scattering flowers, and pipes which would spray perfume on those beneath. The principal banqueting chamber had a dome which revolved continuously both day and night, like the world itself. There were baths running with sea water and spa water. When the house was brought to completion in this style and he dedicated it, he said nothing more to indicate his approval than to declare that he had at last begun to live like a human being.

(Suetonius, *Life of Nero* 31; Suetonius, 2000, p. 211)

Knowing what you now know about Nero and Suetonius, what do you think this description of the Domus Aurea might actually have been intended to convey?

Do any different details stand out on a second reading? Do you now think that this would have been an accurate depiction of the palace?

Discussion

Although the palace might still *sound* awe-inspiring, we can now see that this emphasis on the overwhelming luxury is part of Suetonius' strategy to discredit Nero, and that the reader is meant to see it as evidence of his moral failings rather than of his superior status as an emperor. On a second reading, and with this context in mind, you might also have paused at some of the more mind-boggling details, such as the description of a lake resembling a sea, buildings resembling cities, baths running with sea water, or a dome that resembled the heavens themselves.

If we know that Suetonius was no fan of Nero, then we might see these details in a different light, as a way of suggesting that Nero was trying to convey *too much* personal power in his building project. Confirming this in the final sentence is very much a dig at the emperor's arrogance. We might then also wonder whether these details are themselves somewhat exaggerated by Suetonius in his attempt to give a particular view of Nero; just how big would a lake have to be in order for it to 'resemble a sea'?

This is certainly the approach to Suetonius that modern historians have advocated that we take. As Keith Bradley points out, Suetonius' intention was hardly likely to have been to provide a fully detailed account of the Domus Aurea; rather, 'he has selected those details which are characteristic of the extravagance of the palace since his immediate concern is still to illustrate Nero's *luxuria*' (1978, p. 169). In another passage in Suetonius' biography of the emperor, in which he describes the fire of Rome in 64 CE, his attitude to the emperor is clearer still.

Activity 5

(Allow around 15 minutes to complete this activity.)

Read the following passage from Suetonius and make notes on these questions:

1   Who does Suetonius blame for the fire, and what motivations does he attribute to the perpetrator?

2   How does this contribute to your interpretation of Suetonius' view of the Domus Aurea?

3   Do you think Suetonius' interpretation of events are likely to be accurate?

> Yet he spared neither the people nor the fabric of his ancestral city. When someone in general conversation quoted the Greek phrase 'When I am dead, let earth go up in flames', he responded, 'Rather, "while I live"', and acted accordingly. For, as if he were upset by the ugliness of the old buildings and the narrow and twisting streets, he set fire to the city, so openly indeed that some ex-consuls, when they came upon his servants equipped with kindling and torches on their property, did not stop them. He greatly desired some land near the Golden House, then occupied by granaries, and had them torn down and burnt using military machinery because their walls were made of stone. For six days and seven nights destruction raged and the people were forced to take shelter in monuments and tombs. During that time, besides the enormous number of apartment blocks, the houses of great generals of old, together with the spoils of battle which still adorned them, the temples of the gods, too, which had been vowed and dedicated by Rome's kings and later in the Punic and Gallic wars, and every other interesting or memorable

survival from the olden days went up in flames. Nero watched the fire from the tower of Maecenas, delighted with what he termed 'the beauty of the flames' and, dressed in his stage attire, he sang of 'the Fall of Troy'. And lest he should lose any opportunity of securing spoils and booty even from this, he undertook to have the corpses and ruins cleared at his own expense, allowing no one to come near the remains of their own property. Not merely receiving contributions but extorting them, he bled dry both the provinces and the fortunes of private individuals.

(Suetonius, *Life of Nero* 38; Suetonius, 2000, p. 217)

Discussion

1 Suetonius directly blames the 64 CE fire on Nero himself, accusing him of ordering his own servants to start the fire, and apparently quoting snippets of conversation, which he believes to be incriminating evidence. He is also very clear that Nero started the fire because he wanted to change the appearance of the city, primarily because he wanted to acquire land on which to continue and expand his palace-building projects.

2 This certainly shows that Suetonius could not have been impressed by the Domus Aurea in the way that the brief description that you read in Activities 3 and 4 suggested, at least when taken in isolation. Not only does Suetonius criticise the huge economic impact that Nero's crimes have had (both on 'the provinces and the fortunes of private individuals'), he also laments the fact that the fire destroyed so many 'interesting or memorable survival[s] from the olden days' in the form of old temples, monuments, battle spoils and other structures, all of which would have carried a great deal of importance in shaping and preserving Roman cultural identity.

3 As we saw in the last extract, Suetonius' agenda means that we might have cause to question its accuracy. Given his desire to present a negative depiction of Nero, you might well have stopped to wonder about the accuracy of this version of events – especially given the lurid and rather theatrical detail of Nero apparently dressing up as an actor so that he could sing of the Fall of Troy while he watched Rome burn.

The now notorious detail of Nero's apparent exploits during the fire is certainly a useful piece of evidence for the kind of cultural identity that Nero sought to embody. In fact, the account of him singing of the Fall of Troy gave rise to the well-known expression of Nero 'fiddling [i.e. playing a lyre] while Rome burned', behaviour which has inspired many iconic images of Nero in modern culture, particularly in films; Figure 11 is a poster for an early cinematic adaptation of a famous novel about Nero, *Quo Vadis* (1913). In Suetonius, this behaviour depicts him as a cultured individual, well versed in Greek mythology. But we must be much more sceptical of these explanations as historical evidence, and it would certainly be rare for any modern historian to assign blame to Nero for the fire.

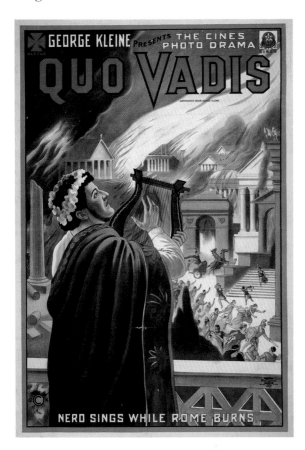

Figure 11 Poster from the silent film *Quo Vadis* (Cines, 1913), dir. Enrico Guazzoni, which tells the story of Nero and the Great Fire of Rome. Photo: Mary Evans/Library of Congress.

In fact, the fire was likely to have been a random event – catastrophic in its scale, but not unusual in a city where fires often blazed in crowded streets, surrounded by many wooden structures. Reading the passage in the previous activity again, you might see more clearly how little it conveys in terms of the facts (e.g. there is no date or location given for the fire). Instead, it focuses on the scandalous details that would support a portrait of Nero as a cruel tyrant, a megalomaniac who apparently burned down the city so that he could build a new one entirely in his own image and name it 'Neropolis' (Suetonius, *Life of Nero* 55; Suetonius, 2000, p. 226). This is not to say that rumours about Nero's culpability might not have been circulating in the aftermath of the fire, but there is no evidence that they were anything more than just rumours.

In case we are tempted to dismiss Suetonius as an isolated voice in this particular demonisation of Nero, let us turn to one last passage, this time from the Roman historian Tacitus, who was writing at about the same time as Suetonius, in the late first and early second centuries CE. His *Annals* are more recognisable to modern readers as a historical account, covering events from the death of Augustus, and his version of the fire is perhaps more circumspect than Suetonius', telling us, for example, that it was a 'rumour' that Nero had sung of the Fall of Troy while the city burned, rather than treating it as fact.

Activity 6

(Allow around 20 minutes to complete this activity.)

Read the following extract from Tacitus' *Annals* and try to answer the following questions:

1   What do you think are the most important characteristics of Tacitus' description of the Domus Aurea, and how does it compare to Suetonius?

2   What kind of judgement on Nero does Tacitus seem to be making?

> Of Rome's fourteen districts only four remained intact. Three were levelled to the ground. The other seven were reduced to a few scorched and mangled ruins. To count the mansions, blocks, and temples destroyed would be difficult. They

included shrines of remote antiquity, [...] the precious spoils of countless victories, Greek artistic masterpieces, and authentic records of old Roman genius. All the splendour of the rebuilt city did not prevent the older generation from remembering these irreplaceable objects. [...]

But Nero profited by his country's ruin to build a new palace. Its wonders were not so much customary and commonplace luxuries like gold and jewels, but lawns and lakes and faked rusticity – woods here, open spaces and views there. With their cunning, impudent artificialities, Nero's architects and engineers, Severus and Celer, did not balk at effects which Nature herself had ruled out as impossible.

[...]

In parts of Rome unfilled by Nero's palace, construction was not – as after the burning by the Gauls – without plan or demarcation. Street-fronts were of regulated dimensions and alignment, streets were broad, and houses built round courtyards. Their height was restricted, and their frontages protected by colonnades. Nero undertook to erect these at his own expense, and also to clear debris from building-sites before transferring them to their owners. He announced bonuses, in proportion to rank and resources, for the completion of houses and blocks before a given date. [...]

A fixed proportion of every building had to be massive, untimbered stone from Gabii or Alba (these stones being fireproof). Furthermore, guards were to ensure a more abundant and extensive public water-supply, hitherto diminished by irregular private enterprise. Householders were obliged to keep fire-fighting apparatus in an accessible place; and semi-detached houses were forbidden – they must have their own walls. These measures were welcomed for their practicality, and they beautified the new city.

(Tacitus, *Annals* 15; Tacitus, 1996, pp. 363–365)

Study note

Don't worry about the specifics of the place names that are mentioned in this extract (such as Gabii and Alba) – although remember you can use online reference tools like the *Oxford Dictionary of the Classical World* to look up such details if you're interested.

Discussion

1 Tacitus does not give a very lengthy description of the palace, but there is an interesting contrast with Suetonius. Tacitus highlights that the Domus Aurea was a remarkable place, not because of its conventional luxuries but because of the way in which it offered an artificial version of the natural world – 'faked rusticity', in Tacitus' words. (Indeed, if you look back at the reconstruction of the complex in Figure 3, you can gain a sense of the extent of its green spaces.)

2 The overall tone in this paragraph certainly seems disapproving – Tacitus describes Nero as 'profit[ing] by his country's ruin', and describes the artificial creation of nature in the palace grounds as 'cunning' and 'impudent'. Nero here – or at least his architects – are effectively being accused of crimes against nature. But you might also have noticed that a little further on in the passage, Tacitus spends some time talking about some positive aspects of Nero's rebuilding of the city after the fire – ensuring that structures were rebuilt in more uniform ways, using fireproof materials and in a timely way, for example – measures that Tacitus says were 'welcomed for their practicality'. This compares interestingly with the extract from Suetonius that you read in the previous activity (Activity 5), which mentions that Nero took responsibility for organising the clearance of debris after the fire, but here with the implication that it was for his personal benefit ('securing spoils and booty'), rather than in order to help the people of the city.

Tacitus' brief description of the Domus Aurea is an interesting additional piece of evidence for how the complex might have been perceived as a new and very deliberate manipulation of urban space. The archaeological record gives us no real insight into what the totality of the palace and its grounds might have been like, but Tacitus suggests that for many Romans of the time, it might have been seen as much *more* than just a palace. By apparently incorporating all these elements of the natural world – lakes, forests and wild animals, for example – it became 'a microcosm of the world in a new paradisiacal existence: a lake surrounded by miniature cities, farms and wild countryside, humans and animals, representing the *Imperium Romanum* [the Roman Empire], with the Mediterranean Sea at its heart' (Mratschek, 2013, p. 52). It was almost as if Nero's ambitions and his sense of his own power and status were so excessive that he sought to make this one corner of the capital city represent the entire world.

2.4 Assessing the evidence

Through exploring the archaeological and textual evidence in the last two sections of this chapter, you have hopefully begun to see some of the challenges in gaining a complete and accurate picture of the Domus Aurea, and the ways in which it was interpreted even in antiquity. Such an ambitious project must have played an important role in the city and dominated Nero's vision of Roman culture, but its limited physical remains make it very difficult to tell what it looked like in its entirety. The textual evidence, while providing valuable pieces of information, also has to be treated very carefully. Look back at the notes that you made on Nero at the beginning of this study week and remind yourself of the catastrophic end to his reign. Having made so many enemies in the latter part of his rule, by the time of his death Nero was deeply unpopular with much of the Roman elite, which explains the view that historians like Suetonius and Tacitus took of him. His bad reputation only solidified as time went on. As we also learn from Tacitus, Nero actually made Christians (at that time a newly emerging religious sect) the scapegoats for the fire and executed many of them in gruesome spectacles in the Circus Maximus (*Annals* 15.44; Tacitus, 1996, pp. 365–366). This persecution would become notorious, to such an extent that Nero was soon regarded as nothing less than the Antichrist himself.

Nero thus becomes subject to a kind of mythologising, in which it became traditional to depict him as a monster, complicating our attempts to know what the historical reality of his reign was. Whatever the emperor intended his remodelling of Rome to communicate, he couldn't fully control its message; especially after his death when the Domus Aurea itself had soon largely disappeared and its memory was preserved – and easily turned against him – in texts written by historians with their own agenda. As the scholar Jaś Elsner explains,

> What is at stake is whether what Nero did [in building the Domus Aurea] was by definition outrageous by every standard of Roman taste and decorum (as the literary sources imply) or whether it *became* the supreme symbol for outrageousness only when (and because) Nero was overthrown.
>
> (1994, pp. 122–123)

The task of a modern historian is therefore to sift through the evidence that we do have in an attempt to come up with a more balanced view.

Activity 7

(Allow around 15 minutes to complete this activity.)

Read the following passage, in which Elsner explains in a little more detail how our interpretation of the Domus Aurea is shaped by the kinds of sources that we have available to us. Then, summarise the key points of his argument in three or four bullet points.

> In effect, Nero only became an outrageous and prodigal builder when he fell from power. Then, the rhetoric of history turned against him and he was condemned in every respect – especially in the most visible and rhetorically potent elements in his reign, his private life and his public works. Essentially, the ancient historians made a brilliant and persuasive job of reversing causalities. Their combined argument was that the outrageous nature of Nero's actions, epitomised by murder and debauchery in private and by buildings and theatrical antics in public, caused his fall. My suggestion is that, at least in the context of his buildings, their outrageousness, and the polemic poured upon them, were not a cause but, in fact, the result of his fall.
>
> By being toppled, Nero did more than end the Julio-Claudian dynasty. He ended also the radical nature of early imperial experimentation with the city of Rome. The *Domus Aurea* became the ultimate, notorious, stage in the Julio-Claudian pattern of luxurious encroachment onto the rest of the city,

begun as early as the extensions of Augustus' house on the Palatine into a palace under Tiberius. As such, and as the supreme monument of an emperor instantly vilified, it was – along with Nero's building projects in general – damned by the rhetoric of history.

(1994, pp. 123–124)

Discussion

The main points that I took from Elsner's argument were:

- Historians writing soon after Nero's downfall decided that his behaviour and lavish building projects were symbols of his scandal and immorality, which directly led to his fall.

- In fact, suggests Elsner, a project like the Domus Aurea was probably not viewed as scandalous and immoral *before* Nero's death. Instead, this negative view was only *retrospectively* applied to it by the historians seeking to discredit Nero.

- The negative impact of the historians' damning verdict on Nero and his building put an end to other emperors attempting similarly ambitious projects.

In this brief tour of one of the most notorious and yet mysterious buildings of ancient Rome, then, we have seen how one ruler attempted to remodel a particular site in the city in order to say something significant about his own power and cultural pre-eminence. At the same time, we have learned some important lessons about the difficulties that modern scholars face in trying to access, reconstruct and understand ancient places. Trying to understand this expression of Roman imperial culture in full presents certain challenges and requires us to tackle different bits of fragmentary evidence in careful, critical ways.

3 The Colosseum

One way that we can make some progress in trying to understand the Domus Aurea – and Roman imperial culture more broadly – is to look at what came after it. In just a few short years, the use of this particular bit of urban space, and the cultural meanings that it would convey, would radically change again.

3.1 Building a new dynasty

As previously mentioned, on Nero's death, the Domus Aurea was regarded as one of the most obvious symbols of this now hated emperor. It was seen to represent a particular version of Roman imperial culture that his successors, unsurprisingly, wanted to distance themselves from. This was a regime in which a huge part of the city could be appropriated and manipulated by the very highest level of society. Even if the city's devastation in the Great Fire was not caused by the emperor, its remodelling was certainly exploited as a means of conveying, in unmistakable terms, his overwhelming power. That said, we must guard against being too quick to assume that the whole expanse of the Domus Aurea was intended only for the imperial court and was totally cut off from the inhabitants of the city.

In your study of Chapter 1 'Athens: places and people', you've already had the chance to see how houses in ancient Athens were not necessarily subject to the same clear distinctions between 'public' and 'private' as we might apply to domestic spaces in the modern world. So too, in Rome, 'imperial palaces were not 'private' in any modern sense of the word' (Elsner, 1994, p. 121). Therefore, it was probably the case that many citizens could roam around Nero's huge parklands, for example, or cross the grounds using the major arterial roads that may have still bisected the area. In so doing, they would have been an important audience for the message that Nero intended the overall palace complex to convey; restricting access to only elite visitors would surely have been a missed opportunity.

Nevertheless, even if the Domus Aurea grounds were more accessible than we might first assume, that didn't stop many elite Romans being alarmed by what Nero's use of urban space represented. (This was especially the case for those who were more conservative and who missed the seemingly more morally upright days of the **Republic**, the political system that had governed Rome for centuries.) Nero's palace complex could be seen as replicating the kind of rural or seaside villas where Romans would go to spend their leisure time (in Latin, *otium*) on a massive scale. Bringing the countryside into the city in this way was seen as a real subversion of political space. It was a conscious choice to emphasise a version of Roman culture that privileged luxury, playfulness, rest and frivolous pursuits. While this might have been welcome to many, it was a far cry from the more conservative, dutiful, militaristic and morally upright version of Roman identity that had been celebrated under the Republic. (Reflecting on Activity 6, this helps to explain Tacitus' disapproving description of the grounds as 'faked', 'cunning', and 'impudent' in their artificial version of nature in the city.)

So when Nero died, his opponents (who had fought against his increasing despotism for some years, and had finally gained the upper hand by overthrowing him) could very easily spin the Domus Aurea as a transgressive, immoral – perhaps even 'un-Roman' – place. The year following Nero's death was politically turbulent. 69 CE is known as the 'Year of the Four Emperors': initially succeeded by Galba, we know that the next two emperors, Otho and Vitellius, continued to inhabit Nero's palace. But the fourth emperor, Vespasian (who came to power by the end of 69 CE and would rule for a decade), had firm ideas about a different fate for the site.

3.2 An amphitheatre for the people

Vespasian's plans were bold. Although there is no evidence to suggest that the Domus Aurea's structures were entirely demolished (indeed, the rooms of the Oppian Wing were probably repurposed as barracks and storage rooms for many years), the area of the grounds that had included the large lake, in the valley between the hills, was now to be the site of a huge **amphitheatre** (Figure 12). For the new emperor, there was no better way to signal that he was returning this large expanse of central Rome to the Roman people.

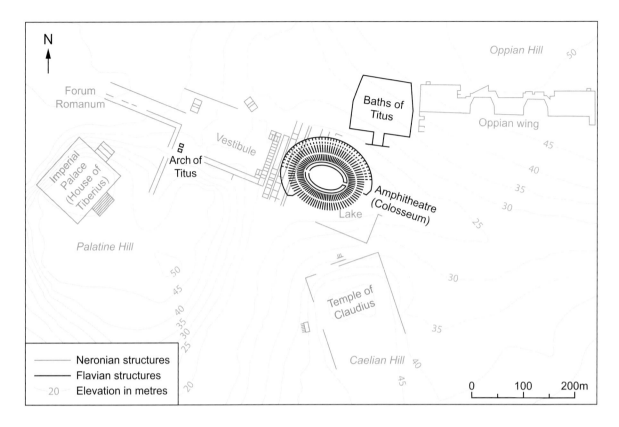

N

Forum Romanum

Oppian Hill   50

Baths of Titus

Oppian wing

45

Imperial Palace (House of Tiberius)

Arch of Titus

Vestibule

40

35

Amphitheatre (Colosseum)

30

25

Lake

Palatine Hill

50

45

40

35
30
25

Temple of Claudius

30

35

Caelian Hill   40

45

20

Neronian structures
Flavian structures
20 — Elevation in metres

0   100   200m

Figure 12 Map showing the likely structures of the Domus Aurea superimposed with the locations of later buildings.

Though we know this building today as the Colosseum (Figure 13) (and sometimes as 'the **Flavian** Amphitheatre'), it was, in antiquity, most likely known as simply 'the Amphitheatre'. It provided (for the first time) a permanent central – and monumental – location in which Romans could enjoy the spectacular shows of the gladiatorial games. After you have read this chapter, we'll explore these games in more detail. By considering the games alongside the building in which they took place, we'll see how some aspects of Roman culture could be much more dependent on mass popular participation than the more elite function of the Domus Aurea. At the same time, it is important to understand that the Colosseum was an important means of political manipulation, just as Nero's palace was. Let's begin to investigate these important themes with a short reading from a book written by the historians Keith Hopkins and Mary Beard.

Figure 13 The Colosseum today. Photo: Givaga/Alamy.

Activity 8

(Allow around 1 hour to complete this activity.)

Turn to Reading 2.1 at the end of this chapter, which is an extract from Hopkins and Beard's, *The Colosseum*. Read it carefully and make notes on the following questions:

1   How had gladiatorial games been staged in Rome before the Colosseum was built?

2   Why were politicians and rulers reluctant to build permanent amphitheatres, especially under the Republic?

3   What kind of role did the permanent amphitheatre take on under the emperors?

You will hopefully have found Hopkins and Beard's discussion to be accessible and informative, and so there is no discussion provided for this activity.

Your reading in Activity 8 has introduced you to the significance of this new building, showing you how it transformed the space that had been previously occupied by the Domus Aurea. This was now a place in which the emperor could come 'face to face with his people' (Hopkins and Beard, 2005, p. 36), rather than being largely set apart from them in an excessively luxurious residence. Although still associated with leisure pursuits, the gladiatorial games were seen as quintessentially Roman, rather than being associated with the Eastern-influenced indolence of a luxurious villa. The games were a valuable means of demonstrating Roman military prowess, virtue and valour (and it is significant that the fact that the construction was funded 'from the spoils of war' was explicitly advertised in an inscription that appeared on its exterior). Moreover, the Colosseum itself became a 'political theatre' exploited 'by the emperor to manipulate his own image, and by the people to express their will' (Coleman, 2006, p. lxxii).

Vespasian died before the Amphitheatre could be completed, but he was succeeded by his son Titus, under whom its inaugural (first) gladiatorial games were held over a period of 100 days in 80 CE. Some valuable textual accounts of those games survive, particularly in a collection of poems generally known by the title *De Spectaculis* ('On the Spectacles'), written by the poet Martial, who was born in modern Spain in *c.*40 CE before moving to Rome in his twenties. His preferred poetic genre was the **epigram**, and he wrote hundreds of these short poems, often witty and satirical in tone, on a multitude of different subjects. He was also what might be called the 'in-house poet of the imperial court' (Hopkins and Beard, p. 24), so it is unsurprising that the tone of *De Spectaculis* is overtly celebratory, as the opening poem in the collection makes clear:

> Let savage Memphis speak not of the Wonders that are her Pyramids; let Assyrian labour glory not in its Babylon; let the soft Ionians win no praise for their Temple of the Crossroads Goddess [Artemis]; let the close-packed altar of antlers lure no crowds to Delos; let not the Carians' immoderate praises elevate their Mausoleum, swaying in empty air, unto the stars. Each labour resigns its title in favour of the Amphitheatre of the Caesars, and Fame shall speak of one marvel in place of all.
>
> (Martial, *De Spectaculis* 1; Martial, 2015, p. 3)

Here, some of the canonical Seven Wonders of the World – from the Hanging Gardens of Babylon to the spectacular Mausoleum of Halicarnassus – are catalogued, but, according to Martial, all are found wanting when set against the new amphitheatre. Its future reputation is secure (almost as if Martial knew how it would still be revered as a symbol of Roman culture in the twenty-first century): the Colosseum is already seen as an embodiment of Roman supremacy, the only thing that 'Fame' need trouble herself with now.

Translating Latin poetry

You might have noticed that, although Martial was introduced as a poet, the first extract that you have just read doesn't look much like a poem! In this recent translation of Martial, Gideon Nisbet chose to translate the Latin poetry as prose, as do a good many other translators of ancient poetry.

There are a number of reasons for this. Some translators may decide that their central aim is to produce a clear, accessible and fluent version of the original Latin, rather than one that reflects its stylistic and formal features.

Latin (and Greek) poetry was based on particular rhythmic structures, or metres, rather than things like rhyme schemes. These metres are often quite complex and can be very difficult to capture or represent in translation. That said, many modern translators have produced poetic versions of ancient literature, which stand out as powerful pieces of literature in their own right. But all translations are aimed at different audiences and have different intentions, and ultimately it is for the translator (and reader) to decide which strategy best suits their needs.

Here are the first few lines of Martial's Latin, to give you a flavour of the original language – but don't worry, there's no expectation that you'd be able to read or pronounce any of this!

Barbara pyramidum sileat miracula Memphis,

Assyrius iactet nec Babylona labor;

nec Triviae templo molles laudentur Iones,

dissimulet Delon cornibus ara frequens

Study note

In the following activity, Martial's poem mentions a few different city locations and structures. You don't need to know any details about them, but the following summaries might help (as will referring back to the map in Figure 12). Note, too, that 'Caesar' is a title that refers to all emperors; here, Martial is addressing Titus.

Colossus of the Sun: the colossal statue of Nero, sometimes interpreted as being in the form of the sun god, Apollo, which stood in the Domus Aurea's grand entrance area.

towering cranes: scholars are uncertain about what this relates to; it may refer to the masts that supported the giant awnings over the Amphitheatre, or perhaps scaffolding that was being used for the construction of the Arch of Titus.

baths: the Baths of Titus opened in 81 CE, probably remodelling the Domus Aurea's baths for public use.

Claudian Portico: located south of the Amphitheatre, the portico was part of a large platform that had been built out from the crest of the Caelian Hill, as the supporting structure for the Temple of Claudius.

Activity 9

(Allow around 15 minutes to complete this activity.)

Now read the next poem in Martial's collection and make notes on these questions:

1   How does Martial continue his celebration of the Flavian Amphitheatre (the Colosseum) in this poem?

2   What kind of opinion of Nero does Martial offer here?

> Here, where the Colossus of the Sun views the stars close at hand and towering cranes rise up in mid-street, the hateful halls of a bestial king once dazzled, when in all Rome stood

just one house. Here, where the spectacular Amphitheatre's
hallowed bulk is being raised up, was Nero's lake. Here,
where we marvel at the baths—gifts to the people, swift in
coming—a regal estate had robbed the poor of their homes.
Where the Claudian Portico spreads out generous shade,
ended the palace's most distant wing. Rome is given back to
herself, Caesar, and under your guardianship her former
master's pleasures belong to her people.

(Martial, *De Spectaculis* 2; Martial, 2015, p. 3)

Discussion

1   The main tactic of this poem is a methodical and repetitive
comparison between what *used* to be on this site (the Domus Aurea)
and what is there *now* (the Colosseum). You might have noticed the
repetition of the phrase 'here, where…', which has the effect of
making us feel like we're standing on the spot with the poem's
narrator, looking in awe at the things that he's pointing out in front of
us – the 'spectacular Amphitheatre' and its associated structures,
such as the baths and the portico. These things are impressive and
welcome in their own right – the Amphitheatre is 'hallowed', the
building of the baths was 'swift', the portico offers shade – but the
praise of the Amphitheatre gains so much more significance by being
explicitly contrasted with what used to be there.

2   In his references to the palace, Martial is clearly taking the same
approach as would later be seen in the written sources you've
already studied, especially those of Suetonius, by using the Domus
Aurea as a symbol of everything that was wrong with Nero and his
regime. Although the palace 'dazzled' – reminding us that it too was
visually impressive – Martial again plays up (or exaggerates?) its
size, pointing out its 'distant wing' and telling us that it was as if one
house had taken over all of Rome, 'robb[ing] the poor of their homes'
in the process. And lest we should be in any doubt about what these
comparisons mean, Martial explicitly refers to the disgraced emperor
as a 'bestial king', living in a 'hateful' palace, before ending with an
address to the new emperor, Titus, praising him for having returned
Rome 'to herself'.

Martial's conclusion to *De Spectaculis* 2, then, outlines how the use of this part of Rome seemed to have radically changed thanks to the new dynasty of Flavian emperors. The provision of pleasures was still its main purpose, as Martial makes clear in the final line of the poem, but these were now pleasures provided for the masses, offering a sense of a shared culture that went far beyond the elite enjoyments housed in the Domus Aurea.

4 Summary

In this chapter, you've had the opportunity to learn about Nero's
Domus Aurea in considerable detail – hopefully realising, in the
process, that we have to be careful not to take the sources that we
have at face value. For such an extensive building project, its
archaeological remains are incomplete and its textual sources are
subject to their authors' particular ideological agendas. Only by
carefully assessing this evidence, and paying attention to what is
missing as much as to what is present, can we arrive at a balanced and
realistic account of what Nero's grand remodelling of the centre of
Rome meant. Nevertheless, despite these challenges, we have begun to
understand just how important this palace was as a means by which
Nero could make bold statements about his personal power and
cultural tastes, and by extension, the overwhelming power and
magnificence of the Roman empire. Moving on to look at how quickly
this imperial vanity project could be replaced by a very different kind
of building, the Colosseum, we've begun to see how an emperor could
make very different decisions about what to do with urban space.

You should now return to the module website to continue your
study of this unit.

References

Ball, L.F. (2003) *The Domus Aurea and the Roman architectural revolution*. Cambridge and New York, NY: Cambridge University Press.

Bradley, K.R. (1978) *Suetonius' Life of Nero: an historical commentary*. Collection Latomus Vol 157. Brussels: Latomus.

Braund, S.M. (2017) *Understanding Latin literature*. 2nd edn. London and New York, NY: Routledge.

Cassius Dio (1925) *Roman History, volume VIII: books 61–70*. Translated from the Greek by E. Cary and H.B. Foster. Loeb Classical Library 176. Cambridge, MA: Harvard University Press.

Coleman, K. (2006) *M. Valerii Martialis Liber spectaculorum*. Edited by K. Coleman. Oxford: Oxford University Press.

Elsner, J. (1994) 'Constructing decadence: the representation of Nero as imperial builder', in Elsner, J. and Masters, J. (eds) *Reflections of Nero: culture, history and representation*. Chapel Hill, NC: University of North Carolina Press, pp. 112–127.

Holland, T. (2015) *Dynasty: the rise and fall of the House of Caesar*. London: Little, Brown.

Hopkins, K. and Beard, M. (2005) *The Colosseum*. London: Profile Books.

Martial (2015) *Epigrams*. Translated from the Latin by G. Nisbet. Oxford: Oxford University Press.

Mratschek, S. (2013) 'Nero the imperial misfit: philhellenism in a rich man's world', in Buckley, E. and Dinter, M. (eds) *A companion to the Neronian age*. Malden, MA and Oxford: Wiley-Blackwell, pp. 45–62.

Pausanias (1935) *Description of Greece, volume IV: books 8.22–10 (Arcadia, Boeotia, Phocis and Ozolian Locri)*. Translated from the Greek by W.H.S. Jones. Loeb Classical Library 297. Cambridge, MA: Harvard University Press.

Pliny (1952) *Natural History, volume IX: Books 33-35*. Translated from the Latin by H. Rackham. Loeb Classical Library 394. Cambridge, MA: Harvard University Press.

Pliny (1962) *Natural History, volume X: Books 36-37*. Translated from the Latin by D.E. Eichholz. Loeb Classical Library 419. Cambridge, MA: Harvard University Press.

Suetonius (2000) *Lives of the Caesars*. Translated from the Latin by C. Edwards. Oxford: Oxford University Press.

Tacitus (1996) *The annals of imperial Rome*. Translated from the Latin by G. Grant. London: Penguin.

Readings

Reading 2.1 *The Colosseum*

Source: Hopkins, K. and Beard, M. (2005) *The Colosseum*. London: Profile Books, pp. 36–41.

The symbolic power of the Colosseum in ancient Rome depended also on political issues that went far beyond the immediate circumstances of its construction. It came to be seen as one of the most important arenas (in the metaphorical as well as the literal sense) in which the emperor came face to face with his people – and to stand as a symbol of the encounter between autocrat and those he ruled. To understand how and why this was so, we need to consider briefly the wider context of the history of Roman politics – and the history of amphitheatres.

For us, the Colosseum is such a well-known part of the Roman skyline that it is easy to forget that, in the AD 70s, the construction of a huge stone amphitheatre in the centre of the city constituted a break with tradition. To be sure, other Italian and provincial cities in the Roman empire had long had amphitheatres of their own: for example, Pompeii (the earliest surviving amphitheatre from about 70 BC), Verona and Milan in Italy, Lyon in France, Merida in Spain and Carthage in Tunisia. And many more were to come as far afield as Jerusalem and London (where remains of the structure roughly contemporary with the Colosseum were discovered under the Guildhall in 1988). In Rome, however, before the Colosseum was built, people had generally watched gladiatorial shows in temporary structures. True, a Roman aristocrat in the reign of the emperor Augustus (31 BC to AD 14) had built a smallish amphitheatre at least partly in stone. But this was hardly grand enough for big shows (certainly the emperor Caligula is reported to have looked down his nose at it) and, in any case, like so much else in the capital, it had been burnt down in Nero's great fire of 64. Standard practice was to build a wooden amphitheatre and take it down when the shows were over, or to make use of public buildings designed with other purposes in mind. Massive shows were occasionally given in the Circus Maximus, where chariot races were held, or in the so-called Voting Pens (or 'Saepta', the vast structure designed to accommodate mass voting by Roman citizens); but both venues were too large for normal displays. More often the gladiators performed in the Forum itself, the audience watching from wooden benches, which would have been dismantled at the end of the day.

Some of these temporary structures, and their fittings, were impressive enough in their own right. Pliny, the insufferable polymath and moraliser who was killed in the eruption of Vesuvius in AD 79, claims that the vast awning which Julius Caesar on one occasion used to cover the whole of the Forum, from one end to the other, was thought more 'amazing' than the gladiatorial show itself. And he tells in gleeful horror of a 'mad fantasy in wood' constructed by one of Cicero's friends in the first century BC. This consisted in two adjacent semicircular wooden theatres, mounted on revolving pivots, which could be swivelled together to make a completely enclosed *amphi*theatre. Apparently, rather like coupling a train with the passengers on board, the whole operation of joining the two halves could be carried out with the spectators in their seats. Pliny was appalled: 'Just imagine the people who have conquered the earth and have subdued the whole world, who govern tribes and kingdoms, who give their laws to the outside world, who are, you might say, a part of heaven on earth – just imagine them balanced on the contraption and applauding their own danger!' Many more Romans, we suspect, would have been impressed at the splendid ingenuity of the device. Certainly, a poet in the reign of Nero imagines two rustics visiting the city overwhelmed by the sight of the emperor's new wooden amphitheatre (even without the mechanical sophistication). They stand 'rooted to the spot, mouth agape' and (in terms reminiscent of Constantius' reported reactions to the Colosseum) they reckon that it is almost as high as the Capitoline hill itself.

Of course, it was not – even if, as Pliny claimed, the largest tree ever seen at Rome, a vast larch that produced a log 40 metres long, was used in its construction. However extravagantly these earlier structures might be written up, in the late first century the Colosseum was something new for the city of Rome itself, in scale and permanence. Why did the innovation of a permanent amphitheatre take so long?

Traditionally, the Roman elite had always been chary of building in Rome a permanent monument to pleasure. It smacked too much of the luxury and decadence that Romans were anxious simultaneously to embrace and to avoid. More importantly yet, in the period of the

Republic (conventionally dated from around 500 to 31 BC), when Rome was governed by elected officials or 'magistrates' and by a Senate made up largely of ex-magistrates – all of them wealthy aristocrats – senators may have been realistically afraid of providing a venue where the mass of citizens could express their views collectively and vociferously. It did not matter much to the Senate what citizens in Pompeii or Bologna thought or did (though a riot in the amphitheatre at Pompeii under the emperor Nero in AD 59 was severely punished by a ten-year ban on gladiator shows). But in Rome itself under the Republic, citizens had a much more direct influence over the passage of laws and the election of senators to further offices. At the same time, citizen voters were also then, potentially at least, soldiers. Their power to vote was a reflection of their power to fight, and vice versa. Mass gatherings, even if apparently for pleasure, must have seemed a dangerous commodity in the eyes of the elite.

That changed in significant ways with the advent of the Roman emperors. By the mid first century BC the Republican system of government had imploded. Out of a series of civil wars, juntas and dictatorships (culminating in the one-man rule and assassination in 44 BC of Julius Caesar), a more-or-less hereditary monarchy emerged, under the first emperor or 'princeps', Augustus. Under the emperors, the bulk of the army was dispersed along distant frontiers and soldiers were recruited predominantly from provincials. The citizens of Italy, with the vital exception of the Palace Guard, were effectively disarmed. And so it became practicable for the emperors to disenfranchise citizens living in Rome. Soon (even if not immediately with the advent of monarchy) elections were transferred from people to Senate. The once warlike 'masters of the [Western] world', as the Roman poet Virgil called them, were – to give it the most cynical spin – gratefully bribed with monthly distributions of free wheat and with frequent shows. This disenfranchisement of the Roman people was probably not part of a magnificently conceived master plan. But, however it evolved, it significantly increased monarchical power. The process is nicely symbolised by the history of the Voting Pens. The emperor Augustus, in honour of Rome's long tradition of popular participation in politics, had erected these to upgrade the old Republican voting enclosure. They were the largest covered building in Rome. If initially citizen voting continued, however, by the end of the first century AD these Pens were no longer used for voting. Instead they had become a venue for large shows, as we have seen, and a giant supermarket for antiques. Democracy, in the traditional sense, was almost dead.

By the time the Colosseum was inaugurated in AD 80, monarchy was so firmly entrenched that emperors could readily risk, even periodically enjoy, confronting their citizen-subjects collectively. More than that, it was essential to their power-base that they should see, and – even more crucially – be seen by, the people at large. Whatever the harsher realities, there was always the ideal or myth that citizens had the right of access to the emperor, to ask a favour, to correct an injustice, to hand in a petition. One illusion on which the Roman monarchy was founded was that the emperor was only the first aristocrat among equals, and one of the emperor's titles right from the beginning cast him in the role of Tribune (or Protector) of the People. No other ancient monarchy, whether in Persia, Egypt, India or China, ever staged such regular meetings between ruler and subjects. In fact, an ancient Chinese visitor to the Roman empire thought the public accessibility of the emperor quite extraordinary: 'When the king goes out he usually gets one of his suite to follow him with a leather bag, into which petitioners throw a statement of their case; on arrival at the palace, the king examines the merits of each case.'

Of course, the Roman people had their fond illusions too: they thought that they could, occasionally at least, collectively influence what the emperor did by letting their rhythmically chanted views be heard.

There were other locations, to be sure, where the emperor could confront his people: in the Forum, for example, or in the Circus Maximus. But the Forum was small by comparison, and the Circus was if anything too huge to concentrate the popular voice. The Colosseum was a brilliantly constructed and enclosed world, which packed emperor, elite and subjects together, like sardines in a tin. Its steeply serried ranks of spectator-participants, watching and being watched, hierarchically ordered by status (by rule, the higher ranks sat near the front, the masses at the back), faced each other across the arena in the round. It was a magnificent setting for a ruler to parade his power before his citizen-subjects; and for those subjects to show – or at least fantasise about showing – their collective muscle in front of the emperor.

The Colosseum was very much more than a sports venue. It was a political theatre in which each stratum of Roman society played out its role (ideally at least; there were times [...] that this – like all political theatre – went horribly and subversively wrong). The emperor knew he was emperor best when cheered by the ovations of an enthusiastic crowd who were seduced by the prospect of violent death (whether of animals or humans), by the gifts the emperor would occasionally have showered amongst the spectators and by the sheer excitement of being there. The Roman elite in the front seats would have paraded their status, nodding to their friends: this surely was where business contracts, promotion, alliances, marriages were first mentioned or followed up. The crowd, usually grateful and compliant, sometimes chanted for the end of a war or for more shows – seeing their power *as the Roman people* all round the arena. It was a vital part of Roman political life to be there, to be seen to be there and to watch the others. Hence the building's iconic status for the Romans, as well as for us.

Chapter 3

Delphi: centre of the Greek world

Written by Emma-Jayne Graham

Contents

1   Introduction

Why is Delphi a useful place for understanding the cultural world of the ancient Greeks? To answer this, we can think about Delphi from two perspectives. First, as a place that can be visited and studied today (Figure 1): that is, a place that provides archaeological and textual evidence that allows some of the cultural priorities and shared practices of ancient Greeks to be identified, reconstructed and explained more than two and a half millennia later. For example, you have already learned about how the archaeological remains of Delphi make it possible to identify its function as a sanctuary by looking at the 'Plan of the Sanctuary of Apollo at Delphi' (Resource 1.3 in the Resources section at the end of this block).

Figure 1 A place for storytelling: a view of the Sanctuary of Apollo at Delphi from the theatre. Photo: INTERFOTO/Alamy.

Second, we can think of Delphi as a place that was hugely significant to ancient people themselves, especially for how they thought about and presented themselves as Greek. It is important to remember that what is commonly described today as 'ancient Greece' did not map to a single definable country with clear territorial boundaries like the modern nation of Greece. As you learned in Chapter 1, ancient Greece was instead composed of a diverse and changeable collection of Mediterranean city-states (*poleis*), which were united by a shared cultural identity (see the map of the ancient Mediterranean, Resource 1.1, in the Resources section at the end of the block). These *poleis*, which were frequently at war with one another, often adopted localised ways of expressing their Greek identity and at times exhibited different forms of government. The specifically Athenian version of Greek cultural identity that you learned about in Chapter 1 offers a good example of this. For reasons that you shall soon discover, Delphi was a place at which the key cultural behaviours shared by these city-states came into sharp focus. To understand Delphi's importance, we therefore need to examine the role it played in what might be described as the Greek cultural imagination. In other words, how it was used to affirm, explain or justify certain types of cultural behaviours and the ideas that were connected with a broadly shared sense of ancient 'Greekness'. Interestingly, ancient primary sources suggest that this was a position Delphi achieved largely through the telling and retelling of different types of story.

You have already encountered one example of cultural storytelling within the fabric of Delphi itself. The list of Greek communities inscribed on the Plataean serpent column (erected in 479 BCE to celebrate Greek military victory in the Persian Wars) presented a very particular story, not only about the outcome of one battle but also who was (and was not) a part of it. In other words, by choosing to publicly display at Delphi which city-states had fought against the Persians, the column presented a quasi-official record of what happened at Plataea. For years afterwards, whenever people told the story of the battle it was to this 'official' Delphic memorial that they deferred for such details. In turn, the column's emphasis on who was actually there effectively turned that story into one about how historical events had determined who the true members of the Greek cultural world were.

At the same time, away from Delphi, stories that wove the Sanctuary of Apollo and its oracle into much broader narratives about 'Greekness' were circulated among Greeks, and non-Greeks, across the Mediterranean. Delphi was therefore a place where it was possible to present stories about Greek cultural identities, as well as being a place that featured within the stories and mythological tales that helped to shape Greek culture itself. To understand more about how this worked, we need to investigate some of these Delphic stories, the varied ways and contexts in which they were told and the reasons for telling them. Only then can we discover quite how central to ancient Greek culture this out-of-the-way place really was.

Figure 2 The stadium at Delphi. Photo: Isidoros Andronos/Alamy.

The Archaic and Classical periods

Your work in this chapter takes you back to a period several centuries before the previous chapter, where your focus was on Rome in the first century CE. Here you will focus primarily on evidence for the Sanctuary of Apollo at Delphi in the sixth and fifth centuries BCE (c.600–400 BCE). This period is often considered to be the heyday of the Delphic oracle and the time during which it played an especially important role in the development of the ancient Greek cultural world.

Awkwardly, it is also a period of time that spans the modern chronological division of ancient Greek history into what is conventionally referred to as the Archaic period and the Classical period:

- Archaic: c.700–480 BCE
- Classical: c.479–323 BCE.

Athens in the Classical period was your focus in Chapter 1. It is important to note, however, that these labels (Archaic and Classical) are modern terms that have been imposed in retrospect, often using memorable historical dates that do not have obvious relationships with changes in artistic style or the ways in which ancient people thought about chronological time.

In this chapter, I will write 'the Classical period' using a capital 'C' to differentiate it from the broader term used for the whole 'classical world' or the whole of 'classical antiquity'. Wherever possible I will use dates (e.g. 479 BCE and the early fifth century BCE) when referring to specific events, texts or objects rather than the broad periods, but you may find that you come across them in your wider reading.

Remember that you can also consult the Classical Studies timeline (Resource 1.2) in the Resources section at the end of this block to contextualise some of the case studies that you will be learning about.

2 The Charioteer's story

Let's start with an example that spotlights the potential for cultural storytelling at Delphi itself. One of the most iconic objects recovered from the excavation of the Sanctuary of Apollo is a bronze statue known as 'The Charioteer' (Figure 3).

Figure 3 'The Charioteer' of Delphi, *c.*470 BCE, bronze sculpture, height 1.8 m. Found at Delphi, Greece. Photo: Constantinos Iliopoulos/Alamy.

Excavated in 1896, 'The Charioteer' was originally commissioned in the 470s BCE by a man called Hieron, who was ruler at Gela (485–478 BCE) and who subsequently ruled as **tyrant** at Syracuse from 478 to 466 BCE (both are Greek colonies in Sicily). It is known from a poem composed by an ancient Greek writer of **lyric poetry** called Pindar that Hieron won horse races at Delphi in 482 and 478 BCE as well as the chariot race in 470 BCE (Pindar, *Pythian* 1; Pindar, 1997, pp. 219–233). The sculpture, which shows a male youth, standing 1.8 m tall, wearing a long, short-sleeved belted tunic and grasping a set of reins in his right hand, is a rare example of a surviving ancient bronze sculpture, since many were later melted down for their precious materials to be reused easily and cheaply.

Figure 4 'The Charioteer' of Delphi, detail of the head, profile, *c*.470 BCE, bronze sculpture, height 1.8 m. From Delphi, Greece. Photo © Luisa Ricciarini/Bridgeman Images.

What makes it especially significant is that its burial in a pit to the north of the Temple of Apollo (perhaps after it was damaged in an earthquake of 373 BCE) also ensured the preservation of its finer details. The eyes are made using glass paste, black stone and brown onyx; copper was used for the eyelashes and lips; the teeth are made from silver; and copper and silver were combined for the hairband (which you can see in Figure 4). The young age of the figure is indicated by his smooth skin and absence of facial hair (in the Greek world, beards were considered a typical indicator of adult male status).

Figure 5 A reconstruction drawing that imagines how 'The Charioteer' may once have looked as part of a much bigger bronze statue group, although the details of its actual arrangement remain unknown. From Roland Hampe *Der Wagenlenker von Delphi* (1941), Munich.

The precious materials signal that this was an elaborate piece of sculpture, even more so when it is put back into its full context. Other fragments found alongside it indicate that the figure of the charioteer himself was originally part of a much bigger statue group comprising a life-sized chariot and a team of four horses, as well as another smaller figure who may have represented a groom or servant (see Figure 5). This statue group perhaps once stood in the open area to the north of the Temple of Apollo, close to where it was eventually buried (see Number 45 on the 'Plan of the Sanctuary of Apollo at Delphi', Resource 1.3). It seems most likely that this statue group was a dedication to Apollo designed to celebrate Hieron's chariot racing victory at Delphi during the Pythian Games of 470 BCE. It was therefore a commemoration of an athletic victory (as we'll examine first), but also an object with religious significance (as we'll go on to see later in this chapter).

Held every four years (as part of a cycle of so-called 'crown contests' comprising athletic and musical competitions held at Olympia, Delphi, Isthmia and Nemea), the Pythian Games were second in importance only to those of Olympia and brought large numbers of aristocratic competitors to Delphi. Traditionally, only aristocratic men were eligible to compete, but the Games were held as part of a much bigger **Panhellenic** festival celebrating the god Apollo, which drew large crowds of spectators (the competitions themselves were considered to be sacred contests and were therefore quite different from the gladiatorial games that provided entertainment in ancient Rome). Apart from general acclaim, the reward for victory was merely a wreath or crown, which was often dedicated by the victor to Apollo as a gesture of thanks for having shown him divine favour. Other offerings might be made as well; **tripods**, like the one on which the Pythia sat (as you will see later, depicted on the drinking cup in Figure 14), proved especially popular. Over time, more elaborate offerings in the form of statues of the victor himself, like 'The Charioteer', were also put up in the sanctuary.

Among the sporting events held during the Pythian Games were chariot and horse races (like those that Hieron competed in). Naked athletes (*gymnos*, the origin of the English word 'gymnasium') also competed to outdo each other at running, jumping and wrestling. It may sound surprising but competing naked was a crucial part of the display of aristocratic forms of Greekness, since it was something that women and slaves were forbidden from doing as well as something no other ancient culture was known to do. This made the Pythian Games an event at which aristocrats from *poleis* across the Mediterranean could actively perform their identity as members of the Greek elite by behaving in very specific Greek ways. Even the Roman emperor Nero, who you met in the previous chapter and who was eager to align himself with a much earlier generation of aristocratic Greek victors, competed in a version of the Pythian Games held during his visit to Delphi in the first century CE, reportedly winning in both athletic and musical competitions (he may have also consulted the oracle).

Activity 1

(Allow around 15 minutes to complete this activity.)

Look back at Figures 3 and 4 and examine them using the background information provided in the main text to help answer the following questions:

1   How would you describe the appearance, pose and expression of 'The Charioteer'?

2   What story might an ancient viewer be prompted to imagine about Hieron when they encountered 'The Charioteer'?

In the second part of this book, Block 2 *Art and power*, you will learn more about how to visually analyse images of objects such as this one. For now, it's fine for your analysis to just be relatively descriptive.

Discussion

1   The individual shown in Figures 3 and 4 has the appearance of a young man, shown by his clean-shaven facial features and the curling locks of hair that cluster by his ears. To me his pose is quite lifelike but also fairly stiff, with the high belt making him appear especially tall. Despite the fact that he is shown driving a chariot he stands very still, with his feet close together rather than braced against its movement. Even his clothes betray little sense of movement, the folds making his body resemble an architectural column. His expression appears to be calm and fixed straight ahead.

2   Showing a charioteer participating in the prestigious chariot race would probably have prompted an ancient viewer to connect Hieron with victory in the Pythian Games. By implication, the main character in that story, Hieron himself, was a member of the aristocratic elite who had travelled from Sicily in order to compete at Delphi. The appearance of the charioteer himself implies that in this story Hieron is a youthful man. The fact that Hieron chose to commission the statue group, either instead of or as well as the customary dedication to Apollo of his victory crown, also told a story about his wealth and social position, reinforced by the use of precious materials. The calm composure of the figure might encourage the viewer to imagine that Hieron was in complete control of his team of horses, or more likely, that this is the moment after his victory when he coolly accepted the cheers of the crowd at the climax of that story.

Figure 6 Identical free-standing marble sculptures of nude male youths (kouroi), *c.*580 BCE. Archaeological Museum, Delphi, Greece. Photo © Ken Welsh/Bridgeman Images. These youths are sometimes referred to as the 'Argive twins', Kleobis and Biton.

The pose of 'The Charioteer' is a consequence of Greek artistic traditions. On the one hand, it echoes in bronze the traditional marble figures of male youths known as **kouroi** produced in the Archaic period, many examples of which were also to be found as dedications at Delphi (compare 'The Charioteer' with the sculptures in Figure 6). Indeed, archaeologist and ancient art historian Richard Neer has suggested that so many kouroi were once erected at Delphi by victors in the Pythian Games that this 'army of kouroi [was] a veritable instantiation of the imagined community of the Hellenic elite' (2007, p. 230).

On the other hand, 'The Charioteer' sculpture begins to demonstrate, in the turn of his head, the gathering of his tunic over the belt, and the detail of his feet, the sort of lifelike naturalism that would come to characterise the art of the Classical period. Produced in 470 BCE, 'The Charioteer' sits right at the point of transition between these two styles. It therefore presents a traditional victory story about wealthy, male, aristocratic superiority, but you might have begun to wonder whether all elements of the story that 'The Charioteer' prompts were entirely true. Did Hieron really look this youthful at the time of his victory? Was he really this calm as he celebrated it? These are questions that can't be answered, nor can we be sure whether a Greek viewer would have cared to ask them: their familiarity with victory dedications possibly meant that these details were part and parcel of how they expected to see a victor presented. Regardless, 'The Charioteer' offers a glimpse into how material objects could tell very public stories about a person's connection with the celebration of Greek cultural life at Delphi that, for want of further information, were difficult to contradict.

2.1 The Charioteer's other story

In fact, there is more to the story of 'The Charioteer' than might initially meet the eye. Like many Greek dedications it was once mounted on a limestone base onto which an **inscription** was carved, outlining the circumstances of its commission. The remains of this inscription (Figure 7) were found in the same pit as the bronze figure. Although the text remains fragmentary, it reveals that the original dedicatory inscription was reworked at a later date, probably in the late 460s BCE, as part of a rededication of the statue group by Polyzalus, Hieron's brother and possible successor. In the process, part of the original text was erased and replaced. If you closely examine the second line of letters on the inscribed stone block shown in Figure 7, you will notice that they have been cut directly into the prepared surface of the stone. This is different from the first line of text, where you should be able to detect that the original prepared surface (and anything that was once cut into it) has been completely chiselled away with horizontal strokes. This has created an indentation across the width of the stone into which has been carved a new line of text (which, interestingly, is also written in handwriting that is slightly different from line two, although you are not expected to be able to spot that!).

Figure 7 The inscribed limestone base that has been associated with 'The Charioteer' statue group. Archaeological Museum, Delphi, Greece, inv. no. 3517. Pierre Amandry, © EFA Photograph number 15917. The first line has been erased and recarved with a new text naming Polyzalus as dedicator.

With careful analysis, some traces of the original text of the first line can still be detected (although, again, don't worry – you are not expected to pick them out!). When translated it appears that the original two-line inscription read:

> [——] he, being ruler of Gela, dedicated
>
> [——] give him glory, noble Apollo

(Adornato, 2008, p. 33)

The first words of each sentence were probably carved on another, now missing, block of stone adjoining this one (the missing words are signalled by the elongated dash in square brackets). By combining historical information about the rulers of Gela with the very faint traces of the original words, the erased first line has been reconstructed by archaeologist Gianfranco Adornato as having once named Hieron as the original dedicator of the statue group:

> Hieron, he, being ruler of Gela, dedicated [this]

(2008, p. 41)

When the first line was replaced about a decade later with the lettering that can more easily be seen in Figure 7, the final two-line inscription came to read:

Polyzalus dedicated me

[——] give him glory, noble Apollo

(Adornato, 2008, p. 33)

Activity 2

(Allow around 15 minutes to complete this activity.)

Carefully reread the English translations of the first and second inscriptions carved on the stone shown in Figure 7. Based on what you know about 'The Charioteer', what new story or stories might the revisions of Polyzalus be using it to tell?

Discussion

By reusing the dedication of his brother, Polyzalus used this very public form of communication dedicated at a site visited by people from across the Mediterranean to tell a story about himself. Since the text does not mention that this is a rededication of an existing statue group (although the obviously erased line of text perhaps suggested it), someone seeing it for the first time would probably assume that Polyzalus dedicated the monument in celebration of his own victory in the Pythian Games. If, on the other hand, they knew that his brother Hieron had originally commissioned the statue group, then they might read into it a story in which Polyzalus was equally victorious, and chose to celebrate both of their victories with the same monument.

It remains unknown whether Polyzalus was ever a victor at the Pythian Games, and if you read the new inscription carefully you might notice that it does not make any claims to an athletic victory – this is merely implied by its juxtaposition with the statue group. 'The Charioteer', then, provides a good example of how multiple Delphic stories might be told and reworked in a single object. Indeed, there may even be another story to be told about this charioteer. Although only aristocrats were eligible to compete in the Pythian Games, and slaves were barred from entering (Crowther, 1992), some historians have suggested that the surviving bronze statue could represent a slave who was responsible for driving the chariot on behalf of its aristocratic owner (Honour and Fleming, 2009, p. 134). This is because the charioteer is shown wearing a tunic, rather than naked as was customary for aristocratic athletes. In this case, victory would still have belonged to Hieron on the basis of having owned and trained such a magnificent team of horses. This remains a matter for debate: although, what is certain is that by reading the combination of the statue group and its inscription in the context of the Sanctuary of Apollo, ancient Greeks would have understood the stories that they sought to tell and found them entirely appropriate to that setting. The question of why they were appropriate leads us back to the bigger picture of Delphi's connection with ancient Greek culture.

Deciphering ancient inscriptions

Inscriptions are useful sources of evidence for Classical Studies. Although inscriptions can appear on all kinds of objects, many were placed in public places where they were used to communicate information. This means that they can provide useful evidence about, for example, who owned or commissioned an object or monument and the circumstances of its creation.

However, because they were written in Greek or Latin, and because constraints of space meant that individual words were often abbreviated or squashed together without any punctuation, inscriptions require some deciphering.

The inscription on the stone base associated with 'The Charioteer' (Figure 7) presents a good opportunity to see how this process works, even if you cannot understand the words themselves (please rest assured that you are not expected to know any ancient Greek for this module!).

When transcribed directly – with spaces added between words to make it a little easier to read – the surviving Greek letters on the stone are revealed as:

ΟΛΥΖΑΛΟΣ Μ ΑΝΕΘΗΚ

ΟΝ ΑΕΞ ΕΥΟΝΥΜ ΑΠΟΛ

If you have time, you might like to examine Figure 7 closely to see if you can recognise any of these letters on the original stone. These letters can then be transliterated into the English alphabet as follows:

OLYZALOS M ANETHEK

ON AEX EUONUM **APOL**

At this point you might be able to start recognising some of the words: **APOL** (Apollo), for example, and **OLYZALOS** (part of Polyzalus).

After this, the abbreviated words can then be expanded and the text can be translated into English:

Polyzalus dedicated me

[——] give him glory, noble Apollo

Although you are not expected to read the original text of any inscriptions that you come across in this module, it can be useful to bear this process in mind, because it explains why the translated text of an inscription often looks very different from the original lettering.

3 Performing religious stories

As you have learned, Delphi was the site of a sanctuary dedicated to the god Apollo, meaning that all Delphic stories were ultimately connected with a particular aspect of ancient Greek culture: religion. In ancient Greece, no separation was made between religious and secular life because the gods were understood to be everywhere and to be involved in everything. This meant that religion effectively underpinned much of ancient Greek civic order and was a central part of social, political and even economic life, becoming caught up in individual and collective decisions about politics, war and the founding of new cities. As a consequence, religious behaviours could happen anywhere – in the home, in the streets, in the marketplace, in the cemetery – but sanctuaries were places specifically set aside for religious purposes. For this reason, religion provides an important context for the stories that were told at and about Delphi. In this section, you will learn a little more about how ancient Greek religion worked, how dedications such as 'The Charioteer' fitted into it, and why the religious setting of Delphi was so appropriate for cultural storytelling.

3.1 A cast of divine characters

Ancient Greek religion was founded on the idea that the 12 Olympian gods (six gods and six goddesses), who lived on Mount Olympus, controlled what happened in the world. Precisely which deities comprised this group varied throughout Greek history, but Table 1 sets out those that appear most often across the whole range of Greek textual sources. You may recognise the names of some of these from your work on Athens, where you encountered buildings in the agora dedicated to different aspects of Apollo, Athena, Hephaestus and Zeus (versions of the Olympian gods were also worshipped in Rome, albeit sometimes under different names: Zeus, for instance, was equated by Romans with Jupiter).

Table 1 shows the most common grouping of the 12 Olympian gods:

Name	Associated with	Family relationship
Zeus	The sky, weather	King of the gods
Hera	Women, marriage	Sister and wife of Zeus
Demeter	Fertility	Sister of Zeus
Hestia	Home	Sister of Zeus
Poseidon	Sea, horses, earthquakes	Brother of Zeus
Apollo	The sun, music, poetry, truth	Son of Zeus and twin of Artemis
Artemis	Wild animals, hunting, moon	Daughter of Zeus and twin of Apollo
Hermes	Messenger of the gods	Son of Zeus
Ares	War	Son of Zeus and Hera
Athena	Wisdom, arts, war	Daughter of Zeus
Hephaestus	Fire, metalworking	Son of Zeus and Hera
Aphrodite	Love, sex, beauty	Daughter of Zeus

It is not necessary to know about all of these gods for your study of this chapter, but it is important to note that Apollo was one of the powerful 12 Olympian gods and, like all gods, he sometimes manifested in relation to one of his particular attributes or areas of concern. You might recall, for example, how some of the deities you were introduced to in Chapter 1 represented a particular version of a god: Apollo Patroos or 'Fatherly Apollo' was specifically associated with the origins of the Athenian people. The version of Apollo who was the focal point for worship at Delphi was strictly known as Apollo Pythios (see Figure 8). 'Pyth-' relates to the verb meaning 'to question', but the **epithet** 'Pythios' was also connected with a Greek myth. This told how the goddess Gaia (who you will learn more about in a moment) had once controlled the oracle at Delphi before Apollo wrested it away from her by killing Python, the giant snake-like creature (sometimes described as a dragon) that she had assigned to guard its location.

Figure 8 Parts of a male chryselephantine statue (a sculpture made from ivory and gold), possibly of Apollo, sixth century BCE, found at Delphi. Archaeological Museum, Delphi, Greece. Photo © Ken Welsh/Bridgeman Images.

Greek gods were anthropomorphic, that is, despite their very non-humanlike divine powers they took human form, and they each had their own individual character. The most powerful was the king of the gods, Zeus. You may recall from the video about the sanctuary on the module website that according to Greek myth Zeus was responsible for determining that Delphi lay at the centre (or navel) of the world, a point marked by the omphalos stone (Figure 9). Like the goddess Gaia, there was also a large number of other gods and goddesses outside of the core group of 12 Olympian gods, not least Dionysus (god of wine and theatre, whose tomb was believed to be located at Delphi) and Hades (god of the underworld), as well as a host of **heroes** such as Heracles and Theseus.

Figure 9 An omphalos stone from Delphi. Photo: Bridgeman Images. This early Roman period version of the stone depicts a rock that has been covered with a woollen mesh, possibly an offering.

Ancient myth told how the Olympians came to power after a battle with the Titans, another family group of beings who were descended from Ouranos (god of the sky) and Mother Earth (Gaia, sometimes referred to as Ge; as I mentioned before, it was this goddess Gaia from whom Apollo later took control of Delphi). After defeating the Titans, the Olympians subsequently fought off the Giants (who, like the snake creature that Apollo defeated, were the children of Gaia) in another battle referred to as the Gigantomachy. This battle appeared frequently in Greek religious art, with dramatic scenes of gods fighting against giants sometimes carved on temples. The fifth century BCE temple dedicated to Athena on the Acropolis at Athens, known today as the Parthenon, featured a Gigantomachy scene. It is a story that also appears on the Siphnian **Treasury** at Delphi, which you will investigate later in this unit (when you return online after this chapter).

As well as being an exciting story, archaeologist John Pedley points out that the Gigantomachy came to be used 'as a metaphor for the victory of civilization over barbarism' (2005, p. 18). Strict artistic tradition dictated that human events should not be presented on monuments sacred to the gods, but by equating the self-proclaimed 'civilised' Greeks with the Olympians, and their enemies with the 'barbarian' giants, the Gigantomachy became a metaphor that could be used to indirectly celebrate human victories. At Delphi, the Gigantomachy was a metaphor with extra significance because it also recalled Apollo's defeat of one of Gaia's other creatures, Python. These metaphorical connections may seem subtle and even convoluted today, but for ancient Greeks these mythological stories structured and explained their cultural world and were easily recognised.

3.2 Religious dedications and competition

Greek gods and goddesses were powerful as well as demanding, and humans were anxious not to offend or displease them. They appeased the divine by building them temples where they could be worshipped (see Figure 10). This included making sacrifices, performing festivals in their honour and giving them offerings, all of which served to glorify and celebrate the supremacy of the gods. As elaborate forms of **votive offerings**, monumental dedications were a public way of giving thanks to a god for their perceived assistance with, or support for, human endeavours. It is in this context that the dedications at Delphi, such as 'The Charioteer' or the Plataean serpent column, can be understood: they advertised the achievements of human individuals and communities, but they also thanked and glorified Apollo for the part he was thought to have played in bringing about their success. For example, the inscription on the base of 'The Charioteer' that we saw earlier makes it clear that the sculpture was a dedication intended to acknowledge 'noble Apollo'.

Greece in this period was nothing if not a competitive world, composed of a collection of *poleis* that were constantly jostling for position and were regularly at war. The Sanctuary of Apollo at Delphi was an ideal place at which this competition could be played out on neutral ground, because although it was a sanctuary much like any other, there were two things that distinguished it. One was its oracle, which we will explore later in Section 4 of this chapter, and the other was its status as an interstate or Panhellenic sanctuary. What this meant is that unlike most sanctuaries, which were controlled by a local *polis* and therefore used as a place to present its own interests and sense of local identity, Delphi was both politically neutral and geographically separate from the main political centres. In fact, for much of its history it was not even controlled directly by the local inhabitants of the city of Delphi itself, but in partnership with a wider group of Greek communities known as an **amphictyony**. This meant not only that Greeks from across the whole Mediterranean could visit and worship at Delphi but that they all had the right to make public dedications there. In addition, the presence of the oracle and the four-yearly Pythian Games ensured that large numbers of people regularly went to Delphi, making it a place at which the public statements made by these religious dedications were guaranteed a large audience.

Figure 10 This image shows a reconstruction of the area immediately outside the Temple of Apollo at Delphi (sometimes called the 'temple terrace'), giving some impression of the scale and decoration of the temple and some of the surrounding dedications. 'The Charioteer' is shown on the middle right of the image, raised up on another terrace. © EFA.

Figure 11 Sphinx of Naxos statue, *c*.570 BCE, marble, height 2.22 m. Archaeological Museum, Delphi, Greece. Photo: Stefano Politi Markovina/ Alamy. *The sphinx would originally have been painted, making details such as its open eyes more obvious.*

A memorable example of this sort of religiously sanctioned public storytelling can be found in the form of two separate dedications erected at Delphi in *c*.422 BCE. Both were dedicated by *poleis* giving thanks for Apollo's divine support: the people of Tegea dedicated their spoils of war, while those of Mantinea erected a statue of Apollo. Both, however, somewhat confusingly did so in order to celebrate victory in the Battle of Laodicea, a battle in which they fought on opposing sides! They could do this because of the sanctuary's Panhellenic status that allowed all Greeks to use the site equally *and* because religious expectations permitted the sort of dedication that allowed them to engage in forms of public storytelling about themselves.

Figure 12 Reconstruction showing how the Naxian sphinx once sat on the top of a tall column at Delphi. Didier Laroche. © EFA.

The Naxian sphinx (see Figures 11 and 12) presents another good example of a dedication that, like 'The Charioteer', was made to the god Apollo, except that this monument was constructed on behalf of a whole *polis* community rather than by an individual.

Activity 3

(Allow around 30 minutes to complete this activity.)

Examine the image of the Naxian sphinx dedication in Figure 11 and the reconstruction in Figure 12 (Number 28 on the 'Plan of the Sanctuary of Apollo at Delphi', Resource 1.3).

Then read the interpretation provided in the extract below before answering the questions that follow.

> Around 570 BC the Naxians offered a sphinx figure, set up between the aire and the cult of Ge [Gaia] area. This was the first monumental offering by an Aegean island and the first in island marble (for both column and sphinx). The sphinx had strong associations with the Naxians: they had dedicated similar sphinxes at Delos [another oracular sanctuary] earlier in the sixth century. At first sight, it seems that the Naxians, like the Eastern dedicators, had taken little notice of the trends of dedication at Delphi (as at Delos) and simply implanted their preferred sculptural dedication, with the expectation that its associations would be understood by Delphi's non-island visitors. Yet closer inspection suggests that the Naxians actually placed their dedication very carefully so that it had both sense and impact within the Delphic context. The impact is clear to see. It alone, by virtue of its height, could be seen at all times from all points in the sanctuary. Its height also put it level (when looking from below) with the entablature of the temple, marking it almost as an *akroterion* [pl. *akroteria*: the ornament at the corner of the roof of a building, or on the end of a gable]. Yet in terms of sense, the sphinx also drew on its relationship to the cult of Ge and the Muses [goddesses upon whom poets, artists, philosophers, and intellectuals depended for the ability to create their works]. The sphinx is often understood as a chthonic animal. Its placement, within the chthonic Ge cult area, and possibly very near the area of Dionysus' mythical tomb, underlined how the meaning of the sphinx was tied to the Earth, to death and to liminality by integrating the dedication into the particular nature of the Apollo sanctuary. The Naxian sphinx introduced Delphi to the Naxians' preferred

choice of iconography, but was also embedded within, and linked closely to, the most sacred areas of Delphi itself.

(Scott, 2010, pp. 46–47 [footnotes removed])

1   List the key features of the form of the creature shown in Figure 11 and the reconstruction of its original setting in Figure 12. You might find it useful to focus on its appearance and pose as well as any details you find particularly striking.

2   In what ways were the Naxians (who offered the sphinx) seeking to be distinctive?

3   In what ways did the Naxians seek to write themselves into the story of Delphi itself?

Study note

This activity is a good opportunity to practise extracting information from both primary sources (like Figure 11) and secondary sources (such as Figure 12 and the extract). You might find it useful to read the extract once for sense and then again more closely, making some notes or jotting down some of the key points that you think relate to each of the questions before you formulate your answers.

Discussion

1   The sculpture is carved from marble and takes the form of a mythical animal hybrid (a sphinx) composed of the head of a human woman with a long braid of hair falling over the left shoulder (another can also just be made out in Figure 11, falling over the right shoulder), the wings and feathered chest of a bird and the body of a lion or other large cat. The sphinx sits on its haunches, its front paws placed on the ground, its legs stiff and straight. Its wings are held upright and together behind the head, which faces forwards. The facial features suggest the presence of a half-smile and the eyes are large. It sits on a marble base shaped like a scroll that is placed on top of a column.

2   The people of Naxos chose to use the symbol of the mythological sphinx because it had meaning to them and their own sense of identity; it was a symbol that they had used to assert that identity elsewhere. Viewers of the monument would therefore immediately

recognise this dedication as belonging to Naxos and, combined with the tall column on which it was placed that ensured it could be seen from across the sanctuary, it allowed them to stand out and draw attention to themselves. They also used marble that came from the island of Naxos itself, effectively implanting a small part of the island into the landscape of Delphi.

3   According to Scott, the iconography and placement of the Naxian sphinx connected it with the mythological origins and religious past of Delphi. It presented visitors with the opportunity to imagine a story that wove these threads together – Gaia, Dionysus, Apollo (via its visual intersection with the roofline of the current temple), the sphinx and Naxos. It therefore laid claim to an especially deep and long-lived relationship between the Naxians and Delphi.

The Naxian sphinx provides a good example of why Delphi was a place of importance for Greek culture, demonstrating how communities capitalised on the opportunities that the sanctuary provided for making public statements about their position within the Greek world. Religious expectations concerning dedications, coupled with the openness of the sanctuary to all Greeks who wished to leave a mark there, meant that it became a location at which both individuals and communities jostled for position and sought to write, and even rewrite, their standing in relation to the wider Greek world. In the next section, we will consider how stories connected with the oracle gave Delphi yet another role within the wider context of that world.

4 Oracle stories

As previously mentioned, one of the main reasons for visiting Delphi was to consult with the oracle. Visitors could ask this priestess, also known as the Pythia, to communicate with Apollo and request an answer to a specific question about how to proceed in a personal or state matter. The process of seeking to understand the will of the gods was known as divination and there were several other oracles located across Greece that were consulted for the same purpose, including those at Didyma and Delos (both linked to Apollo), and at Dodona (linked to Zeus). Delphi, however, was considered the most powerful of them all. It was believed that Apollo spent nine months of the year residing at Delphi, but was only available for consultation on one day in each of those months.

The Roman writer Plutarch (see Figure 13), who was a priest at Delphi in the early second century CE, provides some clues about what happened on the days when the oracle was open in his collection of essays and speeches known as the *Moralia*. The need to act in accordance with strict tradition when consulting the Delphic oracle meant that the occasions Plutarch describes probably only varied in small ways from those that took place in the sixth and fifth centuries BCE. According to Plutarch, the Pythia would purify herself by washing with the sacred waters of the Castalian Spring located just outside the Sanctuary of Apollo, before entering the temple and arranging herself on top of a tall bronze tripod (see Figure 14). The tripod was placed in an area of the temple that may have featured a crack in the natural rock that emitted gases or vapours, which allowed Apollo to communicate through her. This area was known as the *adyton* (a sort of inner shrine), but where it was within the structure of the temple remains unknown.

Figure 13 Marble bust of a man from Delphi, once identified as the Greek historian Plutarch (43–120 CE) but now labelled as 'a philosopher'. Archaeological Museum, Delphi, Greece. Photo © Luisa Ricciarini/ Bridgeman Images.

In order to approach the Pythia, the enquirer also purified himself (no women were allowed to consult the oracle), paid the fee (in the form of the *pelanos*, a small sacrificial cake bought from the Delphians and then burned on the altar outside), and performed a sacrifice, probably of an animal, at a hearth inside the temple. When it was his turn, he entered the *adyton* and posed his question before writing down the response (or having it written down for him) and leaving. The response itself might be read out loud in front of the temple. Anyone who was not a citizen of Delphi had to be accompanied throughout the process by a local representative (*proxenos*).

Figure 14 By the Kodros Painter, Attic red-figure *kylix* (drinking cup) showing King Aegeus in front of the Pythia, *c.*440–430 BCE, ceramic. Found at Vulci, Italy. Now in the Altes Museum, Berlin. Photo: Adam Eastland/ Alamy.

The order in which these consultants entered the temple was strictly fixed, with citizens of Delphi always permitted to be the first in the queue. After this came Greeks from cities that belonged to the amphictyony, followed by all other Greeks and, finally, non-Greeks. Within each of these categories however, those who had been granted *promanteia* (the right to consult the oracle before others) were able to skip the queue to the front of their group. This was considered a real privilege and was usually a sign that they had done something particularly important to support or embellish the sanctuary. This was the case for the people of the island of Chios, who were rewarded with *promanteia* for constructing a magnificent altar outside the Temple of Apollo around the beginning of the fifth century BCE (Figure 15).

Figure 15 The altar of the Chians (early fifth century BCE) outside the Temple of Apollo at Delphi. Photo: Manuel Cohen/Scala, Florence.

From looking at textual sources, such as those by Greek writers Herodotus and Thucydides (who you will explore in more detail in Section 4.2), it becomes clear quite how often the oracle was consulted and the reasons for doing so. For instance, the citizens of Athens consulted Delphi on at least 28 occasions before 300 BCE, often to confirm their decision to go to war, as part of the process of founding new cities or responding to crises such as plagues (Bowden, 2005, p. 6). By spotlighting the role of the Delphic oracle in some of the major events of Greek political and cultural history, these textual sources also provide evidence for another form of Delphic storytelling, revealing that widely circulated stories about Delphi were central to the ways in which Greeks understood the world in which they lived. More specifically, they reveal that being seen to consult the oracle meant that a Greek community was also seen to be acting in a specifically Greek way, with the stories that subsequently circulated about those consultations reinforcing how being Greek meant making sense of the world with divine help (Kindt, 2016, p. 10).

4.1 Writing about Delphi

In Table 2, I have provided some information about a sample of primary textual sources, written by 12 ancient writers, that feature Delphi and its oracle (although this is far from an exhaustive list!). The dates for each refer to the lifetime of the author, where this is known. You might recognise some of the authors from your work on Athens and Rome in the previous chapters.

Table 2 Some of the ancient textual sources that mention the Delphic oracle

Author	Work	Genre	Period	Extra information
Aeschylus	Consultations of the Delphic oracle appear in: *The Libation Bearers*, *Prometheus Bound, Seven against Thebes*	Greek tragedy (drama)	*c.*525–456 BCE	
Pindar	*Pythian Odes*	Lyric poetry	*c.*518–438 BCE	
Sophocles	Consultations of the Delphic oracle appear in: *Electra*, *Oedipus at Colonus, Oedipus the King*	Greek tragedy (drama)	*c.*497/6–406 BCE	
Herodotus	*Histories*	History	*c.*484–430 BCE	Covers the Greco-Persian wars of 490 and 480–479 BCE
Euripides	*Ion* is set in Delphi; consultations of the Delphic oracle also appear in: *Andromache, Iphigenia in Tauris, Electra, Orestes, Medea, Phoenician Women, Suppliant Women*	Greek tragedy (drama)	*c.*485–406 BCE	

Author	Work	Genre	Period	Extra information
Thucydides	*History of the Peloponnesian War*	History	*c.*471–396 BCE	Covers the war between Athens and Sparta, 431–404 BCE
Xenophon	*Apology*	Philosophy, in the form of a legal speech	*c.*430–355 BCE?	An account of the trial of Socrates in 399 BCE, when he was charged with impiety
Xenophon	*Hellenica* (also known as *History of Greece*)	History	*c.*430–355 BCE?	Covers the period 411–362 BCE
Plato	*Apology*	Philosophy, in the form of a legal speech	*c.*428/7–348/7 BCE	A speech that purports to be that which Socrates used for his defence at a trial in 399 BCE, when he was charged with impiety
Strabo	*Geography*	Geography	*c.*64 BCE–25 CE	Description of the known world, in 17 books
Plutarch	*Moralia*, with separate books on: *The E at Delphi*, *The Oracles at Delphi No Longer Given in Verse*, *The Obsolescence of Oracles*	Essays	*c.*45–120 CE	Plutarch served as a priest of Apollo at Delphi from *c.*95 CE

Author	Work	Genre	Period	Extra information
Pausanias	*Description of Greece*	Geography	c.115–180 CE	A sort of sacred travel guide to the traditional religious sites of Greece; Pausanias was working during the Roman period but came from Greece and wrote in Greek

Activity 4

(Allow around 20 minutes to complete this activity.)

Look at the information provided in Table 2. I chose to include these sources because they offer examples that demonstrate the range of different genres and the long period of time over which the Delphic oracle remained influential.

Without needing to read the sources themselves, what do you think can be learned from this collection of writings about the importance of the Delphic oracle? You might find it useful to think about the implications of the different types of textual sources that are represented here (their genre) and the dates at which they were produced.

Discussion

Two broad points might have emerged. First, these sources cover a wide variety of genres, ranging from poetry, literature and plays to historical, geographical and philosophical works. They therefore have the potential to offer a wide range of voices, styles and types of information or opinions, and suggest that the Delphic oracle was so embedded in ancient culture that it was appropriate to mention it in relation to all manner of different contexts.

Second, the fact that the oracle appears in textual sources from the early fifth century BCE (e.g. Aeschylus and Pindar) and continues to do so even into the second century CE (the period of the Roman Empire) also suggests that its influence and cultural importance was long-lived.

You might have also noticed that the genre of these sources changes over time, with a shift away from poetry and drama towards historical or geographical works in later periods. This can be explained by broader cultural changes: the heyday of Greek tragedy (which was closely associated with Classical Athens) eventually ended, and writers working during the Roman period, such as Pausanias, appear to have been especially interested in exploring historical aspects of the sacred landscape of Greece. Let's now examine some of these sources in more detail.

Activity 5

(Allow around 20 minutes to complete this activity.)

Now read the following extract from the work of ancient writer Pausanias, which is taken from his *Description of Greece*, written in the second century CE (the final entry in Table 2).

Before you start, you might find it useful to know that in Greek mythology the god Apollo was often connected with birds and laurel trees, and that Trophonios and Agamedes were legendary architects of the heroic past, believed to have lived before the Trojan War (thought by the Greeks to have taken place around the thirteenth or twelfth century BCE). Do not worry about all the other names in the extract and who all the people were; focus instead on the description of the early temples at Delphi.

> Tradition, however, reports no other man as prophet, but makes mention of prophetesses only. They say that the most ancient temple of Apollo was made of laurel, the branches of which were brought from the laurel in Tempe. This temple must have had the form of a hut. The Delphians say that the second temple was made by bees from bees-wax and feathers, and that it was sent to the Hyperboreans [a mythical race of giants] by Apollo. Another story is current, that the temple was set up by a Delphian, whose name was Pteras, and so the temple received its name from the builder. After this Pteras, so they say, the city in Crete was named, with the addition of a letter, Aptereï. The story that the temple was built of the fern (*pteris*) that grows on the mountains, by interweaving fresh stalks of it, I do not accept at all. It is no wonder that the third temple was made of bronze, seeing that Acrisius made a bedchamber of bronze for his daughter, the Lacedaemonians [Spartans] still possess a sanctuary of Athena of the Bronze House, and the Roman forum, a marvel

for its size and style, possesses a roof of bronze. So it would not be unlikely that a temple of bronze was made for Apollo. The rest of the story I cannot believe, either that the temple was the work of Hephaestus, or the legend about the golden singers, referred to by Pindar in his verses about this bronze temple:

Above the pediment sang

Golden Charmers.

These words, it seems to me, are but an imitation of Homer's account of the Seirens. Neither did I find the accounts agree of the way this temple disappeared. Some say that it fell into a chasm, in the earth, others that it was melted by fire. The fourth temple was made by Trophonius and Agamedes; the tradition is that it was made of stone. It was burnt down in the archonship of Erxicleides at Athens, in the first year of the fifty-eighth Olympiad, when Diognetus of Crotona was victorious. The modern temple was built for the god by the Amphictyons from the sacred treasures, and the architect was one Spintharus of Corinth.

(Pausanias, *Description of Greece* 10.5.9–13; Pausanias, 1935, pp. 395, 397 [footnotes removed])

When you have finished reading, answer the following question:

What is your immediate response to this as a primary source for Delphi, and do you think it can be used to understand anything about the types of stories that were told about Delphi?

Discussion

Pausanias tells a story about Delphi that includes elements that he says even he does not believe, so it is difficult to read this account of temples made from branches, beeswax and feathers at face value. You know from Table 2 that Pausanias wrote in the second century CE, which also means that a very long time had elapsed between the early days of the sanctuary as described here and the time when he was writing. For this reason, even if it was not so fantastical, you might already feel uncertain about its potential accuracy.

It is not possible to use this as a source of direct historical information. Instead, however, it can be used to think about the types of story that were told about Delphi, even into the Roman period, and how these sought to emphasise its mythological origins and connections. Delphi's close relationship with Apollo is reinforced here by a tale involving specific building materials (feathers and laurel) and a really deep sense of history mixed with mythology (mythistory) is presented through the supposed connection to the Hyperboreans and legendary architects. That the mythical origins of Delphi were still a topic of interest in Pausanias' time also suggests the enduring power of these stories.

4.2 Tales about the oracle

Although the temples that Pausanias describes in his *Description of Greece* are unlikely to represent reality, his account points towards a role for Delphi in the stories that Greeks told about their shared origins and customs. This is revealed further by the ways in which authors writing in the centuries before Pausanias wove the Delphic oracle into the historical narratives that they used to explain their cultural present. Good examples can be found in the *History of the Peloponnesian War* by the Athenian general Thucydides (which can also be found in Table 2), in which he describes multiple occasions when the Greeks consulted the oracle at Delphi.

Activity 6

(Allow around 45 minutes to complete this activity.)

Turn to Reading 3.1 at the end of this chapter and read the three extracts from Thucydides' *History of the Peloponnesian War*. Then answer the following questions:

1   Under what circumstances was the Delphic oracle consulted in each of the three extracts?

2   How would you describe the way in which Thucydides presents these consultations and what do you think this suggests about the role of the Delphic oracle in the affairs of Greek communities?

Discussion

1   **Extract 1** concerns the relationships between different Greek communities, specifically whether the Epidamnians should concede their city to the people of Corinth in order to help protect them from barbarian attack.

Extract 2 concerns the question of whether the Spartans should go to war against Athens.

Extract 3 concerns the question of whether the Spartans should found a new colony at Heracleia.

2   In all three instances the Delphic oracle confirms the appropriate action, and Thucydides describes this in a very matter-of-fact way. The Epidamnians had already decided that they needed to concede to the Corinthians, but were determined to check with the oracle that this was the right thing to do. The fact that their situation then improved, combined with the account of the failure of their previous attempts to resolve the situation on their own, confirms the oracle's authority.

Similarly, the oracle confirms the decision that the Spartans had already made about going to war. Here, Apollo's statement that he would have been on their side regardless also effectively confirms that the gods were responsible for upholding order within the world. Finally, in the last extract, the Spartans have already spent time debating whether to go ahead with the proposed colony at Heracleia, and have established very good reasons for doing so. Nevertheless, they still seek approval from Delphi. In all three extracts the oracle is presented as ratifying human decisions, ensuring that they align with the expected order of the world.

In the three extracts from Thucydides, which you have now examined, humans are essentially described as having already made a decision that they seek to have the Delphic oracle endorse. This same pattern is repeated at other moments throughout the *History of the Peloponnesian War*. Accounts like these reveal that, within the Greek world, consulting an oracle was often a fairly normal and accepted thing to do before any major undertaking. The consultation process not only allowed the leaders of *poleis* communities to proceed without their decision prompting dissent but also meant that all members of that community and, crucially, the other communities of the wider Greek world who heard or read these stories, knew that for them to not proceed would mean a dangerous contradiction of divine order. The stories themselves, and the fact that they repeatedly underpin Thucydides' narrative, therefore confirm that oracular consultation was simply what you should do if you were a Greek community with a potential problem. In this way, consulting the oracle was established by

Thucydides as a key element of Greek cultural norms and behaviours, and Delphi was the place at the very heart of that.

4.3 Understanding oracle stories

Stories about the Delphic oracle appear most frequently in a text known as *Histories* (sometimes referred to as *The History of Herodotus*), which was composed by the historian Herodotus in the mid fifth century BCE (and can also be found in Table 2). Once again, the stories that he tells reveal Delphi to be deeply entangled with how Greeks understood the world and identified themselves. Crucially, these are histories that intend to make a point, not merely to recount events. At the centre of Herodotus' work lie encounters between Greeks and non-Greeks, and he includes tales that underscore the cultural differences between them. Engagements with Delphi are fundamental to this enterprise because the ways in which Greeks and non-Greeks are shown to respond to the oracle allows Herodotus to highlight these differences, confirming to his largely Greek audience what it meant to behave as a Greek.

The story of the relationship between Delphi and Croesus (an incredibly wealthy king of **Lydia** shown in Figure 16) is probably one of the most famous of all oracle narratives. It is told as an extended story across much of Book 1 in the *Histories*, so I shall summarise the key elements for you here. Herodotus describes Croesus as the:

> first of all the Barbarians of whom we have knowledge, [who] subdued certain of the Hellenes [Greeks] and forced them to pay tribute, while others he gained over and made his friends.

> (Herodotus, *Histories* 1.6; Herodotus, 1890)

It is clear from the start that this man was not considered to be culturally Greek. Croesus is described by Herodotus as consulting the Delphic oracle on several occasions, not by visiting himself but by sending delegates on his behalf.

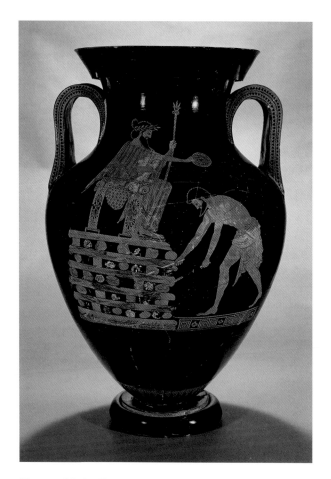

Figure 16 Attributed to the so-called Myson painter, Attic red-figure belly amphora depicting Croesus on his pyre, *c*.500–490 BCE, ceramic. Found at Vulci, Italy. The Louvre, Paris, France. Photo: © Peter Willi/Bridgeman Images.

On the first occasion, in 560 BCE, Croesus sought to test the Delphic oracle as part of a wider trial of oracles across the eastern Mediterranean. He did this by sending delegates to all of them at the same time. According to Herodotus he did this so that:

> he might try the Oracles and find out what knowledge they had, so that if they should be found to have knowledge of the truth, he might send and ask them secondly whether he should attempt to march against the Persians.

(Herodotus, *Histories* 1.46; Herodotus, 1890)

In short, Croesus wanted to determine which oracle was the most reliable. So, on the hundredth day after they all left Lydia, Croesus arranged for his delegates to ask the oracle to which they had been sent what he was doing on that very day. Herodotus continues:

> Now what the other Oracles prophesied is not by any reported, but at Delphi, so soon as the Lydians entered the sanctuary of the temple to consult the god and asked that which they were commanded to ask, the Pythian prophetess spoke thus in hexameter measure [a poetic metre, comprising six metrical feet in each line and a combination of short and long syllables]:
>
> "But the number of sand I know, and the measure of drops in the ocean;
>
> The dumb man I understand, and I hear the speech of the speechless:
>
> And there hath come to my soul the smell of a strong-shelled tortoise
>
> Boiling in cauldron of bronze, and the flesh of a lamb mingled with it;
>
> Under it bronze is laid, it hath bronze as a clothing upon it."
>
> (Herodotus, *Histories* 1.47; Herodotus, 1890)

Knowing the day on which the question would be posed, Croesus made sure to do something especially unusual, making a stew of tortoise and lamb in a bronze casserole pot. This was something that nobody could possibly have guessed a king would do! Delphi was the only oracle to accurately describe his actions. Having tested the oracle and, 'judging that the Oracle at Delphi was the only true one, because it had found out what he himself had done' (Herodotus, *Histories* 1.48; Herodotus, 1890), Croesus then sought to garner favour with the oracle by making huge and very costly sacrifices to Apollo and by sending elaborate offerings to Delphi, including a statue of a golden lion (Herodotus, *Histories* 1.50; Herodotus, 1890). After this he sought two further predictions from Delphi, one concerning the length of his family's reign over Lydia, to which the oracle replied that his monarchy would last until 'it cometh to pass that a mule of the Medes [people from the area of ancient western and northern Iran] shall be monarch' (Herodotus, *Histories* 1.55; Herodotus, 1890). He famously misinterpreted this as meaning that his family would have a long rule, assuming that by 'mule' the oracle meant an animal. Cyrus, the man who defeated him not long after this prophecy was uttered was in fact half Mede and half Persian, making him mixed race, which ancient people described using the term 'mule' (which would now be considered racist).

Even more famously, Croesus also misinterpreted the other consultation, one that led him into the war with the Persians that would end in his defeat. Asking the Delphic oracle (as well as another oracle at Amphiaraus) whether he should wage war on Persia, Herodotus says that:

> the answers of both the Oracles agreed in one, declaring to Crœsus that if he should march against the Persians he should destroy a great empire: and they counselled him to find out the most powerful of the Hellenes and join these with himself as friends.
>
> (Herodotus, *Histories* 1.53; Herodotus, 1890)

Assuming this meant that he was guaranteed a glorious victory, Croesus chose not to make a treaty with the Greeks, went to war, and destroyed his own empire.

Activity 7

(Allow around 30 minutes to complete this activity.)

Reading 3.2 is another extract from Herodotus' *Histories*. Read it through and compare the actions of the Athenians with those of King Croesus, which you have just read about. How do they behave differently?

As you read, think about how the two stories allow Herodotus to use Delphi to comment on the essence of Greekness in comparison with non-Greek culture.

You might find Herodotus' text a little dense in places, so for the purposes of this activity don't worry about being able to identify all the details or characters. Focus instead on the overall narrative – what the Athenians do – and how this reading compares with the story Herodotus tells about Croesus.

Discussion

Although the (Greek) Athenians' rejection of the first response from the oracle – and their seeking of a second, more positive one – might initially seem to parallel the sort of excessive self-confidence displayed by (the non-Greek) Croesus, you may have spotted two main differences between the stories.

First, one of the reasons for rejecting the oracle's initial response was because, to the Athenians, it simply wasn't clear what Apollo was advising them to do. Their fate was sealed, Athens would fall, temples would be destroyed and 'from the topmost roof to the pavement / Dark blood trickles, forecasting the dire unavoidable evil', says the Pythia. But how they should respond to this was still not clear. Unlike Croesus, when they sought a second response, the Athenians did not wish to test the power of the god. The second (accepted) response predicts an equally disastrous outcome, albeit one which suggests (rather ambiguously as it turns out) that there may be a way for the Athenians to act that won't mean complete disaster. What can be seen in this story is the (Greek) Athenians seeking to better understand what Apollo wants them to do. As Herodotus tells it, (the non-Greek) Croesus made no such attempt, ignorantly interpreting his own responses in the way that he wanted.

Second, the Athenians take the response from Delphi back to Athens and discuss its meaning collectively. Again, this contrasts with Croesus, who displays (in the eyes of Herodotus) a typically barbarian and monarchical arrogance by assuming that he alone can decipher the meaning of the oracle's words. The actions of the Athenians in this equally famous story of the 'bulwark of wood' or 'the wooden walls' are not only typically Greek; they also speak directly of the cultural and political landscape of Athens itself and the emergence of the more collective forms of democratic government that you learned about in Chapter 1.

4.4 How to tell an oracle story

Just as interesting as what the stories about Croesus and the Athenians reveal about the significance of Delphi is the fact that they are reminiscent of another central aspect of ancient Greek culture: **oral traditions**. Ancient Greeks rarely wrote things down, at least not with the intention of recording everything as often happens today. That is not to say that they never wrote anything down, or that they did not also engage in very public forms of writing, such as the inscriptions placed on dedications. It is important to acknowledge, however, the significance of oral traditions in Greek storytelling, traditions that stretched back beyond the epics of the poet **Homer**.

You may have noticed that many of the oracle stories you have read, by both Thucydides and Herodotus, adopt a very similar format to each other. Classicist Lisa Maurizio describes them as presenting common 'framing narratives with an almost invariable plot structure – crisis, consultation, interpretation, action, confirmation or refutation of interpretation made evident in the oracle's fulfilment' (1997, p. 311). Both Croesus and the Athenians are, for example, faced with war, so they ask the oracle what they should do, (mis)interpret the response and act accordingly, with the consequences revealing the divine predictive powers of the oracle. This strongly suggests that something has caused these tales to follow the same narrative structure, and it is now widely agreed that this is the result of oral transmission. That is, this structure makes for the best way to tell an oracle story because it is one that is most effectively remembered and retold. By looking closely at the sources that report these narratives, Maurizio was able to conclude that most of these stories were probably circulated by word of mouth for at least a generation before they were finally written down and recorded (1997, p. 313). Evidently there was something about these stories that appealed to those who repeatedly told and listened to them.

Summary

Your study of the Sanctuary of Apollo at Delphi in this chapter has focused on exploring just some of the ways in which this ancient place provided the setting for stories connected with ancient Greek cultural behaviours. Sometimes these were stories that capitalised on the distinctive characteristics of the sanctuary as a location in which an individual could publicly present themselves as behaving in a typically Greek manner, as in the instance of 'The Charioteer'. Other examples included stories that were told both at Delphi and further afield about Greek communities or city-states, such the Naxians, the Athenians, the Spartans and the Epidamnians. In these cases, connections with Delphi were used by Greek communities to align themselves with the religious practices and expectations of a much wider Greek cultural world.

Your examination of the oracle stories recounted by Thucydides and Herodotus also showed how interactions with Delphi could reveal crucial cultural differences between Greeks and non-Greeks, at the same time as such tales explain why Delphi was so central to Greek ways of understanding how the world worked. In the process, what has become clear is that Delphi was a place that fostered and encouraged different methods of ancient storytelling in both written and material forms, which allowed ancient Greeks to signal to one another that they had a shared understanding of the importance of the behaviours that underpinned their particular culture. Such stories also provide ancient historians, classicists and archaeologists with crucial evidence for those behaviours, making it possible to better understand what was important to the ancient Greeks and their sense of cultural identity.

You should now return to the module website to continue your study of this unit.

References

Adornato, G. (2008) 'Delphic Enigmas? The Γέλας ανασσων, Polyzalos, and The Charioteer statue', *American Journal of Archaeology*, 112(1), pp. 29–55.

Bowden, H. (2005) *Classical Athens and the Delphic oracle: divination and democracy*. Cambridge: Cambridge University Press.

Crowther, N.B. (1992) 'Slaves and Greek athletics', *Quaderni Urbinati di Cultura Classica*, 40(1), pp. 35–42.

Herodotus (1890) *The history of Herodotus*. Translated from the Greek by G.C. Macaulay. London and New York, NY: Macmillan. Available at: http://www.sacred-texts.com/cla/hh/hh7140.htm (Accessed: 10 January 2020).

Honour, H. and Fleming, J. (2009) *A world history of art*. Rev. 7th edn. London: Laurence King Publishing.

Kindt, J. (2016) *Revisiting Delphi: religion and storytelling in ancient Greece*. Cambridge: Cambridge University Press.

Maurizio, L. (1997) 'Delphic oracles as oral performances: authenticity and historical evidence', *Classical Antiquity*, 16(2), pp. 308–334.

Neer, R. (2007) 'Delphi, Olympia, and the art of politics', in Shapiro, H.A. (ed.) *The Cambridge companion to Archaic Greece*. Cambridge: Cambridge University Press, pp. 225–264.

Pausanias (1935) *Description of Greece*. Loeb Classical Library 297. Translated from the Greek by W.H.S. Jones. Cambridge, MA: Harvard University Press.

Pedley, J. (2005) *Sanctuaries and the sacred in the ancient Greek world*. Cambridge: Cambridge University Press.

Pindar (1997) *Olympian odes, Pythian odes*. Loeb Classical Library 56. Translated from the Greek by W.H. Race. Cambridge, MA: Harvard University Press.

Scott, M. (2010) *Delphi and Olympia: the spatial politics of Panhellenism in the archaic and Classical periods*. Cambridge: Cambridge University Press.

Thucydides (2013) *The history of the Peloponnesian War*. Translated from the Greek by J. Mynott in *Thucydides: the war of the Peloponnesians and the Athenians*. Cambridge: Cambridge University Press. Available at: https://www-cambridge-org.libezproxy.open.ac.uk/core/books/thucydides/B3A64B95579E3B2E88C423168C17ED2F (Accessed: 29 January 2020).

Readings

Reading 3.1 *The History of the Peloponnesian War*

Extract 1

Source: Thucydides (2013) *The history of the Peloponnesian War*, 1.24–25. Translated from the Greek by J. Mynott in *Thucydides: the war of the Peloponnesians and the Athenians.* Cambridge: Cambridge University Press. Available at: https://www-cambridge-org.libezproxy.open.ac.uk/core/books/thucydides/B3A64B95579E3B2E88C423168C17ED2F (Accessed: 29 January 2020).

The oracular consultation described here took place in 435 BCE. The numbers at the beginning of paragraphs show you where each new 'chapter' begins.

24. Epidamnus is a city on the right as you sail into the Ionian gulf. The neighbouring population are Taulantians, barbarians of the Illyrian race. The city was colonised by Corcyraeans but the founding father was Phalius son of Eratocleides, a Corinthian descended from the line of Heracles, who was invited there from the mother-city very much in accordance with ancient practice. Some Corinthians and some other Dorians were also among the colonists. As time went on the Epidamnians became very powerful with a large population; but after internal conflicts lasting many years, it is said, they were decimated as a consequence of a war with the neighbouring barbarians and were deprived of much of their power. Finally, just before our present war, the common people there expelled the leading men, who then joined the barbarians in attacking the inhabitants of the city and harried them both by land and sea. When the Epidamnians in the city found themselves hard pressed they sent envoys to Corcyra as their mother-city, petitioning them not to look on while they were being destroyed but to reconcile the exiles with them and bring the war with the barbarians to an end. This petition they made sitting as suppliants at the temple of Hera. The Corcyraeans refused their supplication, however, and sent them away empty-handed.

25. When the Epidamnians learned that no help would be forthcoming from Corcyra they were at a loss how to deal with the crisis and sent to Delphi to ask the god whether they should make the city over to the Corinthians as their original founders and try to obtain some assistance from them. The god responded that they should do so and should make the Corinthians their leaders. So the Epidamnians went to Corinth in accordance with the oracle and committed the city to them, pointing out that their founder was from Corinth and revealing the terms of the oracle. They petitioned them not to look on while they were being destroyed but to come to their defence. The Corinthians undertook to give assistance, both as a matter of right, since they regarded the colony to be at least as much theirs as the Corcyraeans', and also out of hatred for the Corcyraeans, since although they were colonists of theirs they were failing to show them respect. They did not present the traditional gifts of honour at their common festivals [the Isthmian Games were held at Corinth], nor did they bestow the first portion of the sacrifices on a Corinthian as the other colonists did. Instead, the Corcyraeans looked down on them: for in terms of financial power the Corcyraeans were at that time the equals of the richest of the Greeks and in terms of military resource they were even stronger, sometimes boasting of their great superiority at sea and citing the earlier occupation of Corcyra by the famed naval power Phaeacia (which led them to build up their naval strength all the more and become no mean power – having 120 triremes [ships] available when they began the war).

Extract 2

> **Source:** Thucydides (2013) *The history of the Peloponnesian War,*
> 1.118. Translated from the Greek by J. Mynott in *Thucydides: the*
> *war of the Peloponnesians and the Athenians.* Cambridge: Cambridge
> University Press. Available at: https://www-cambridge-org.
> libezproxy.open.ac.uk/core/books/thucydides/
> B3A64B95579E3B2E88C423168C17ED2F (Accessed: 29
> January 2020).
>
> The oracular consultation described here took place in 431 BCE.

Not many years after this there then took place the events that have
already been narrated: the episodes at Corcyra and at Potidaea and all
the things that constituted the occasion for this war. All these activities
of the Greeks, both in relation to each other and to the barbarians,
took place in this period of about fifty years between the retreat of
Xerxes [leader of the Persians] and the start of the present war. In that
time the Athenians established their empire on a stronger basis and
greatly advanced their own power. The Spartans were aware of this but
did little to check them. For most of the time they remained passive,
being ever slow to go to war unless forced to do so, and partly too
being hampered by wars of their own at home, until the power of the
Athenians was finally clear for all to see and their actions were
beginning to impinge directly on the Spartan alliance. Then they could
bear it no longer, and decided they must commit themselves totally to
the cause and break the might of Athens, if they could, by undertaking
this war.

The Spartans, then, had decided in their own minds that the treaty had
been broken and that the Athenians were the ones at fault, but they
sent to Delphi to enquire of the god if war was the best course for
them. The god responded, it is said, that if they fought the war with all
their strength victory would be theirs, and added that he himself would
support them, whether bidden or not.

Extract 3

Source: Thucydides (2013) *The history of the Peloponnesian War*, 3.92. Translated from the Greek by J. Mynott in *Thucydides: the war of the Peloponnesians and the Athenians*. Cambridge: Cambridge University Press. Available at: https://www-cambridge-org. libezproxy.open.ac.uk/core/books/thucydides/ B3A64B95579E3B2E88C423168C17ED2F (Accessed: 29 January 2020).

The oracular consultation described here took place in 426 BCE.

At about the same time the Spartans founded Heracleia, their colony in Trachis, with the following purpose in mind. The people of Malis taken as a whole divide into three separate groups: Paralians, Hiereans and Trachinians. Of these the Trachinians had suffered very badly in a war with their neighbours the Oetaeans and first thought of attaching themselves to the Athenians; but they then became afraid that they could not trust them and instead approached the Spartans, sending Teisamenus there as their envoy. The Dorians, from the mother-city of Sparta, joined in this mission too and with the same requests, since they were also suffering at the hands of the Oetaeans. The Spartans listened to their appeals and were minded to send out a colony. They wanted to support both the Trachinians and the Dorians, and at the same time the city seemed to them well placed for their war with Athens: a fleet could be made ready there for an attack on Euboea with only a short crossing to make, and it gave useful access to Thrace. All in all, they were very eager to found a settlement there.

So they first consulted the god at Delphi and with his approval sent out settlers, drawn both from their own citizens and the 'outsiders', and they invited to join them any other Greeks who so wished, except for Ionians, Achaeans and some other peoples. Three Spartans were the founding leaders of the colony: Leon, Alcidas and Damagon. They established and fortified anew the city that is now called Heracleia, located some four and a half miles from Thermopylae and just over two miles from the sea. They began building dockyards and also blocked off the side facing Thermopylae, right at the pass, to make the place easier to defend.

Reading 3.2 *The History of Herodotus*

Source: Herodotus (1890) *The history of Herodotus*, 7.140–7.142. Translated from the Greek by G.C. Macaulay. London and New York, NY: Macmillan. Available at: http://www.sacred-texts.com/cla/hh/hh7140.htm (Accessed: 10 January 2020).

The oracular consultation described here took place in 480 BCE. The Athenians are facing imminent attack from the Persians and need to make a decision about whether to flee Athens or to stay and defend it. The numbers at the beginning of paragraphs show you where each new 'chapter' begins.

140. For the Athenians had sent men to Delphi to inquire and were preparing to consult the Oracle; and after these had performed the usual rites in the sacred precincts, when they had entered the sanctuary and were sitting down there, the Pythian prophetess, whose name was Aristonike, uttered to them this oracle:

"Why do ye sit, O ye wretched? Flee thou to the uttermost limits,
Leaving thy home and the heights of the wheel-round city behind thee!
Lo, there remaineth now nor the head nor the body in safety, –
Neither the feet below nor the hands nor the middle are left thee, –
All are destroyed together; for fire and the passionate War-god,
Urging the Syrian car to speed, doth hurl them to ruin.
Not thine alone, he shall cause many more great strongholds to perish,
Yes, many temples of gods to the ravening fire shall deliver, –
Temples which stand now surely with sweat of their terror down-streaming,
Quaking with dread; and lo! from the topmost roof to the pavement
Dark blood trickles, forecasting the dire unavoidable evil.
Forth with you, forth from the shrine, and steep your soul in the sorrow!

141. Hearing this the men who had been sent by the Athenians to consult the Oracle were very greatly distressed; and as they were despairing by reason of the evil which had been prophesied to them, Timon the son of Androbulos, a man of the Delphians in reputation

Timon the son of Androbulos, a man of the Delphians in reputation equal to the first, counselled them to take a suppliant's bough and to approach the second time and consult the Oracle as suppliants. The Athenians did as he advised and said: "Lord, we pray thee utter to us some better oracle about our native land, having respect to these suppliant boughs which we have come to thee bearing; otherwise surely we will not depart away from the sanctuary, but will remain here where we are now, even until we bring our lives to an end." When they spoke these words, the prophetess gave them a second oracle as follows:

"Pallas [Athena] cannot prevail to appease great Zeus in Olympos,
Though she with words very many and wiles close-woven entreat him.
But I will tell thee this more, and will clench it with steel adamantine:
Then when all else shall be taken, whatever the boundary of Kecrops
Holdeth within, and the dark ravines of divinest Kithairon,
A bulwark of wood at the last Zeus grants to the Trito-born goddess
Sole to remain unwasted, which thee and thy children shall profit.
Stay thou not there for the horsemen to come and the footmen unnumbered;
Stay thou not still for the host from the mainland to come, but retire thee,
Turning thy back to the foe, for yet thou shalt face him hereafter.
Salamis, thou the divine, thou shalt cause sons of women to perish,
Or when the grain is scattered or when it is gathered together."

142. This seemed to them to be (as in truth it was) a milder utterance than the former one; therefore they had it written down and departed with it to Athens: and when the messengers after their return made report to the people, many various opinions were expressed by persons inquiring into the meaning of the oracle, and among them these, standing most in opposition to one another:–some of the elder men said they thought that the god had prophesied to them that the Acropolis should survive; for the Acropolis of the Athenians was in old time fenced with a thorn hedge; and they conjectured accordingly that this saying about the "bulwark of wood" referred to the fence: others on the contrary said that the god meant by this their ships, and they advised to leave all else and get ready these. Now they who said that the ships were the bulwark of wood were shaken in their interpretation by the two last verses which the prophetess uttered:

"Salamis, thou the divine, thou shalt cause sons of women to perish,
Or when the grain is scattered or when it is gathered together."

In reference to these verses the opinions of those who said that the ships were the bulwark of wood were disturbed; for the interpreters of oracles took these to mean that it was fated for them, having got ready for a sea-fight, to suffer defeat round about Salamis.

Postscript

Eventually, thanks to the intervention of the politician Themistocles, the Athenians reached the consensus that by 'a bulwark of wood' the Pythia did indeed mean the Athenian fleet. The Athenians fled the city and although it was largely destroyed by the Persian invaders, their ships were able to engage the Persians in battle at Salamis with great success.

Block 1 Resources

Resource 1.1
Map of the ancient Mediterranean

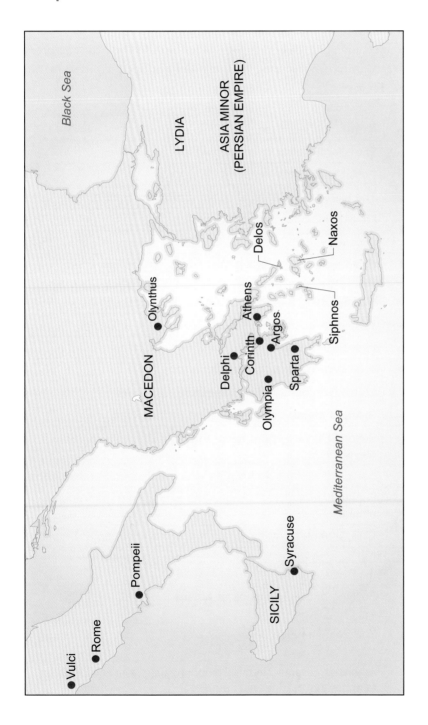

Resource 1.2
Classical Studies timeline

There are a number of events on the following timeline that are not directly studied in A112, but they have been included in order to give you a more comprehensive sense of the wider historical context in which they took place.

Date	Event
c.1500 BCE	The site of Delphi is first settled
c.1260 BCE	Possible date of a historical Trojan War
c.800 BCE	The site of Delphi first acquires a religious significance
776 BCE	First Olympic Games at Olympia
753 BCE	Legendary date of Rome's foundation
750–580 BCE	Greek colonisation in the Mediterranean and Black Sea
c.700 BCE	Homer's *Iliad* and *Odyssey* possibly composed
c.650 BCE	The first temple in honour of Apollo is built at Delphi
c.590 BCE	First Sacred War
586 BCE	First athletic games at Delphi
509 BCE	Foundation of the Roman Republic
490 BCE	Battle of Marathon ends the First Persian War
480 BCE	Second Persian War begins; Persians attack the Sanctuary at Delphi
479 BCE	Battles of Plataea and Mycale end the Second Persian War
478 BCE	Foundation of Delian League and beginning of the Athenian empire
c.470 BCE	'The Charioteer' statue commissioned and put up at Delphi
448 BCE	Second Sacred War; Pericles leads the Athenian forces in the Battle of Delphi
447–432 BCE	Building of the Parthenon at Athens
431–404 BCE	The Peloponnesian War
404 BCE	Athens is defeated in the Peloponnesian War; end of Delian League and the Athenian empire

Date	Event
373 BCE	An earthquake destroys the Temple of Apollo at Delphi
359–336 BCE	Rise of Macedon under Philip II
336–323 BCE	Reign of Alexander the Great and Macedonian conquest of the Persian empire
191 BCE	Delphi comes under Roman control
44 BCE	Assassination of Julius Caesar
31 BCE	Battle of Actium leaves the Emperor Augustus supreme in Rome
19 BCE	Publication of Virgil's *Aeneid*
14 CE	Death of Augustus, accession of Tiberius as emperor
37–41 CE	Rome is ruled by the Emperor Caligula
41–54 CE	Rome is ruled by the Emperor Claudius
54 CE	Death of Claudius, accession of Nero as emperor
64 CE	Great Fire of Rome
68 CE	Death of Nero
69 CE	Year of the Four Emperors
69–79 CE	Rome is ruled by the Emperor Vespasian
79–81 CE	Rome is ruled by the Emperor Titus
80 CE	Completion of the Colosseum

Resource 1.3
Plan of the Sanctuary of Apollo at Delphi

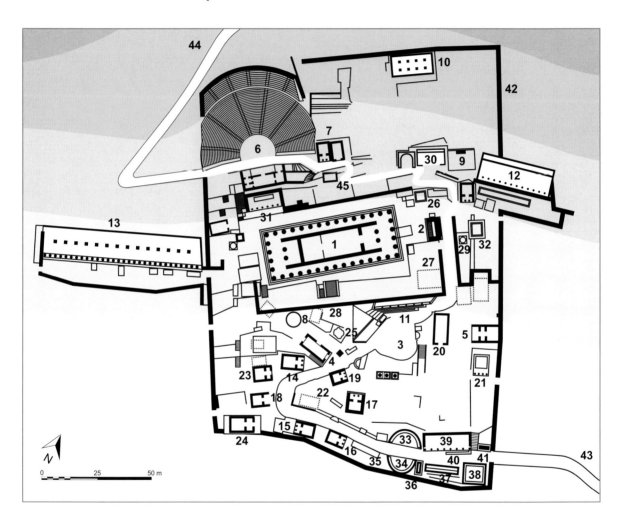

Key for the plan	
1. Temple of Apollo	24. Treasury of the Thebans
2. Altar of the Chians	25. Rock of Delphic Sibyl
3. Aire	26. Column and statue dedication of Prusias II
4. So-called 'bouleuterion'	27. Column and statue dedication of Aemilius Paullus
5. Treasury	28. Column with sphinx dedication of the Naxians
6. Theatre	29. Plataean serpent column
7. Buildings of uncertain function	30. Statue of group dedication of Daochus
8. Possible Sanctuary of Gaia	31. Enclosure and statue group dedication of Craterus
9. Cult area of Neoptolemus	32. Column with chariot statue dedication of the Rhodians
10. Lesche of the Cnidians	33. First exedra and statue group dedication of the Argives
11. Stoa of the Athenians	34. Second exedra and statue group dedication of the Argives
12. Stoa of Attalus	35. Statue group dedication of the Tarentines
13. West Stoa	36. Trojan horse statue dedication of the Argives
14. Treasury of the Athenians	37. Statue group dedication of the Athenians
15. Treasury of the Siphnians	38. Statue group dedication of the Spartans
16. Treasury of the Sicyonians	39. Stoa of the Spartans
17. Treasury of the Aeolians	40. Statue group of the Arcadians
18. Treasury of the Boeotians	41. Bull dedication of the Corcyraeans
19. Treasury of the Cnidians	42. Temenos wall
20. Treasury of the Corinthians	43. Start of the Sacred Way
21. Treasury of the Cyrenians	44. Road to the stadium
22. Treasury of the Megarians	45. Possible location of the Charioteer statue group of the Hieron of Gela and Syracuse
23. Treasury of the Potidaians	

Block 2:

Art and power

Edited by Clare Taylor

Introduction

Written by Clare Taylor

Welcome to Block 2 and to your study of Art History and Visual Cultures. In this block you will be exploring visual imagery, one of the most powerful means in which cultural identity is established. You'll be looking at artworks from diverse cultural traditions, from across Britain, wider Europe, India and Mexico, and at how artists have challenged European models in their art. Throughout, you will be building your skills in how to look at, and analyse, artworks. You'll also be reading examples of writing about art – from exhibition catalogue extracts to museum websites – in order to understand more about how viewers have understood visual messages, both in the past and today.

Study note

A112 uses the term 'Art History' as shorthand to refer to the expanded field of study of Art History and Visual Cultures.

The term 'artwork' is an umbrella term used in this module to encompass all types of visual, material and spatial culture ranging from paintings, prints and buildings to designed or sculpted objects.

1 Introducing the block theme: Art and power

'Art and power' is the theme of this block as it allows you to study both the art of powerful groups and how this dominance has been challenged. One of the ways it has been challenged is through the sorts of artworks we study. It's worth saying that we use the term art history *and* visual cultures today because the study of art covers a much wider definition than it has done previously. Formerly, to be recognised as an artwork meant that the work needed to conform to established ways of being made and presented, and in Europe these were often rooted in the revival of the antique, and in Italy in particular. The idea of what art was (and who could make it) was also largely limited to what we now call 'fine art': painting, sculpture and architecture. This model has been challenged not only by art historians but also by artists, particularly since the nineteenth century.

Many of the artworks associated with the powerful, such as portraits of rulers like Elizabeth I or buildings like Buckingham Palace in London, fall into these 'fine art' categories. These artworks survive by being collected and exchanged among powerful social elites. Since the nineteenth century, private ownership, and control, of art has expanded with the creation of public art museums; curators have therefore taken an increasingly important role in defining art and who can be an artist. The rise of museums has also changed how we can view art. Artworks collected by public museums like the National Galleries around the British Isles are displayed away from their original context (in private collections) and gain a new power, as artworks alone, isolated from the spaces they were created for.

Art historians today are also interested in artworks that were in the past labelled as part of the 'lesser arts'. These include the so-called decorative or applied arts: textiles, ceramics, furniture and other designed objects. The fact that many are anonymous (their designer or maker is unknown), has also led them to be seen differently to a painting signed by a well-known artist. Today, we see these diverse artworks as part of the visual and material culture of societies and communities. Many of these objects are now more accessible to, and owned by, many more people, and art historians can use them to challenge the hierarchies around fine art. By asking different questions about art, we work with a wider range of creative works. For example, printed images have frequently been regarded of lesser status than a supposedly unique, painted artwork. However, prints have played an important role in exchanging visual ideas across cultures. Publications such as Owen Jones's 1856 design sourcebook *The Grammar of Ornament* circulated prints that could be used to create new designs. The circulation of visual culture often leads to it being reimagined and adopted in new ways, and these changes can represent the exercise of power by new users of art for their own purposes, not previously determined by the original work.

Another way in which we can understand the relationship between art and power emerges from looking at how different cultures prioritise types of artworks. For example, as you will see in Chapter 1, it was miniature painting, not large-scale painting in oils, which was the medium of choice for portraiture in India's Mughal Empire, so this is the type of artwork we need to examine to understand how this imperial court asserted their identity. Paying attention to material culture also challenges a hierarchy of materials based on classical models: sculpture of mixed media, incorporating natural materials or textiles, claim our attention as much as marble and bronze.

Today, when we consider the relationship between art and power, we also have to acknowledge the levels of exploitation that many artworks embody, particularly through histories of colonisation. The imperial legacies that have shaped the built environment and material culture in Britain continue to be highly visible in major port cities and in country houses. Whereas many country houses follow the classical tradition and adopt the models of ancient Roman buildings, Sezincote in Gloucestershire (Figure 1) adopts aspects of the built environment of India. Sezincote's design shows how the owners not only used the capital accumulated in India to purchase landed estates and build a new home in which to display material goods, but also, more unusually, its design appropriated ideas from Hindu and Muslim architecture, leading it to be labelled 'Neo-Mughal'. The presence of a colonial-era use of Mughal style in the imperial heartland of England expresses very different meanings to us now, in the visibility of the origins of the wealth that created it, compared to the hidden sources of wealth behind many classical country houses built from the profits of the British Atlantic trade in enslaved people.

Figure 1 Sezincote, Gloucestershire, designed by Samuel Pepys Cockerell for Charles Cockerell, 1805–1807. Photo: Clare Taylor.

Knowledge of these various hierarchies is also crucial if we are to understand artworks that challenge the powerful, be that religious bodies, nations, political movements or cultural institutions such as museums. As you will see in Chapter 3, such artworks may be found in protest movements, in organised artistic or community groups, and in the work of those who sit outside the accepted training and career of 'being an artist' or who reject the art market. In order to examine how groups who are marginalised around categories of otherness – including gender, ethnicity, sexuality, mental and physical ability, disabilities and other differences – represent themselves (rather than being represented by outsiders), art historians now seek to identify and study artworks produced by groups who are under-represented, if not invisible, in older histories of art.

2 What will you study in this block?

In the following three chapters, you will be looking at the theme of art and power through the lens of artworks representing individuals, ideas and the landscape around them as well as the monuments and buildings they create. You will examine three different case studies, which allow you to study the relationship between art and power from different angles. These will also enable you to study how rulers were portrayed, how country houses were built to convey power and status, and conversely how individuals and groups have used art to resist and challenge the powerful.

In the first chapter on portraiture, you will begin by looking at individuals, building on the work you have done on the Grand Tour portraits (in Block 1, Unit 4 on the module website). You will explore portraits associated with rulers from the 1400s to the 1600s, not only from Italy but from across Europe, and from the Ottoman and Mughal Empires, challenging artistic hierarchies that have in the past prioritised the art of Italy. You'll learn about the role of portraiture as part of interactions between cultures, and the ways in which portraits may be read by viewers in the past and today, taking account of marginalised groups as well as the powerful.

The second chapter turns to buildings and the individuals who created them, looking at the country house in Elizabethan England through the lens of a single site, Hardwick in Derbyshire. As well as examining the design of the two houses on this site, this chapter builds on your study of interiors in Block 1 to examine the contribution of the 'lesser arts', including textiles and furniture, to show how Hardwick was designed to articulate the dynastic power and cultural status of its female patron. You will also explore the enduring power of the country house; how sites such as Hardwick were used as models by country house builders in Victorian Britain as well as their place as heritage attractions today.

Like the first, the third and final chapter in this block looks across place and time to examine how artists have used artworks to challenge and subvert inequalities in power using prints, photography and posters. You will learn how artists adopted satire and propaganda to challenge political and cultural positions. These artworks took as their subject images of war or of the oppression of marginalised groups, including artists themselves, across Spain, Germany and the contemporary period in Britain. The discussion also returns to the issue of display, and looks at how the art market and museums can reinforce or challenge existing hierarchies around art and power.

In Unit 4 (on the module website) you will have the opportunity to explore a range of ideas about portraits beyond art history. How, for example, were portraits of emperors circulated in the classical world? And how do writers in the past and today use real and imagined portraiture as a device in their work?

3   What skills will you develop?

The activities in this block are designed to help you to develop your skills of analysing artworks as well as the close reading of written texts. The visual analysis toolkit (Resource 2.1 in the Resources section at the end of this block) will also help you grasp the tools and terms that art historians use to analyse artworks. You have already met this toolkit in the introduction to A112 (Week 1 of the module) and used it in your work on the Grand Tour portraits in Block 1. If you have time, you could take this opportunity to look at the visual analysis toolkit in more detail by reading the 'Introduction' and 'Approaching artworks' sections. Don't worry too much about any terms that are new to you (although you may like to highlight them), as throughout this block, and indeed the module, you will be referred back to the toolkit to complete certain activities.

Digital communications driven by graphics and images are playing an increasing role in our lives. Gaining an understanding of the visual power of art, how it is used, by who and for what purpose, is a key skill. Studying this block will not only help you to articulate this world, it will also enable you to reflect on contemporary debates about how the powerful use visual imagery and equally how marginalised groups seek to represent themselves.

Chapter 1

Portraits of power: from Italian princes to Mughal emperors

Written by Leah R. Clark

Contents

1 Introduction

What is a portrait? Portraiture is a particular genre or form of art that can be executed in various media from sculpture to painting. This chapter will look primarily at portraits during the period 1400–1600 in Europe (mostly Italy and England), but it will also examine the genre in the Ottoman and Mughal empires. Portraits could serve a number of functions, but it is important to remember that unlike today, when we can take a quick photograph with our phones or digital cameras and immediately share it with friends and family, portraits took time and money to produce in the **Renaissance**. During this period, portraits would include hiring an artist and often paying for the required materials (canvas, paint, etc.). This meant that only those in the middle to upper classes of society (such as wealthy families, merchant-bankers, ambassadors and rulers) could afford portraits. Having one's portrait done at this time was therefore in itself a sign of prestige.

Beyond the element of prestige, what functions did portraits serve? On a basic level, they were commemorative, serving to record a likeness for future generations. Indeed, we only have an idea of what famous individuals from the past looked like because of the portraits that have survived. Portraits were often discussed as a way of making absent friends present. They could be used to assert power, act as propaganda and were also used in diplomacy. Additionally, portraits were often employed in marriage negotiations, so that either party could be made aware of what potential partners looked like. They could be collected and displayed to show one's alliances or show off one's powerful friends. Portraits were also used in devotional images, to demonstrate piety and act as a form of devotion. We will be looking at specific functions in more depth throughout this chapter. In particular, we will examine the circulation, collection and display of portraits and what they can tell us about the relationship between art and power (state power primarily, but other concerns around religion, gender and race also feature).

What was the Renaissance?

The term 'Renaissance' is usually used to refer to a period in time (*c.*1400–1600) traditionally associated with the revival of classical antiquity in arts and culture in Europe, but it can also be applied to any culture that has a period of flourishing. Debates in the field of Renaissance Studies have questioned whether the Renaissance should be called the Renaissance at all, as it often suggests a closed European phenomenon, sometimes restricted just to Italy and the rebirth of a local, classical antiquity (associated with the rise of humanism, a cultural and educational movement).

Other terminology, such as the '**early modern**' period, has been employed to denote a more neutral, all-encompassing approach, which recognises that there were a series of 'Renaissances' flourishing all over the world, without the Eurocentric connotations. Early modern also suggests a broader time period, but this is debated; some scholars understand this to include the medieval period and the Renaissance, while others limit it to 1600–1850. In this chapter, I use the term 'Renaissance' to refer to the period roughly between 1400–1600 (not restricted to Italy), and 'early modern' to refer to the larger period, 1400–1750, which also assumes a global scope.

Portraits are products of particular cultures, so learning to interpret a portrait not only tells us something about the sitter but also about the larger culture that it was produced in. Another key theme throughout this chapter is **cultural translation**, and we will be looking at how certain forms of portraiture and objects used to display power were employed across cultures.

Art historians use particular skills of visual analysis to look at images and art objects, and throughout this chapter you will be learning these skills. You will also build on skills such as textual analysis, which you began developing in Block 1 and will develop further throughout this module. The visual analysis toolkit (Resource 2.1 in the Resources section at the end of this block) will be a useful guide throughout this unit. Now, let's have a look at a portrait and think about what art historians call the formal qualities.

Figure 1 Hans Holbein the Younger, *Jane Seymour*, 1536, oil on panel, 65 × 41 cm. Kunsthistorisches Museum, Vienna, Inv.No.: Gemäldegalerie, 881. Photo: © Bridgeman Images.

Activity 1

(Allow around 15 minutes to complete this activity.)

1. Look at Figure 1 of Jane Seymour (r.1536–37) and write down what you see at first glance. To begin with, you might find it difficult to describe anything beyond a woman standing.

2. Now spend some time looking closely and consider the following elements, with the help of the 'Paintings' section of the visual analysis toolkit (Resource 2.1 in the Resources section at the end of this block):

- Clothing: does it look expensive or cheap?

- Setting: are there any indicators of what sort of space this is?

- Stance and emotion: is the sitter standing or sitting? Is she in profile, or three-quarter? Does she engage the viewer? Does she look poised, nervous, alert, angry, happy, sad?

- Other accessories: are there other objects in the room? Does the sitter wear jewellery, a hat or other accessories? What might these say about her?

- Light: is the sitter in darkness or light? Are there shadows?

Discussion

You might have noticed that, in the portrait, Jane Seymour wears rings as well as a very large necklace. She also has jewels stitched onto her gown, mainly around her collar and waist, and her necklace brooch shows the letters 'IHS' (not easily discernible). Her hat also sports jewels, framing her face. She is in three-quarter view, meaning that she is not entirely in profile nor does she look directly at the viewer. She is also depicted just below the waist up: it is not a full portrait, but it is also not just a head shot (or **bust**). She is not smiling but she is not frowning either. Her lips are pursed, as if she might speak if spoken to. Her dress shows varied textures of expensive textiles: from the red velvet to the embroidered silver and gold threads, which were all costly materials for the time. Finally, there is no background; she is presumably in an interior space, and Holbein has suggested some depth by depicting her shadow.

Jane Seymour would appear to be a wealthy woman to a contemporary viewer. But how can we tell that? One part of Art History is not only looking but also situating the work within the historical context. Contemporary viewers would have been able to estimate the costs of the jewels and these would be clear symbols that she had money. The 'IHS' on her necklace brooch are the first letters of **Jesus Christ**'s name in Greek. The reference to Christ would underline her piety, something especially praised in women of the time (women were encouraged to model themselves on Mary, the mother of Jesus). She has her hands clasped in front of her, a demeanour that would have been seen as a respectable stance for a woman. By not looking directly at the viewer, she would have been read as a virtuous woman, as guidance for women of the time instructed them not to look directly at men. So, while she is represented as a powerful woman, she also had to be depicted in a way that conformed to decorum for women.

The art historian, Harry Berger, discusses portraits in terms of telling a story, and this can be a useful way to approach portraits (1994). He argues that in the early modern period, portraits were performed; this **performance** was staged not only by the sitter but also, and often largely, by the artist. 'Performance' here, as it is often employed more broadly in the humanities, refers not to a theatrical performance but to the way in which our identities are performed or 'staged'. However, it is important to note that, unlike the theatre, we cannot just choose any identity, because the identities we perform are played out within a culture's norms and behavioural expectations. Indeed, in the case of portraits, these expectations and norms are usually heightened to show an idealised self.

As a result, Berger suggests that we approach portraits and the stories they tell in four modes:

1   The sitter's social, political and/or professional status, as well as their 'character', which might be their moral quality or state of mind.

2   The painter's characterisation of the sitter and how the artist produces this.

3   The sitter's pose and appearance.

4   The archival data: the historical information that we gather to confirm or support 1, 2 and 3, which helps us understand things about the lives, behaviours and practices of sitters and painters.

These 'modes' might seem complex, but we will be working through them as we make our way through this chapter. Berger (1994) reminds us of the 'fiction of the pose'; that is, while a portrait might look like a real person, it is of course a portrayal or representation of that person. Portraits are not objective but subjective portrayals, based on what the artist, sitter and/or patron wants the viewer to see. We should read portraits then as ways in which norms for a particular society or group are visualised and communicated. This helps us to understand how the powerful project their power through portraits; they use cultural artefacts (such as portraits) to produce a particular reading of themselves.

2 Staging portraits

What was involved in staging a portrait and creating the 'story' for the viewer? Artists and sitters would have had to decide on the particular clothing, jewels and other accessories that they were to be portrayed in. A good example of this is the portrait of Francesco Maria I della Rovere, Duke of Urbino (1490–1538) by the well-known Venetian artist Titian (*c*.1490–1576) (Figure 2).

Figure 2 Titian, *Francesco Maria I della Rovere, Duke of Urbino*, *c*.1537, oil on canvas, 114 × 103 cm. Galleria degli Uffizi, Florence, Inv.1890 n.926. Photo: Scala, Florence – courtesy of the Ministero Beni e Att. Culturali e del Turismo.

How is the Duke of Urbino portrayed here? You might say he looks rather stiff in his armour, but we need to think about why he would have chosen to be depicted that way, and historical evidence also helps us to recreate the parameters of how such a portrait was created or 'staged.' Many Italian rulers were **condottieri**, or military commanders. The dukes of Urbino were particularly well known for their military prowess and would sell their military abilities as captains to other states – essentially, they were for hire. Francesco Maria I della Rovere succeeded his uncle Guidobaldo da Montefeltro as ruler of Urbino. Francesco was one of Italy's most important military leaders of the time and frequently served the **Republic** of Venice.

How might his position as duke and *condottiere* be conveyed in the painting? The choice to be depicted in armour was concerted and indeed convoluted. Titian did not take the duke's portrait in person; instead, the armour was shipped to Urbino and put on by an assistant in bare legs (as the sketch by Titian attests; Figure 3)! The loaning of items was a fairly common occurrence, such as in 1549 when the well-known Netherlandish portraitist Anthonis Mor (*c*.1516–1577) was lent rings, chains, jewels and precious garments belonging to King Philip II of Spain (r.1556–1598) to be inserted into his portraits (some of which are shown in Figure 4, such as the chain or collar of the **knightly Order** of the Golden Fleece and his garments).

Underneath the armour in Figure 2, the Duke of Urbino is wearing black and yellow, the colours of the Montefeltro house, underscoring his descent from this family and thus his right to rule. On the shelf behind him, to the left, is a helmet topped by a dragon and on the right, the batons of command of the papacy, Florence and Venice. The motif of the oak branch also references his bloodline and the house of della Rovere (*rovere* means 'oak' in Italian), and notably its most illustrious member, his uncle, Pope Julius II (r.1503–13). The portrait is thus a staged reference to his right to rule, his military power and his family connections. Titian underscores the theatrical effect by using a red velvet cloth as the backdrop, showcasing the instruments on display and contrasting them with the dark armour. The duke's stance tells the viewer he is a force to be reckoned with, especially with the baton in his right hand thrusting out into our space.

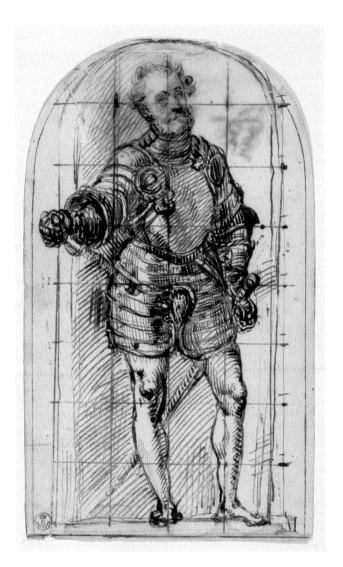

Figure 3 Titian, *Study for the Duke of Urbino*, *c*.1536, pen and ink on paper, 24 × 14 cm. Gabinetto dei Disegni e delle Stampe degli Uffizi, Florence, n. 20767 F. Photo: Scala, Florence – courtesy of the Ministero Beni e Att. Culturali e del Turismo.

Figure 4 Anthonis Mor, *Portrait of Philip II in Armour*, 1557, oil on canvas, 186 × 82 cm. Monasterio de San Lorenzo, El Escorial, Madrid. Photo: Album/Scala, Florence.

Titian's portrait of Francesco delle Rovere is actually part of a **pendant**, made as a pair with his wife's portrait, Eleonora Gonzaga (1493–1550) (Figure 5). Eleonora was described in Baldassare Castiglione's *Book of the Courtier* (first published in 1528) as embodying 'wisdom, grace, beauty, capacity, tact, humanity and every other gentle quality' (2003, p. 242 [the fourth book]).

Figure 5 Titian, *Eleonora Gonzaga Duchess of Urbino*, *c*.1537, oil on canvas, 114 × 103 cm. Galleria degli Uffizi, Florence, Inv.1890 n.919. Photo: Scala, Florence – courtesy of the Ministero Beni e Att. Culturali e del Turismo.

Activity 2

(Allow around 10 minutes to complete this activity.)

How does Eleonora's portrait (Figure 5) differ from her husband's (Figure 2)? Does Castiglione's text about Eleonora support her portrait? Consider how gender plays a role.

You can also revisit Berger's four 'modes' to consider how they work here:

1   The sitter's social, political and/or professional status, as well as their 'character', which might be their moral quality or state of mind.

2   The painter's characterisation of the sitter and how the artist produces this.

3   The sitter's pose and appearance.

4   The archival data: the historical information that we gather to confirm or support 1, 2 and 3, that helps us understand things about the lives, behaviour and practices of sitters and painters.

(This fourth mode will be more difficult, but you can draw on Castiglione's text as a primary source.)

Discussion

In contrast to the duke, Duchess Eleonora sits primly in her chair, immobile. Detailed attention is paid to the rendering of her court dress and jewels, and she is certainly not in armour (Mode 2 and 3).

Castiglione's description suggests he is characterising all the things that a noble woman should be (Mode 4). We might note beauty and grace in a portrait, but how does an artist communicate 'wisdom', 'capacity' or 'tact' (Mode 1)?

You might have found that disentangling all the 'modes' can be difficult, as they are closely related. In terms of the sitter's appearance, we can be sure of what the painting looks like, but we cannot be sure of whether this accurately depicts the sitter.

Art historians have interpreted the portrait of Duchess Eleonora in contrasting ways. On the one hand, it can be read as a sign of the limitations of women in the **courts**, who were often used as marriage pawns within male political and diplomatic networks and were made to proscribe to ideal feminine behaviour. This might be underlined by the dog, who is a symbol of fidelity, and thus Eleonora's portrait could be read as embodying the perfect bride and court consort: devoted to her husband and securing the future line of legitimate male heirs (Mode 4). Others have interpreted this as evidence of Eleonora's cultural role at court, emblematised in her inclusion in Castiglione's famous text. Women in the courts could hold a certain amount of political power, sometimes serving as regents when their husbands were abroad. Titian's landscape (seen through the window in Figure 5) is vast, which has been read as untraversable, marked by a church tower in its idealised blue distance, yet landscapes often appeared in the backgrounds of portraits, especially those of male rulers, referring to their domains and their power over their lands. These portraits, while staged, also demonstrate that there isn't always just one clear message conveyed by a portrait. It is also likely that contemporary viewers may have brought to them both the social conventions of the time and multiple viewpoints in reading them.

These dual portraits (Figures 2 and 5) also point to the tradition of **double portraits**, particularly at Urbino, drawing upon a famous double portrait from the fifteenth century of Federigo da Montefeltro (r.1444–1482) and Battista Sforza (r.1460–1472), Duke and Duchess of Urbino (Figure 6). In this way, the double portrait as a format also connected Francesco and Eleonora to past rulers of the city, underlining the family's legacy as military commanders (Federigo was one of the most well-known *condottieri* of the fifteenth century) and underscoring their right to rule Urbino.

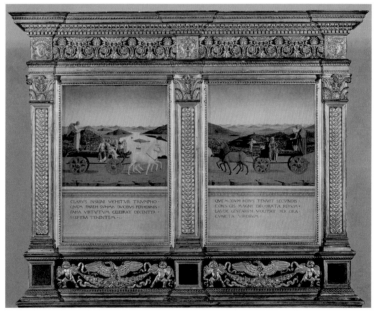

Figure 6 Piero della Francesca, *Battista Sforza and Federigo da Montefeltro* (obverse) and *Triumphs* (reverse), *c.*1473–75, oil on wood, each panel 47 × 33 cm. Galleria degli Uffizi, Florence, Inv. 1890 nn. 1615, 3342. Photo: Scala, Florence. Not in original frame.

3 Circulating images of power

As well as serving dynastic or hereditary claims, portraits were used to circulate images of the powerful. This section will look at some of the various functions of portraits, with a particular focus on their political and public aspects.

Study note

The following three activities connect together and will build on your skills of visual analysis, contextual analysis and comparison, respectively. Art historians often knit together historical texts and other forms of visual culture with a work of art to understand its context, and you will be learning how to do this in the following activities.

Activity 3

(Allow around 10 minutes to complete this activity.)

First, look closely at Figure 7 (the portrait of the Italian noblewoman Bianca Capello) and apply your skills of visual analysis utilising the visual analysis toolkit (Resource 2.1 in the Resources section at the end of this block). Write down what you see (your answer should relate to Berger's Modes 2 and 3).

Discussion

The sitter looks out at the viewer, calm yet attentive, her face framed by a delicate lace collar. The artist, Scipione Pulzone, has taken particular delight in portraying the lustre of the pearls, with dabs of white paint, mimicked in her glossy eyes. Arranged neatly in her bosom is a red carnation, carefully placed. She is in three-quarter view and it is a bust portrait. There is no clear background, so that the emphasis is on Capello's face, and this provides a stark contrast between the dark background and the white lace. From the caption, we can tell that it is a fairly small portrait, so it would have required the viewer to get quite close to it to be able to pick out the painterly details, such as brushstroke and how the pearls are rendered.

Figure 7 Scipione Pulzone, *Bianca Capello*, 1584, oil on canvas, 57 × 47 cm. Kunsthistorisches Museum, Vienna, Inv.No. Gemäldegalerie, 1138. KHM-Museumsverband.

Now let's consider the context for the commission of Figure 7 and its viewership. In 1585, the Venetian nobleman Francesco Bembo visited Bianca Capello in Florence, where he saw Pulzone's portrait of her. Bembo was so taken with the portrait that he commissioned a copy from Pulzone (Kessel, 2010). This second version was sent to him in Venice, where Bembo (as he informed Capello in a letter) immediately sat in front of the picture for two hours contemplating it. Eventually, he covered it in a cloth and took it upstairs to show to the women of the house, where he notes:

I lifted up the cloth with which I had it covered. And as if the curtain of a scene was dropped, the people were full of admiration. When the cloth fell, these Women were left stupefied and completely and totally satisfied.

(quoted in Kessel, 2010, p. 280)

Bembo had received the painting on 8 March 1586 and by May of that year as many as 700 visitors had allegedly come to see it. Guests viewing the painting acted in a similar way to how devotees acted in front of religious images at the time, such as kissing it, and when Bianca later fell ill, viewers came to pray for her well-being in front of it.

Activity 4

(Allow around 10 minutes to complete this activity.)

For this activity, think about what the reception of the image in Bembo's home tells us about the function and circulation of portraits such as Figure 7.

By reading the previous quote and the summary of the context, think about how the painting's contemporary viewers behaved in front of it and write down some of your thoughts (your answer should relate to Berger's Mode 4).

Discussion

The context demonstrates that the painting had a complex history, which highlights the multiple and very public functions of portraits. It underlines that copies or replicas of portraits were fairly common and that there was a theatricality involved, which involved particular forms of behaviour in viewing such paintings. Viewers acted in a similar manner to how they acted in front of a holy image, underscoring how some portraits were thought to have a presence, just as a human would – they stood in for the person.

Bembo's story immediately forces us to ask the question: who was Bianca Capello and why was there such a devotion to her image? Answering this question requires us to reconstruct the story of the sitter and the commissioner, and forces us to do some historical research to better understand the context. Our visual analysis can only get us so far, but understanding the context can tell us more about the sitter, and further historical research might also tell us about the symbolism of the painting, revealing whether her attire (and other markers) might have another level of meaning.

From historical documents, we know that Bianca Capello was a rather notorious character in sixteenth-century society. She was from a wealthy, powerful Venetian family, but at the age of 15 she eloped with the young accountant Pietro Bonaventuri to his home town of Florence against her father's will. It was in Florence that she was taken under the wing of Francesco I de' Medici, the heir to the grand-ducal throne of Tuscany. Francesco took a liking to Bianca, and the two secretly married in 1578 after both their spouses had died. A year later they were married in public, making her the grand duchess of Tuscany. While once a disgrace to Venice, Bianca was now celebrated in her home city with numerous ceremonies, where her father and brother were invited into the Palazzo Ducale and knighted by the doge (chief magistrate of Venice). It was clear that she now had diplomatic value for Venice. Bembo also came from a wealthy Venetian family, and it was on diplomatic business representing the Republic of Venice in Florence that he became acquainted with Bianca (and her portrait) and a friendship was formed. As you may have guessed, Figure 7 is the copy that Bembo then ordered and showed off in his home.

As a grand duchess, numerous portraits were made of Bianca. Commenting on the Venetian painters who tried to copy the portrait, Bembo wrote: 'Many want a copy, and few, or rather none, of these painters will make it. Tintoretto has started one, but it turns out to be very dissimilar, for [the original] looks more like a living person than a painted one, and its diligence misleads all' (Kessel, 2010, p. 282). In comparing the portrait to others that were made by Pulzone, including one possibly by a female artist (see Figure 8), it is clear that the detailed emphasis on the clothing and pearls enhances the 'lifelike' quality of the version that Bembo commissioned.

Figure 8 Lavinia Fontana (attributed), *Bianca Capello*, *c*.1585. Collezioni comunali d'arte, Bologna.

We are now going to take a closer look at what Capello is wearing in her picture in order to situate her portrait within other forms of visual culture. Figures 9 and 10 show two prints from Cesare Vecellio's sixteenth-century costume book. The book articulates strict regulations on what women could wear according to status: not only social status but also marital status. It depicts clothing and adornments that would clearly signal whether the wearer was married, widowed or single (or even a courtesan). The book also detailed behaviour to accompany status. Unmarried noble girls should be guarded by their fathers and could only leave their homes occasionally to go to church or for holy days, and when they did so they had to wear a silk veil. Once married, noble women were allowed to enter the public sphere by being beautifully dressed and could enjoy dancing or balls.

Figure 9 (left) Christoph Krieger, 'Young married woman of the Venetian nobility' and **Figure 10 (right)** Christoph Krieger, 'Married woman' woodcut from Cesare Vecellio, *De gli habiti antichi, e moderni di diverse parti del mondo libri due [...]*, Damiano Zenaro, Venice, 1590. Metropolitan Museum of Art, New York, Rogers Fund, 1906, transferred from the Library, Accession No. 21.36.146.

Activity 5

(Allow around 10 minutes to complete this activity.)

Now compare Figure 7 with the two prints from Vecellio's sixteenth-century costume book (Figures 9 and 10) and consider it in relation to the text that accompanied these prints about the appropriate behaviour of women (summarised in the previous paragraph). You might want to return to your visual analysis from Activity 3 and compare what you noticed in the painting with what you see in the prints.

Write down your thoughts on how a costume book like this one provides evidence for the art historian and also any problems it raises as a source of evidence.

Discussion

By comparing the portrait with sixteenth-century prints depicting Venetian women, it is clear that Pulzone has used the lace collar and pearls to portray Capello as a married noblewoman. From the textual evidence accompanying the prints, the book also suggests that there were articulated social mores for women and their behaviour.

It is important to also question the primary text: this was written by Vecellio, a man who generalises female behaviour. By doing so, he creates expectations and largely reinforces social norms for women, but did all women and families subscribe to these ideas? By looking at Bianca's portrait in relation to the prints and text, it has helped us understand better the expectations placed on women, and that portraits would often subscribe to those ideals.

We can now look at this portrait (Figure 7) through these key identifiers and tell a story. We can conclude that items of clothing worn on the body were social markers, signifiers that contemporaries would have understood to be read (Berger's Mode 4). Having more information about Bianca's story, however, demonstrates that she exercised some sort of authority to break away from those prescriptions. But why would Bembo want her portrait? We will have to speculate, but it is likely that one of the main reasons was to help his own status by showing off his close friendship with the grand duchess of Tuscany. The circulation of her image in the form of a copy worked to enhance his own reputation in Venice, and the theatrical display of it ensured that it was talked about.

As previously mentioned, the act of asking for a copy or getting a portrait copied was fairly common practice. While portraits were works of art, we need to also think of them as ways of communicating a message. We often think of works of art as singular masterpieces that cannot be replicated, as there is always an 'original' and then a 'copy.' These categories do not entirely work for portraits, as we know that artists were often commissioned to produce a portrait and would then have to be prepared to create multiple 'replicas' because of demand.

The portrait of Jane Seymour that we saw in Figure 1 is based on this original drawing by Holbein (Figure 11). The drawing and the portrait are an identical match in terms of measurements, which indicates that a tracing process must have been used to transfer a precise reproduction of the drawing onto the panel. While this could have been done to alleviate the sitter from having to sit too long (sitters were notorious for complaining about how hard it was to sit still for hours), it also enabled Holbein to be able to use the original drawing for future portraits, should they be required. We know that this was common practice for Holbein. Indeed, this particular study of Jane Seymour was used by Holbein for a number of portraits, including a full-length portrait in a now-lost Whitehall mural (surviving as a copy, see Figure 12).

Figure 11 Hans Holbein the Younger, *Jane Seymour*, *c*.1536–37, black and coloured chalks, pen and ink on pale pink prepared paper, 50 × 29 cm. Royal Collection Trust © Her Majesty Queen Elizabeth II, 2020, RCIN 912267. Photo: © Bridgeman Images.

Figure 12 Remigius van Leemput (copy of a now lost Holbein), *Henry VII, Elizabeth of York, Henry VIII and Jane Seymour*, 1667, oil on canvas, 89 × 99 cm. Hampton Court Palace. Royal Collection Trust © Her Majesty Queen Elizabeth II, 2020, RCIN 405750. Photo: © Bridgeman Images.

Jane Seymour was the third wife of Henry VIII (r.1509–47) and mother of Edward VI (r.1547–53). Her portrait would have been in demand by those who wanted to show acquaintance with the royal family (to enhance their status) and those who wanted to show allegiance. Others might keep portraits to give away upon request. In 1550, a Milanese official wrote to Cardinal Antoine Perrenot of Granvelle, stating that he had heard Granvelle had many portraits of himself and asked for one, which he would keep 'for my contemplation and for the decoration of my house' (quoted in Campbell, 1990, p. 183). The portraits in question were probably by the well-known portraitist Anthonis Mor (and his workshop) and were copies of Figure 13.

Figure 13 Anthonis Mor, *Portrait of Cardinal Antoine Perrenot of Granvelle*, 1549, oil on panel, 105 × 77 cm. Kunsthistorisches Museum, Vienna, Inv.No. Gemäldegalerie, 1035. Photo: © Bridgeman Images.

4 Currency of fame

We have seen how portraits could be exchanged and circulated through painted copies, but portraits circulated in other media too. In the fifteenth century, two new ways to circulate portraits emerged: the portrait medal and the printed portrait.

Figure 14 Pisanello, Portrait medal of Leonello d'Este. Obverse: bust of Leonello d'Este. Reverse: singing lion. 1444, cast bronze, diameter: 10 cm. Victoria and Albert Museum, London, A. 165-1910. © Victoria and Albert Museum, London. (There are multiple copies in collections around the world.)

In Italy, the portrait medal emerged as a response to renewed interests in antiquity. They were not as small as coins, but they were similar to, both physically and conceptually, ancient Greek and Roman coins, which were collected in abundance in the Renaissance (you will be familiar with ancient coins from your work on representations of the Colosseum in Block 1 Unit 2). Medals were commemorative and, like coins, they were round and two-sided, consisting of an **obverse** (front) and a **reverse** (back) and were often made in multiples. Medals were frequently made in bronze, a material prized at the time. Many rulers exchanged their medals and they were shown off to visitors in collections, placed in special cabinets or kept in velvet bags, while some were pierced and strung up around the library or study (evidence of which is visible in the tiny hole at the top of the medal in Figure 14). The more medals you had of important people, the more connected you could show you were.

The portrait medals by the artist Pisanello (1394?–1455) were made for court rulers and are some of the most famous examples. They often reflect a scholarly, humanist, courtly circle, and the reading or interpretation of the medal requires knowledge of the ruler and members of their court. Pisanello's medal of Leonello d'Este (r.1441–50) is one of the earliest portrait medals of the Renaissance (Figure 14). Leonello d'Este was the Marquis of Ferrara, a court that was renowned for its humanist learning. This medal was made to commemorate his marriage to Maria d'Aragona, the daughter of King Alfonso d'Aragona (V of Aragon/I of Naples) in 1444.

On the obverse of the medal, we find a profile portrait of Leonello with a stylised mane of hair, likely a pun on his name ('little lion' in Italian). Encircling him are his name and titles, including his new status as son-in-law of a king (of Aragon) in abbreviated form: GE[nerus] R [egis] Ar[agonum]. The Latin is an obvious nod to antiquity and would have required a humanist education to decipher it. The reverse of the medal is where you often find quite complex symbolism.

Activity 6

(Allow around 5 minutes to complete this activity.)

Look closely at the reverse side of the medal in Figure 14 and write down what you see. Have a guess at the meaning of the symbolism.

Discussion

On the reverse side of the medal is a lion, king of beasts, which is again a pun on Leonello's name. There is an eagle on a branch and you might have made out a billowing sail, but the meaning of these is certainly not obvious. You might have also noticed the date in Roman numerals (MCCCCXLIIII) and the artist has signed his name in Latin 'OPVS PISANI PICTORIS' (roughly translated as 'the work of Pisanello the painter').

Through further historical study, we can better understand the iconography and meaning of the medal. The lion on the reverse of the coin in Figure 14 is being taught to sing by Cupid, alluding to the taming power of love. The presence of the eagle on a bare branch is not entirely clear, but probably references the Este family's symbol of the eagle. The billowing sail on the pillar behind Cupid is the Este emblem referencing the Latin motto *festina lente* ('proceed cautiously'), together with fortitude, symbolised by the pillar.

Figure 15 Giovanni Cristoforo Romano, portrait medal of Isabella d'Este. Obverse: bust of Isabella d'Este. Reverse: winged female figure with staff and palm branch; in front of her is a snake and above her the zodiac sign Sagittarius. *c.*1495–98. Gold with diamonds and enamel, diameter 7 cm, Kunsthistorisches Museum, Vienna, Inv.Nr. Münzkabinett, 6833bβ. KHM-Museumsverband.

Such a portrait medal (as the one shown in Figure 14) would have served as a conversation piece in a collection, sparking discussion and debate as to the interpretation. The multiple interpretations and the challenge of deciphering meaning was part of the enjoyment in viewership. The messages conveyed, such as those of power and fortitude and Leonello's connections to the Aragonese family, would have been ones that Leonello would have been eager to have people reveal as they deciphered the symbolism. Some of the most famous collectors of the Renaissance had medals made of themselves, such as Isabella d'Este (r.1490–1539), whose addition of jewels to the obverse made it a particularly unique and precious object (Figure 15).

Figure 16 Sandro Botticelli, *Portrait of a Man with a Medal of Cosimo de' Medici*, 1474, tempera and oil on panel with a gilded gesso medal, 58 × 44 cm. Galleria degli Uffizi, Florence. Photo: Scala, Florence.

The extent to which such medals were used to show alliances is evident in a portrait of an unidentified man by Sandro Botticelli (1445–1510) (Figure 16), who holds up a medal of Cosimo de' Medici, who was the head of the Medici Bank and de facto ruler of Florence (1389–1464) (Figure 17). What is extraordinary is the way in which Botticelli has attached a replica medal to the painting. By making a **gesso** cast, **gilding** it and attaching it to the wood panel, he added a three-dimensional quality. In the fifteenth century, Florence was a republic, where there were different factions (those who supported the powerful Medici family, and those who did not), and viewers would have been aware of who the sitter was loyal to. Medals became so sought after by rulers as a way to propagate and circulate their fame that the Ottoman Sultan Mehmed II (r.1444–46, 1451–81) had Italian artists execute them for him (which will be further explored in Section 6 of this chapter, see Figure 34).

Figure 17 Bertoldo di Giovanni, Portrait medal of Cosimo de' Medici. Obverse: bust of Cosimo de Medici. Reverse: Peace. *c.*1480–1500. Galleria Estense, Modena. Photo: Finsiel/Alinari Archives. Reproduced with the permission of Ministero per i Beni e le Attività Culturali. (There are multiple copies in collections around the world.)

By the sixteenth century, portraits increasingly made their appearance in printed books, usually modelled on known painted portraits. In the 1530s, the historian Paolo Giovio began constructing a villa at Como in Italy, which would form his 'museum', housing his collection of approximately 400 portraits (a precursor to the National Portrait galleries we know today). Each portrait was accompanied by a small piece of parchment outlining a short biography of the sitter. In 1546, these biographies were published in Venice but with no accompanying portraits. Giovio stated that it would be too difficult to accurately depict the portraits in print, and that his descriptions would have to suffice for the reader. It was not until 1575 and 1577, after Giovio's death, that portrait accompaniments were published with his text based on those in Como (Figures 18 and 19).

Figure 18 (left) 'Francis I' from Paolo Giovio, *Elogia virorum bellica virtute illustrium*, P. Pernae, Basil, 1575. Bibliothèque nationale de France, Paris, K-122 (3). **Figure 19 (right)** Cristofano dell'Altissimo, *Portrait of Francis I, King of France*, from the Como series, Galleria degli Uffizi, Florence. Photo: The Picture Art Collection/Alamy.

A close acquaintance of Giovio was the famous author and artist Giorgio Vasari, whose *Lives of the Artists* was the first book dedicated to the biographies of artists. The 1568 edition contained portraits to accompany and support the colourful biographies (Figure 20). Therefore, print became a new medium to circulate portraits and biographies of illustrious individuals.

Figure 20 'Portrait of Rosso Fiorentino', woodcut from Giorgio Vasari, *Le vite de' piu eccellenti pittori, scultori, e architettori* (The Lives of the Most Excellent Painters, Sculptors and Architects), 1568. Houghton Library, Harvard University, Cambridge, Massachusetts. Photo: © Bridgeman Images.

5 Collecting and display

Figure 21 Andrea Mantegna, Camera Picta (also known as *Camera degli Sposi*), 1465–74, fresco. Castello San Giorgio, Palazzo Ducale, Mantua. Photo: akg-images/Mondadori Portfolio/Antonio Quattrone.

Multiple portraits painted and displayed together were common in the Renaissance and are known as portrait cycles. Fifteenth-century portrait cycles often came in the form of painted frescoes on walls, where the painted portraits would greet visitors to a palace. A famous example is a group portrait by the court artist of Mantua, Andrea Mantegna (1431–1506), featuring his patrons, the Gonzagas, rulers of the **city-state** (see Figure 21). It was executed from 1465–75 and became known as the Camera Picta (painted chamber), a room that could serve as a bedchamber, an entertaining space and a private study.

By looking closer at the portraits in the Camera Picta (shown in Figures 22, 23 and 24) it is possible to discern who might be a member of the ruling family (the Gonzagas), who might be a **courtier** and who might be a servant, determining a clear hierarchy. Above the fireplace (to the right in Figure 21) the ruling family sits (which you can see in more detail in Figure 22). Facing them on the adjacent wall we find the male members of the Gonzaga family with other princes, accompanied by horses and dogs (seen in Figure 23). The painting brings to life the court of the Gonzaga, but also conveys messages on how to behave within such spaces and underlines the hierarchy of the court. The courtiers painted on the steps (in Figure 22) act as a boundary between the 'inside' of the court and the 'outside', delaying the admission of a few men who eagerly await the privilege of admittance.

Figure 22 Andrea Mantegna, detail of Marquis Ludovico Gonzaga with his wife, Barbara of Brandenburg, and members of the court in the Camera Picta (also known as *Camera degli Sposi*), 1465–74, fresco. Castello San Giorgio, Palazzo Ducale, Mantua. Photo: © Bridgeman Images.

As mentioned, above the fireplace Marquis Ludovico Gonzaga (r.1444–78) appears with his wife, Barbara of Brandenburg (1433–78), their children, and members of the court (Figure 22). Ludovico (the man in light red on the left with a hat) turns to a messenger who has recently handed him the letter in his hand. Scholars have deliberated about what this letter might signify; whether mundane affairs of state or a significant political event, or even perhaps a request for his portrait, we are likely never to know, but what is clear is the entire room evidently celebrates the Gonzaga dynasty and the magnificent creations produced under it, such as this frescoed room by their renowned court artist. It is also very much a political work of art, documenting the prestige and ambitions of the Gonzaga family, which is to be perpetuated through the male line, so carefully executed in the portraits of Gonzaga men (the scene now called *The Meeting*; Figure 23).

Figure 23 Andrea Mantegna, *The Meeting* in the Camera Picta (also known as *Camera degli Sposi*), 1465–74, fresco. Castello San Giorgio, Palazzo Ducale, Mantua. Photo: © Mondadori Portfolio/Electa/Antonio Quattrone/ Bridgeman Images.

When commissioning a group portrait, who you left out of the scene could be just as important as who you included. Absent from the scene is Duke Galeazzo Maria Sforza of Milan, whose family were the chief employers of Gonzaga military forces (who were *condottieri*, like the rulers of Urbino). The Duke of Milan noted his displeasure in having his portrait left out of the room while the artist had included the Holy

Roman Emperor and the King of Denmark, who according to him were 'two of the worst men in the world' (quoted in Manca, 2007 p. 52).

Figure 24 Andrea Mantegna, the oculus in the Camera Picta (also known as *Camera degli Sposi*), 1465–74. Castello San Giorgio, Palazzo Ducale, Mantua. Photo: akg-images/Mondadori Portfolio/Electa.

Inclusion and exclusion also raise the issue of invisibility, underscored when you look up into the **oculus**, where servants stare down at the viewer (Figure 24). It is a reminder of those who were physically present at court but who were often invisible. Their portraits were rarely rendered, except in representations such as this, where they were anonymous and on the outside, made to perform a sort of spectacle, represented beside *putti*. Of particular note is the anonymous black slave wearing a striped turban. While we don't know the identity of the Gonzaga slave, there is a rare example of a drawing of a black African woman by German artist Albrecht Dürer (1471–1528), who we can actually identify and therefore give her an identity. Dürer records her as Katharina, a servant or possibly a slave, who the artist encountered in Antwerp in the house of one of his patrons, João Brandão, a Portuguese factor (mercentile agent) who used to trade goods (Figure 25).

Figure 25 Albrecht Dürer, *Katharina*, 1521. Silverpoint drawing on paper. Gabinetto dei Disegni e delle Stampe degli Uffizi, Florence. No. 1060 E. Photo: Scala, Florence.

In a fresco such as the Camera Picta, where the emphasis is on display, the female slave would have been perceived by contemporaries as a visible exotic object, comparable to the peacock, demonstrating the wealth of the Gonzaga. Relegated to the oculus, she is also meant to signal what historian Peter Erickson calls 'a seen-but-not-heard' subservience (2009, p. 24).

In other instances, black children appear alongside courtly portraits as prized possessions, such as in the portrait of Laura dei Dianti, from the court of Ferrara (Figure 26). It is a reminder that the history of portraiture is largely a history of white identities of a particular class, which tells us only one side of the story that conceals the realities of many people and the inequalities of Renaissance power.

Figure 26 Titian, *Portrait of Laura dei Dianti, c.*1522–23, oil on canvas, 119 × 93 cm. Collection Heinz Kisters, Kreuzligen, Switzerland. Photo: akg-images.

In *The Meeting* scene (Figure 23), to the right of the doorway in the Camera Picta, the political ambitions of the family are clearly visible. Here Ludovico greets his son, Francesco Gonzaga, who had just been made a cardinal in 1461, thus securing the family a highly sought-after connection at the papal court. Rather than a record of a real meeting, however, this is fictitiously contrived. The King of Denmark (the man in black, to Francesco's right, who had married the marquis's sister-in-law, Dorothea of Brandenburg), and the German Holy Roman Emperor Frederick III (facing Francesco) are likely painted from known portraits. As far as we know, Frederick never visited Mantua.

The array of profiles is reminiscent of portrait medals – a collection of the Gonzaga's acquaintances and family members. As a whole, the room is a publicity stunt, showcasing the family's aspirations and political connections while rebuffing others.

Portraits could speak to family pride, but they were also part of a growing culture of collecting, which included the collection and display of a variety of objects from classical sculpture to contemporary paintings. The collection of ancient busts was part of a tradition of **uomini famosi** (or famous men), which drew on classical literature that spoke of the display of ancestral busts in Roman houses. The Roman authors Pliny the Elder and Cicero both discussed the need to honour these effigies of ancestors to perpetuate the memory of famous men who could act as **exemplars**.

The display of portraits was part of the culture of collecting, an activity that drew on the classical past as a model. The particular genre of writing about art (which was revived in the Renaissance) also looked to classical examples, demonstrating a larger phenomenon of looking to the ancient past that was widespread in arts and culture, and underscoring the need in Art History to often work across disciplines. In Vasari's *Lives of the Artists,* he discusses the work of the Venetian painter Giovanni Bellini (*c.*1435–1516) (an example of whose painting you can see in Figure 27) in relation to the tradition of portraiture:

> And having devoted himself to making portraits from the life, he introduced into Venice the fashion that everyone of a certain rank should have his portrait painted either by him or by some other master; wherefore in all the houses of Venice there are many portraits, and in many gentlemen's houses one may see their fathers and grandfathers, up to the fourth generation, and in some of the more noble they go still farther back—a fashion which has ever been truly worthy of the greatest praise, and existed even among the ancients. Who does not feel infinite pleasure and contentment, to say nothing of the honour and adornment that they confer, at seeing the images of his ancestors, particularly if they have been famous and illustrious for their part in governing their republics, for noble deeds performed in peace or in war, or for learning or any other notable and distinguished talent? And to what other end, as has been said in another place, did the ancients set up images of their great men in public places,

with honourable inscriptions, than to kindle in the minds of their successors a love of excellence and of glory?

(Vasari, 'Life of Giovanni Bellini', 1912, pp. 182–183)

Figure 27 Giovanni Bellini, *The Doge Leonardo Loredan*, 1502, oil on poplar, 62 × 45 cm. The National Gallery, London, Acc. No.:4531. Photo: © The National Gallery, London/Scala, Florence.

Furnishing a palace with portraits displayed the owner's wealth and connections, but it was also linked to humanist ideas about exemplars. Duke Federigo da Montefeltro's study in Urbino from the 1470s exemplifies a new kind of collecting space that emerged in fifteenth-century Italy. This was often referred to as a ***studiolo***, which could serve as a library, museum and social space. Here, Duke Federigo (who we encountered in Figure 6) commissioned a series of portraits not of family members but of famous men, as a way to exemplify his learning and erudition (see Figure 28). Below each portrait was an inscription that linked the individual to Federigo, creating a sort of mythical lineage, connecting him to great men of the past. In addition, he placed his own image with his son in the room, underlining the permanence of his dynasty and his worldly claims of power (Figure 29). Here, he wears the knightly Order of the Ermine's cloak and collar as well as the Order of the Garter (intentionally visible on his exposed leg), symbolising his links with both the King of Naples and the King of England.

Figure 28 (left) *Studiolo* of Urbino, 1470s. Galleria Nazionale delle Marche, (Palazzo Ducale), Urbino. Photo: AGF Srl/Alamy. **Figure 29 (right)** Justus of Ghent, probably reworked by Pedro Berruguete, *Federigo da Montefeltro and His Son, Guidobaldo*, about 1476. Galleria Nazionale delle Marche, (Palazzo Ducale), Urbino. Photo: Scala, Florence – courtesy of the Ministero Beni e Att. Culturali e del Turismo.

Displaying portraits in one's house (where visitors would see your acquaintances, both familial and political) worked to convey power and status, just as the objects on display did. For example, Hans Holbein the Younger's *The Ambassadors*, (Figure 30) is recorded in a '*grand' salle*' (large room) in a 1589 inventory of the Château of Polisy in France (the home of Jean de Dinteville, one of the ambassadors in the painting). There were other portraits of the family throughout the palace, including one where Jean de Dinteville and his brothers appear in the guise of Biblical figures in *Moses and Aaron before Pharaoh* (Figure 31). This is a reminder that these paintings, unlike the ones in museums today, did not stand alone but were part of the architectural decorations and the larger schemes of entire palaces.

Figure 30 (left) Hans Holbein the Younger, *The Ambassadors*, 1533, oil on oak, 207 × 210 cm. The National Gallery, London Acc. No.: NG1314. Photo: © The National Gallery, London/Scala, Florence.
Figure 31 (right) Unknown artist, *Moses and Aaron before Pharaoh: An Allegory of the Dinteville Family*, 1537, oil on wood, 177 × 193 cm. Metropolitan Museum of Art, New York, Wentworth Fund, 1950, Acc. No.: 50.70.

6 Cross-cultural dialogues and signs of power

This section of the chapter will draw upon two main symbols used in portraits in both the East and West: the **equestrian portrait** and the **globe**. This section expands on what you have already learned about portraiture in the European context to demonstrate how portraiture is not just a Western art tradition but, as will be explored here, Ottoman and Mughal rulers also utilised portraits to convey their power. A key point to note is that such symbols are not simply borrowed from one culture to another, but often involve a form of cultural translation.

Figure 32 (left) Bronze statue of Marcus Aurelius, *c.*173–76 CE. Capitoline Museums, Rome. Photo: Vito Arcomano/Alamy. **Figure 33 (right)** Antonio Pollaiuolo, *Study for the Equestrian Monument to Francesco Sforza*, Duke of Milan, early to mid 1480s, pen and brown ink, light and dark brown wash; outlines of the horse and rider pricked for transfer, 28 × 25 cm. Metropolitan Museum of Art, New York, Robert Lehman Collection, 1975, Acc. No.: 1975.1.410.

Equestrian portraits have been well known as instruments of power since antiquity. The bronze equestrian portrait of Marcus Aurelius (r.161–80 CE) (thought to be of Constantine in the Renaissance) was a prominent public monument in Rome (Figure 32) and acted as a model for Renaissance portraits. While many large-scale equestrian sculptures were planned in the Renaissance, most of them did not get finished due to the high costs of execution (Figure 33 shows a sketch of a sculpture that was never completed). Many equestrian portraits, however, survive in other media from paintings to medals, and horses were symbols employed in both the East and West, as seen already in the Gonzaga frescoes in Mantua (Figure 23). Horses were symbolic in themselves: they were costly symbols of power, which were exchanged between princes, used to broker alliances and secure trade deals. In Europe they also had associations with the East, as some of the best breeds came from 'Arab' lands. Cultural translation, then, can occur over time, such as in the reuse of classical symbols in Renaissance culture (the translation of past artefacts into the present) and also in how contemporary cultures exchange symbols and practices, and in turn translate them into new cultural contexts.

Figure 34 Costanzo da Ferrara, Portrait medal of Mehmed II. Obverse: bust of Mehmed II. Reverse: equestrian portrait of Mehmed II. 1481, bronze, diameter 12 cm. Ashmolean Museum, University of Oxford, HCR8016. Photo: Bridgeman Images. (There are multiple copies in collections around the world.)

Figure 35 After Pieter Coecke van Aelst, 'Procession of Sultan Süleyman through the Atmeidan' woodcut of the frieze *Ces Moeurs et fachons de faire de Turcz* (Customs and Fashions of the Turks) (detail), Mayken Verhulst, Antwerp?, 1533. Metropolitan Museum of Art, New York, Harris Brisbane Dick Fund, 1928, Acc. No.: 28.85.7a, b.

The Ottoman Sultan Mehmed II had his equestrian portrait included on the reverse of his medal (Figure 34). His profile portrait was situated on the obverse (attention to his turban is key here, underlining how important clothing was in constructing identity). Mehmed II's medal reveals the cross-cultural dialogues both in its imagery as well as in its execution. It was made by Costanzo da Ferrara (1450– after 1524), an Italian artist who was likely sent to the Ottoman court following a request from Mehmed II to King Ferrante (Ferdinand I) of Naples for a suitable artist to help with the decoration of his new palace. The medal is an Ottoman artefact, delivered in a Western-European tradition, depicting a symbol of the equestrian portrait that had currency in both East and West. Indeed, the Sultan on horseback became *the* formulaic representation of the 'Turk', copied and subsequently used for generations as a symbol of Eastern power (see Figure 35). The equestrian portrait of Mehmed II thus circulated through a wide range of media, working to become an 'icon' that is instantly recognisable.

It is often common to find depictions of equestrian portraits with the rider in armour. This underlines the power of the subject as a military commander, able to control both humans and nature. In a portrait by Titian (who painted many of the portraits that we saw in Section 2) of Charles V (Holy Roman Emperor, 1519–56; King of Spain as Charles I, 1516–56; and Archduke of Austria as Charles I, 1519–21), he is depicted at a specific battle, the Battle of Mühlberg in 1547. This was an important triumph for Charles and his defence of the Catholic faith against the Reformed church, led by the Lutheran Philip of Hesse. The horse is a Spanish-type cross between a European and an Arab 'race'.

Activity 7

(Allow around 10 minutes to complete this activity.)

Consider this famous portrait of Charles V (Figure 36). How is he dressed and what might this portrait convey to the viewer? Draw on what you have learned about armour in Section 2 of this chapter.

Figure 36 Titian, *Charles V at Mühlberg*, 1548, oil on canvas, 332 × 279 cm. Museo del Prado, Madrid, Inv. No.: P000410. Photo: akg-images/Rabatti & Domingie.

Discussion

The portrait shows Charles V as if in a real battle situation in armour. His lance is poised and he looks as if he is in movement heading towards battle. He looks like a commander ready to take on what is necessary, powerful and alert. Armour, as you have seen previously, was a way to 'stage' a portrait and perform a particular identity. Instead of being depicted in robes of state as a king, Charles V is choosing to depict himself as a military commander.

Contemporaries noted that in this portrait (Figure 36), Charles V is depicted as he was: wearing his own armour and riding that particular horse. It celebrates **Habsburg** power by situating the painting within a particular historical moment. The painting has been interpreted by historians Lisa Jardine and Jerry Brotton (2000) as conveying a message of triumph, not only over Protestantism but also Charles's ability to control the Muslim East in terms of the Arab horse (during his reign there were numerous campaigns against the Ottoman Empire). As Charles was king of Spain, it can also be seen as a representation of Spanish imperialism. Under Charles V, Spain continued to expand its possession of the so-called 'New World', including the conquest of Mexico and Peru. Such a portrait underlines how power can mask the bleaker side to these works of art and the messages that they convey.

As mentioned, another clear symbol of power utilised in portraits was the globe, which was also translated across cultures as a sign of power and knowledge. In September 1617, the English ambassador to the Mughal court, Sir Thomas Roe, presented the Emperor Jahangir with gifts, which included the geographer/cartographer Gerardus Mercator's latest edition of the maps of the world. Following this, globes frequently appear in portraits of the Mughal emperor, such as in the **Darbar** *of Jahangir*, where the emperor rests his feet on a globe (Figure 37; also see Figures 38 and 39). But rather than this being a simple import of the 'European' globe into a Mughal **miniature** portrait, the insertion of this globe needs to be situated within the complex intercultural dialogues of the early seventeenth century.

Figure 37 Abu'l Hasan, *Darbar of Jahangir*, *c*.1615, opaque watercolour, gold and ink on paper, 17 × 12 cm. Freer Gallery of Art, Smithsonian Institution, Washington, D.C.: Purchase — Charles Lang Freer Endowment, F1946.28.

The Mughal Empire (1526–1857)

The Mughal Empire was founded by Babur after his successful invasion of northern India in 1526. Babur descended on his father's side from Timur Lang (Tamerlane), a Mongol ruler, and on his mother's side from Genghis Khan, and therefore had close social and political ties with Central Asia. He was succeeded by Humayun, who was followed by four great emperors, under whom the Mughal Empire reached its peak: Akbar (r.1556–1605), Jahangir (r.1605–27), Shah Jahan (r.1628–58) and Aurangzeb (r.1658–1707).

The Mughals were Muslims who expanded their territory across the Indian subcontinent (what is now India, Pakistan and Afghanistan), and their main seats of power were located in Fatehpur Sikhri, Agra (the site of the famous Taj Mahal built by Shah Jahan), Delhi and Lahore. Akbar introduced administrative systems, recruiting Persians, Indian Muslims and Hindu Rajputs, and is known for his religious tolerance. Under the Mughals, there was a great flourishing of the arts, particularly in the art of the book as well as architecture.

Activity 8

(Allow around 25 minutes to complete this activity.)

Now turn to Reading 1.1 and read the three extracts, which are summaries of Sir Thomas Roe's embassy to the Emperor Jahangir.

As you will see, the extracts are presented in their original seventeenth-century English, but I have also provided modern translations alongside the text.

As you read through both versions, consider how Mercator's map book was perceived by the emperor, according to the English. Also consider how we use these as sources and any questions they might raise.

Discussion

From the three extracts, we are given an English perspective that the Mughal emperor was displeased. Reading between the lines, we could say that this displeasure was because the map was Eurocentric and that Jahangir's title of 'world conqueror' was not reflected in the map book. The use of 'conceit' by Edward Terry suggests that the Mughal emperor had too big an opinion of himself and his territories. This raises more questions: should we take this at face value? What were the English doing at the court and what political agendas did they have?

Rather than just reading this narrative of the Mughal court's ignorance and distaste for maps, it is important to situate it within its historical context. The reports that we have of the event are written by Englishmen at the Mughal court, who were serving a particular political and economic agenda. England's reputation as a country with little significance to Mughal trade and diplomacy became very clear to Sir Thomas Roe upon his arrival. His presence at the Mughal court was a type of performance. As art historian Mehreen Chida-Razvi has argued, Roe needed to engage in the politics of display and presentation to make himself seem more important than he was, and his textual accounts were part of that creation (2014, p. 268). It is here that the visual sources can reveal some more about the Mughal interest in geography and what art historian Ebba Koch calls the 'cartographic dialogue' between Europe and the Mughals, which can complicate our reading of the textual sources (2012, p. 563).

Figure 38 Abu'l Hasan, *Allegorical Representation of Emperor Jahangir and Shah 'Abbas of Persia*, *c.*1618, opaque watercolour, gold and ink on paper, 24 × 15 cm. Freer Gallery of Art, Smithsonian Institution, Washington, D.C.: Purchase — Charles Lang Freer Endowment, F1945.9a.

Activity 9

(Allow around 10 minutes to complete this activity.)

Now look at Figure 38. This image shows Jahangir (who is depicted on the right) and his rival and cousin Shah Abbas I (r.1587–1629) (ruler of the Safavid dynasty in Iran), by the famous painter Abu'l Hasan (*c.*1588/9–1628).

How is the globe being employed here and what power dynamics might be at play? Where are the figures positioned on the globe?

Discussion

In this miniature portrait, we get a clearer picture of how the Mughals utilised cartography (the practice of drawing maps) for their own purposes. Abu'l Hasan has depicted Jahangir embracing his Safavid rival, Shah 'Abbas. Particularly obvious is Jahangir's triumph over his rival through his body language (they hug, but Jahangir is overwhelmingly the bigger one here) and the symbolism of the animals at their feet (Jahangir is the strong lion, while Shah 'Abbas is the doting lamb). They are standing on a globe, where their territories are delineated. This is not a Eurocentric globe but a world in which Jahangir's territories dominate, underscoring his name, which means 'world conqueror'. The lion sprawls across Persia and much of Central Asia, where Shah 'Abbas's territories have been reduced to some small ones around the Mediterranean.

As the historian Sumathi Ramaswamy (2007) has argued, Figure 38 is a 'painting back', a visual retort that challenges European cartography and provincialises Europe instead. Jahangir came to employ the globe to speak of Mughal dominance in a number of paintings (as can also be seen in Figure 39). It should be noted too that globes had been produced in the Muslim world as early as the eleventh century, but mostly in the form of celestial spheres, and were exchanged as diplomatic gifts. The insertion of the globe then in such an image as the *Darbar of Jahangir* (which we saw in Figure 37), could speak to cross-cultural traditions of gift-giving, knowledge and power.

Figure 39 Hashim and Abu'l Hasan, *Jahangir and Jesus*, *c.*1610–20. Chester Beatty Library, Dublin, CBL In 07A.12. © The Trustees of the Chester Beatty Library, Dublin.

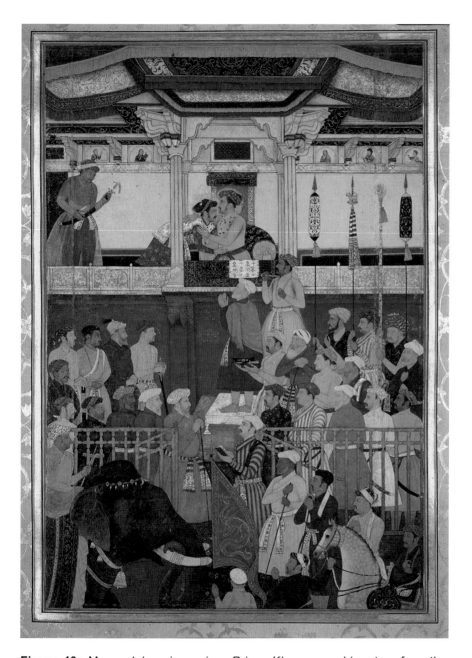

Figure 40a Murar, *Jahangir receives Prince Khurram on his return from the Mewar campaign (19 February 1615)*, 1656–57, opaque pigment and gold on paper. Royal Collection Trust © Her Majesty Queen Elizabeth II, 2020, RCIN 1005025.am. Photo: © Bridgeman Images.

Figure 40b Detail of Christian images from the top of Figure 40a. On the right an image of Mary, the Mother of Jesus, and to the left an image of Jesus holding a globe.

The Mughal court was well known for its interests in the arts, not only the famous miniatures made within Mughal workshops but also for the works collected from Europe. During the celebrations of **Nawruz** in March 1616, Roe notes that portraits of James I, Elizabeth I and others were on display at the darbar. The display of these portraits is evident in Mughal paintings that show the presence of images of Mary and Jesus on display in the **jharoka** (see the frieze near the ceiling in Figure 40a and the detail in 40b) or in the miniature that displays a portrait of King James I among other rulers (you can see these rulers in the bottom-left corner of Figure 41).

We can conclude, then, that the presence of the globe in many of Jahangir's portraits spoke to an international and global phenomenon, which was used by rulers to demonstrate their power. This should not be read as simply copying a European symbol but as a form of cultural translation, whereby the globe is made local and relevant. It also points to another important issue regarding maps and globes: that they are not solely protoscientific objects but, as Jerry Brotton (1997) notes, they can be used as prestige objects, symbols of worldly power and ideological constructions. Globes and their representations in paintings (just like equestrian portraits) became part of the instruments of exercising state power and the growing trade and diplomatic routes that became necessary to sustain that power.

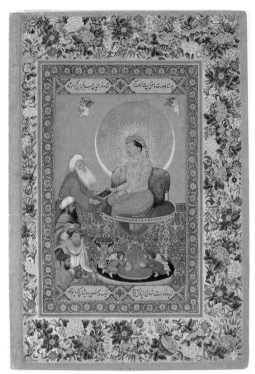

Figure 41 Bichitr, *Jahangir Preferring a Sufi Shaykh to Kings*, from the St. Petersburg Album, *c.*1615–18, (detail on the right), opaque watercolour, gold and ink on paper, 25 × 18 cm. Freer Gallery of Art, Smithsonian Institution, Washington, D.C.: Purchase — Charles Lang Freer Endowment, F1942.15a.

While claiming to represent the world, maps and globes can also serve very local, immediate needs. For example, the portrait of Elizabeth I (r.1558–1603) known as the 'Ditchley portrait', presents Elizabeth standing on a globe (Figure 42). Specifically, she stands on Oxfordshire, a county of particular relevance to the portrait. It was commissioned by Sir Henry Lee to commemorate the queen's visit to his house at Ditchley in Oxfordshire. Through the use of the globe, Lee is not only showcasing Elizabeth I's power but also his own, as the portrait attests to his acquaintance with the queen and forever memorialises her visit to his house.

Figure 42 Marcus Gheeraerts the Younger, *Queen Elizabeth I* ('The Ditchley portrait'), *c.*1592, oil on canvas, 241 × 152 cm. National Portrait Gallery, London, NPG 2561. © National Portrait Gallery, London.

The globe also appears as one of the important objects in the middle of Holbein's painting of *The Ambassadors* (which you can see a close-up of in Figure 43). Here the painting points to the local ambitions of Jean de Dinteville, as 'Polisy' (the château and surrounding land belonging to Dinteville's family) is clearly visible on the map. This is an up-to-date globe, which depicts the **Line of Demarcation** established by Spain and Portugal in 1494, after the 'discovery' of the New World by the explorer Christopher Columbus in 1492. This line essentially divided the world, with Portugal claiming all undiscovered lands to the east of the Atlantic, while Spain claimed everything to the west. Prominently displayed on the globe is 'AFFRICA' and yet, as Erickson (2009) has argued, Africa is markedly absent from the image – no objects or people associated with the continent are present. The globe here points to the global ambitions of growing European empires, of which the slave trade was one of the main driving forces. It is important to note what is and isn't visible in portraits, and to always consider from what perspective such images are commissioned and interpreted.

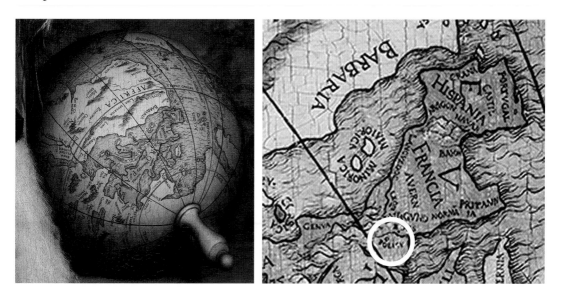

Figure 43 Hans Holbein the Younger, *The Ambassadors* (Figure 30; detail showing the globe and Polisy), 1533, oil on oak, 207 × 210 cm. The National Gallery, London Acc. No.: NG1314. Photo: © The National Gallery, London/Scala, Florence.

7 Summary

This chapter has examined how portraits are products of particular cultures and that they work to assert, underscore and even establish certain cultural norms and ideals, from Republican Venice to the Mughal court. Returning to Berger and his four 'modes' (as discussed at the start of this chapter), we have seen how sitters use portraits to tell certain stories about themselves. By looking closely at portraits, we have analysed how early modern individuals used symbols, objects, clothing and stance to convey these stories and a particular identity. By utilising both close-looking skills and historical evidence, we are able to construct a better understanding of the lives of the sitters, and also the conditions in which they lived and how art and power were closely connected. We have also seen that this power was largely at the expense of other voices not being heard and the exploitation of marginalised groups.

> You should now return to the module website to continue your study of this unit.

References

Berger, H. (1994) 'Fictions of the pose: facing the gaze of early modern portraiture', *Representations*, 46, pp. 87–120.

Brotton, J. (1997) *Trading territories: mapping the early modern world*. London: Reaktion Books.

Campbell, L. (1990) *Renaissance portraits: European portrait-painting in the 14th, 15th, and 16th centuries*. New Haven and London: Yale University Press.

Castiglione, B. (2003) *The book of the courtier*. Mineola, NY: Dover Publications Inc.

Chida-Razvi, M.M. (2014) 'The perception of reception: the importance of Sir Thomas Roe at the Mughal court of Jahangir', *Journal of World History*, 25(2/3), pp. 263–284.

Erickson, P. (2009) 'Invisibility speaks: servants and portraits in early modern visual culture', *Journal for Early Modern Cultural Studies*, 9(1), pp. 23–61.

Jardine, L. and Brotton, J. (2000) *Global interests: Renaissance art between East and West*. Ithaca, NY: Cornell University Press.

Kessel, E. van (2010) 'Staging Bianca Capello: painting and theatricality in sixteenth-century Venice', *Art History*, 33(2), pp. 278–291.

Koch, E. (2012) 'The symbolic possession of the world: European cartography in Mughal allegory and history painting', *Journal of the Economic and Social History of the Orient*, 55(2), pp. 547–580.

Manca, J. (2007) *Andrea Mantegna and the Italian Renaissance*. New York, NY: Parkstone.

Ramaswamy, S. (2007) 'Conceit of the globe in Mughal visual practice', *Comparative Studies in Society and History*, 49(4), pp. 751–782.

Roe, T. (1899) *The embassy of Sir Thomas Roe to the court of the Great Mogul, 1615–1619*. Edited by W. Foster. London: Hakluyt Society.

Vasari, G. (1912) *The lives of the most eminent painters, sculptors and architects*. Translated from the Italian by De Vere, G. London: Macmillan and Co and the Medici Society.

Readings

Reading 1.1 The embassy of Sir Thomas Roe

Extract 1

Source: Roe, T. (1899) *The embassy of Sir Thomas Roe to the court of the Great Mogul, 1615–1619*. Edited by W. Foster. London: Hakluyt Society, pp. 413–414.

[In September 1617, Roe tells us that the Jahangir rode past his house and the following exchange took place:]

I rode out to meete him. The custome is, that all men by whom hee passeth neare their gate make him some Present, which is taken as a good signe, and is called *Mombareck*, good Newes or good Success. I had nothing to give, nor might fitly goe with nothing, nor stay at home without discourtesie; which made mee venture upon a faire Booke well bound, filleted and gilt, Mercators last Edition of the Maps of the world, which I presented with an excuse that I had nothing worthy, but to a great King I offered the World, in which he had so great and rich a part. The King tooke it in great courtesie, often laying his hand on his breast, and answering: Every thing that came from mee was welcome.

Modernised version (Leah R. Clark)

I rode out to meet him. The custom is that if he passes the gate near your residence you have to offer him a present, which is taken as a good sign, and it is called Mombareck, good news or good success. I had nothing to give, but I didn't want to give him nothing, nor stay at home and not be courteous; so I decided to give him a fine book, expensively bound and decorated in gold, Mercator's latest edition of the maps of the world, which I presented with an excuse that I had nothing worthy, but to a great King I offered the world, in which he had so great and rich a part. The King took it with great courtesy, often laying his hand on his breast and said that everything that came from me was welcome.

Extract 2

Source: Roe, T. (1899) *The embassy of Sir Thomas Roe to the court of the Great Mogul, 1615–1619*. Edited by W. Foster. London: Hakluyt Society, pp. 416–417.

[On 25 September, Roe became ill and Jahangir sent him wine and food.]

Then he [Jahangir] sent for the Map-booke, and told me he had shewed it his *Mulaies* [teacher or doctor of the law], and no man could reade nor understand it; therefore if I would I should have it againe. I answered: At his pleasure; and so it was returned.

Modernised version (Leah R. Clark)

Then he [Jahangir] sent for the Map-book [Mercator's book of maps], and told me he had showed it to his Mulaies [teacher or doctor of the law], and no man could read or understand it; therefore if I wanted I could have it back. I responded by saying that it was as he pleased; and so it was returned.

Extract 3

Source: Ramaswamy, S. (2007) 'Conceit of the globe in Mughal visual practice', *Comparative Studies in Society and History*, 49(4), pp. 757–758.

[In addition to Roe, we have the version of the story from his chaplain, Edward Terry:]

The Mogol feeds himself with this conceit, that he is Conqueror of the World; and therefore [...] having at that time nothing left which he [Roe] thought fit to give him, presented him with Mercators great book of Cosmography (which the Ambassador had brought thither for his own use), telling the Mogol that that book described the four parts of the world, and all several countreys in them contained. The Mogol at the first seem'd to be much taken with it, desiring presently to see his own territories, which were immediately shewen unto him; he asked where were those countreys about them; he was told Tartaria and Persia, as the names of the rest which confine with him; and then causing the book to be turn'd all over, and finding no more to fall to his share but what he first saw, and he calling himself the Conqueror of the World and having no greater share in it, seemed to be a little troubled, yet civily told the Ambassadour, that neither himself, nor any of his people did understand the language in which that book was written, and because so, he further told him that he would not rob him of such a jewel, and therefore returned it unto him again. And the truth is that the Great Mogol might very well bring his action against Mercator and others who describe the world, but streighten him very much in their maps, not allowing him to be lord and commander of those provinces which properly belong unto him.

Modernised version (Leah R. Clark)

The Mughal [Jahangir] tells himself that he is Conqueror of the World and therefore [...] since Roe had at that time nothing left, which he thought suitable to give him, Roe presented him with Mercator's great book of Cosmography (which the ambassador had brought there [to India] for his own use), telling the Mughal that the book showed the four parts of the world, and all different countries in those four parts. The Mughal at first seemed to be much taken with it, wishing right away to see his own territories [on the map], which were immediately shown to him. He asked what were those countries which surrounded his own territories, and he was told Tartary [term used by Europeans to describe a large area of Central Asia from the Caspian Sea to the Pacific Ocean] and Persia, as the names of those which surround him; and then ordering the book he looked it over completely, and finding no more lands belonging to him than what he saw at first sight, and he calling himself the Conqueror of the World and having no greater part of it, he seemed to be a little troubled, yet politely told the Ambassador, that neither himself, nor any of his people understood the language in which that book was written, and because of that, he further told him that he would not rob him of such a jewel and therefore returned the book to him. And the truth is that the Great Mughal might be angry with Mercator and others who present his territories as too small on their maps, not acknowleding him to be lord and commander of those provinces which properly belong to him.

Chapter 2

Building seats of power: the country house

Written by Clare Taylor

Contents

1 Introduction

Figure 1 Samuel Hieronymus Grimm (1733–1794), Hardwick Hall (east front), 1781, watercolour. Photo: © The National Trust.

The focus of this chapter is Hardwick in Derbyshire. I have chosen this site because it allows you to study how the country house expresses messages about power, identity and status, both in the past and today, but there are other reasons too. First, there is Hardwick's patron, Elizabeth Talbot, Countess of Shrewsbury (*c*.1521–1608), or 'Bess of Hardwick'. We will examine how her identity has been constructed in relation to the elite culture of the Elizabethan period. Second, there is the evolving design of the two halls at Hardwick: Hardwick Old Hall (built *c*.1587–1591) and the new hall, known as 'Hardwick Hall' (begun in 1590 and occupied from 1597). Both buildings show how the site articulated power and status in relation to knowledge of other houses that were constructed at around the same time. Third, studying Hardwick allows us to look beyond architecture to the decoration and objects that survive inside it (including textiles and furniture), and how their designs were informed by wider European culture and were used to convey ideas about both personal and family identities.

2 Country houses as seats of power

Why do country houses such as Hardwick occupy such an enduring place in British cultural life? Frequently built on a grand scale, these houses have survived in the landscape long after smaller scale dwellings (constructed of less robust materials for more modest purposes) have disappeared. Preserved by aristocratic dynasties or by institutional custodians, such as the National Trust and National Trust for Scotland, British country houses often remain standing long after the estates of which they formed a central part (and whose productive land and rents were central to their economy) have been separated from the house itself, and even after their contents have been sold. In Britain, a remarkable number of country houses survive in comparison to mainland Europe, where the effects of two world wars resulted in many being destroyed, or their contents lost, during periods of wartime fighting or occupation. Similarly, in Ireland many country houses have also been destroyed, either by being burned down as symbols of colonial oppression during the War of Independence and the Civil War between 1916–23, or as a result of the subsequent redistribution of estates.

The status of the country house is not only about its position in the landscape. They also derive authority from their associations with key figures in national life, such as politicians and writers. One example is Sir Winston Churchill's (1874–1965) country house at Chartwell in Kent (Figure 2), or Blenheim Palace in Oxfordshire, whose building was funded by the nation after the Battle of Blenheim (1704) but which was also Churchill's birthplace.

Surviving country houses have also come to occupy a place in contemporary British cultural life through their commercial opening to visitors. This is not a recent development (in 1920, Hardwick already had around 4000 visitors per year) but it is one that has become more significant since the 1950s. In 1953, Hardwick was one of four 'stately homes' chosen by the BBC's North of England service for a weekly TV feature on Sunday outings. Growth in car ownership, National Trust and English Heritage membership, as well as the sheer number of country houses opening for visitors (through organisations such as the Historic Houses Association), have all contributed to increasing numbers visiting country houses, their parkland and estates. The National Trust is also a major landowner in the UK, with over 200 historic houses in its property portfolio and over 26 million visitors per year to its sites, some 279,000 of whom visited Hardwick Hall in 2017–18 (The National Trust, 2017/18, p. 5). It therefore has a significant responsibility for enabling, as well as shaping, the visitor experience.

Figure 2 Winston Churchill, *View of Chartwell*, *c.*1938, oil on canvas, 61 × 91 cm. Chartwell, The Churchill Collection, National Trust, Coombs 286. Reproduced with permission of Curtis Brown, London, on behalf of Churchill Heritage Limited © Churchill Heritage Limited. Churchill was a keen artist for much of his long life, and took lessons from painters including Sir Walter Sickert.

The country house also occupies a place in the cultural imagination of Britain as the backdrop to fictional events in literature, film and on TV. For writers from Jane Austen to Elizabeth Gaskell, Agatha Christie to Kazuo Ishiguro, the country house often features in novels, particularly as the setting for crime fiction. The 2019 film *Downton Abbey*, and the globally successful TV series that preceded it, revolved around the workings of the fictitious country house after which the series was named (Downton is in fact based on a Neo-Elizabethan country house, Highclere Castle, in Hampshire). This, and other historical dramas based around interpersonal 'upstairs/downstairs' narratives (*Upstairs, Downstairs* is the title to an earlier TV series that focused on relations between owners and servants in an aristocratic London house), rather than between people and objects, arguably also create visitor expectations that country houses will be rooted in personal stories (Cox, 2018).

Critics of those who view the country house as a national treasure have argued that this perspective takes away from funding (as well as visitors) to other areas of culture, such as the promotion of industrial heritage or contemporary art. They also argue that culture is shaped by an elite whose control extends to preserving the types of heritage that conform to their own ideas of heritage (of which the country house is one example). Accordingly, the country house can be seen as preserving an aristocratic way of life.

Activity 1

(Allow around 10 minutes to complete this activity.)

Read the extract below, which is taken from the historian Peter Mandler's book, *The Fall and Rise of the Stately Home*. Then jot down your thoughts on what Mandler is saying about the 'elite' country house:

> Elite culture is not something apart from or floating above the social, economic, political and cultural history of the nation: it is shaped by the marketplace, by government, by popular attitudes and prejudices as well as by the internal culture of the élite itself. This is particularly true of those elements of high culture that are proposed to the nation as *its* heritage, and more true still of the country house. For the country house on its estate has never been solely a matter of taste: it is also an economic unit subject to the vicissitudes of agriculture and the land and art markets, an asset subject to taxation, a target for political attacks on the rich and privileged and an object of planning law and government intervention.

> (Mandler, 1997, p. 2)

Discussion

Mandler argues that elite culture is itself shaped by the world around it and 'by popular attitudes and prejudices'. He claims that this is especially so in relation to the country house, detailing some of the economic and political reasons why he believes this is the case.

Country houses are certainly not immune to changing economic fortunes or taxation regimes. Hardwick Old Hall and Hardwick Hall came to the Ministry of Works (now known as English Heritage) and the National Trust respectively in 1959 as part of a settlement of death duties, that is, inheritance tax on the estate of the 10th Duke of Devonshire. However, in other ways, Mandler's use of the term 'high culture', often seen in opposition to 'popular culture', is problematic, since it perpetuates some of the issues concerning the role of country houses as part of national heritage. In recent years this role has been further problematised, particularly the ways in which their building and decoration was funded. Key to this is the legacy of the exploitation of people through the British Atlantic slave trade. One example concerns the profits from raw materials such as sugar, which was cultivated on plantations worked by enslaved people in the Caribbean and was available for Bess of Hardwick's descendants to buy from nearby towns by the 1650s. Country houses were also built on the profits of materials closer to home, such as the mining of coal and iron ore. Hardwick's profits came from the rental income from tenants farming its estate land.

In the last four decades, the visitor's experience of the country house has also been shaped by the shifting interest in the lives of those who worked in service (in order to run and maintain it) as well as members of the elite families that owned it. Innovative interpretation could be seen at Erddig (a National Trust property in North Wales) in the 1980s, where visitors entered the house from the service areas, rather than that used by the family, and viewed information not just about the family that built the house but also the individuals and their families who worked in it and on the estate (see Figure 3).

Figure 3 Photograph of the servants against the garden front at Erddig, Wrexham, 1912. Photo: © National Trust/John Bethell. This image is part of a tradition of painting and photographing the servants at Erdigg (note where a head has been pasted on). Each servant holds an object related to their work, while members of the family who owned Erdigg appear in the window.

Another area of growing interest is the role played by women (like Bess of Hardwick) in the design and running of country houses, a role that has often been ignored by a narrative centred on male owners. This can be seen in the following quote, in which Mark Girouard describes the country house (I have used '[sic]' to indicate where the use of 'his' can be found in the original text):

[The country house] was the headquarters from which land was administered and power organised. It was a show-case, in which to exhibit and entertain supporters and good connections. In early days it contained a potential fighting force. It was an image-maker, which projected an aura of glamour, mystery or success around its owner. It was visible evidence of his [sic] wealth. It showed his [sic] credentials—even if the credentials were sometimes faked.

(Girouard, 1980, p. 3)

This chapter considers these issues of class, hierarchy and gender in relation to Hardwick. We will return to the work of Girouard, an expert on the country house and on Hardwick in particular, who has family links to the house and has done much to enable its rediscovery. We will also consider more recent work on the house and the contribution of the **patron**, artists and craftsmen to its decoration and furnishing. This will not only enable us to understand some aspects of Elizabethan culture but also to reflect on the (inevitably different) cultural values attached to the country house today.

3 Bess of Hardwick's houses

The story of Hardwick is intimately bound up with the iconic status of its female patron. Bess began life as a member of a modest gentry family who had lived in a manor house on the site of what is now Hardwick Old Hall for generations. She died as a countess and the second wealthiest woman in England, after Elizabeth I, outliving her four husbands. Her reputation, however, has been mixed. On the one hand, her four marriages (and the increased wealth and position of each of her husbands) has contributed to a reputation that she was an ambitious and avaricious woman. How far can this reputation be justified? Her first step on the social ladder was not an unusual one, as she became a gentlewoman in the household of another Derbyshire family. In *c.*1543, when she was in her mid twenties, she married Robert Barlow (d.1544) who was probably a member of the same aristocratic household. After Barlow's death, her second marriage in 1547 was to Sir William Cavendish (1505–1557) and took place when she was part of a much grander household. This marriage was of a quite different order; Cavendish was a former auditor responsible for the sale of church lands following the **Dissolution of the Monasteries**, so brought not only wealth but connections at court too. Together they bought Derbyshire estates, including Chatsworth. After Cavendish's death in 1559, Bess then married Sir William St Loe (1518–1565), a favourite courtier of Elizabeth I and another wealthy landowner. This enabled Bess to strengthen her position close to royal power as a gentlewoman of the privy chamber.

Figure 4 Rowland Lockey (*c*.1567–1616), *Mary, Queen of Scots*, 1578, oil on panel. Hardwick Hall. Photo: © National Trust Images/John Hammond. This portrait still hangs in the Long Gallery.

Finally, in 1567 she married Sir George Talbot, 6th Earl of Shrewsbury
(1528–1590), as part of a joining together of the two families with two
marriages between the sons and daughters of Bess and Shrewsbury's
earlier marriages. Shrewsbury was one of the wealthiest men in
England who controlled large areas of the northern Midlands.
Moreover, from the late 1560s he was given custody of Mary, Queen
of Scots (r.1542–1567; Figure 4), who represented the greatest threat to
Elizabeth I's regime. Although Bess reached the status of countess and
became a major figure in her own right through this final marriage, it
was strained by the cost and pressures of Shrewsbury's position
guarding Mary, and the marriage ended in bitterness in 1584. Bess's
ambition that her granddaughter and ward, Arbella Stuart (1575–1615;
Figure 5), had claims to the throne also contributed to this situation
(Girouard, 1989, pp. 8–9).

Through marriage, Bess certainly climbed the social ladder,
accumulated estates and became closer to life at court. However, all of
her marriages, except the last, are thought to have been happy. Her
position might have been founded on her husbands' wealth and land,
but it was not just the accumulation of lands themselves that brought
her wealth, since her skills in managing rents and income were also
significant. Another side to her reputation portrays her as a woman
familiar with the culture of Renaissance Europe, as she was a prolific
letter writer and builder. In the next section of this chapter, we are
going to consider the ways in which Bess's building and decoration
projects asserted her power and status, but we are going to start by
looking at how she herself was portrayed by artists.

Figure 5 Unknown artist, *Arbella Stuart*, 1589, oil on panel. Hardwick Hall.
Photo: © National Trust Images/Robert Thrift. This portrait still hangs in the
Long Gallery.

3.1 Portraying Bess of Hardwick

Figure 6 Follower of Hans Eworth (*c.*1525–1578), *Elizabeth Hardwick, Countess of Shrewsbury*, *c.*1560, oil on panel. Hardwick Hall. Photo: © National Trust Images.

Figure 7 Attributed to Rowland Lockey (*c.*1565–1616), *Elizabeth Hardwick, Countess of Shrewsbury*, after 1590, oil on canvas. Hardwick Hall. Photo: © National Trust Images/John Bethell.

Activity 2

(Allow around 10 minutes to complete this activity.)

Look at Figure 6, a portrait of Bess when she was in her early forties, and Figure 7, painted some 20 years later. Both portraits remain at Hardwick Hall.

Apply the 'Paintings' section of the visual analysis toolkit (Resource 2.1 in the Resources section at the end of this block) to compare and contrast how the artists have conveyed the sitter's status, thinking back to your work on portraiture in the previous chapter. These images can be seen in more detail in the online gallery on the module website.

Jot down notes on the sitter's stance, clothing and other accessories (and ignore the later inscription above Bess's shoulder in Figure 6).

Discussion

Both artists show a three-quarter length view of the sitter. In the earlier portrait (Figure 6), Bess's determined gaze is turned to her left, slightly away from the viewer, her hands clasped over her skirt in a pose that demonstrates decorum. Rowland Lockey's later portrait (Figure 7) is quite different in its visual effects. Bess is now turned towards her right, meeting the viewer's gaze, her right hand outstretched to rest on a table.

In the earlier portrait, Bess is shown dressed in a fur-lined overgarment with slashed sleeves over an embroidered shirt, her cap is decorated with pearls, and she is wearing many gemstone rings, conveying both wealth and a taste for costly textiles and jewels. In the later portrait, Bess is depicted wearing a dark dress. The blackness of her garment and the background is lifted only by a five-strand pearl rope into which her left thumb is linked, her starched ruff and cuffs, and her red hair that frames her pale face. This may be an image of a widow in old age, but it is one that conveys not only wealth but authority. Bess's hairstyle may also have reminded you of portraits of Elizabeth I.

It's been suggested that the gloves Bess clasps in Figure 6 may indicate that this *c.*1560 portrait was linked to her marriage to Sir William St Loe, since a pair of leather gloves was a traditional wedding gift. However, the pose adopted in the later 1590s portrait, standing with her right hand resting on a table, imitates that adopted by royal women (as you have seen in Mary, Queen of Scots's portrait in Figure 4) and embodies her own dynastic claims:

> The portrait would have been read more as a portrayal of a dynast than as a painted commemoration of an aristocratic woman in old age. Bess's deliberate portrayal as a widow marked a significant moment in her late biography, and revealed her as virtuous, authoritative and legally independent of a 'superior' male partner. As an old woman, she may appear like the queen; in terms of legacy, however, Bess was quite unlike her. Her widow's attire and pearls signified Bess's marriages and children and her success as a progenitor.
>
> (Taylor, 2016, p. 74)

Significantly, this later portrait of Bess coincided with the start of the building of Hardwick Hall. Just like the portraits, this building was conceived in order to serve Bess's personal and dynastic ambitions as the seat of a Cavendish dynasty, under her younger and favoured son, William Cavendish (1551–1626), who would inherit the property after her death.

4 Building Hardwick Hall

By the time Bess returned to Hardwick, she was an experienced builder at Chatsworth and elsewhere with her second husband, Sir William Cavendish. She would also have been familiar with the latest models in architecture and design from her travels to country houses around Britain and the libraries of printed books that she had seen there. It was as a patron-builder that she would now seek to cement her reputation and that of her intended dynasty.

4.1 The relationship with Hardwick Old Hall

Figure 8 North (garden) front, Hardwick Old Hall, photograph by Herbert Felton in 1953. Historic England Archive.

Hardwick's site was one that contemporaries remarked upon, including the **antiquarian** William Camden (1551–1623) on his tour of England, Scotland and Ireland. Camden uses seventeenth-century language in describing the approach to the house, so after reading the following passage you may like to read my own (rough) modern translation.

Higher yet in the very East frontier of this County, upon a rough and a craggy Soile standeth Hardwic, which gave name to a Family in which possessed the same: out of which descended Lady *Elizabeth* Countesse of *Shrewesbury*, who beganne to build there two goodly houses joyning in manner one to the other, which by reason of their lofty situation shew themsleves, a farre off to be seene, and yeeld a very goodly prospect.

(Camden, 1637, pp. 555–556)

Modern translation

Higher yet in the very east frontier of this county, upon a rough and craggy soil stands Hardwick, which gave its name to a family who possessed the site: from whom descended Lady Elizabeth, Countess of Shrewsbury, who began to build there two well-designed houses close to each other, which by reason of their lofty situation are visible from a long way off, and provide a very pleasant view.

Camden's account conveys both the remoteness of the position on the edge of a rocky plateau and its long association with Bess's family. This family history and the prominent position of the site are the building blocks of the assertion of power that the architecture represents. Camden describes 'two goodly houses' joined together, houses that can both be seen from a distance. Although Hardwick Old Hall and Hardwick Hall are not physically linked, they stand a few hundred yards apart and, as we shall see, are related to each other in design terms too.

Bess had gained experience of building projects when she oversaw extensive works at Chatsworth from the 1550s onwards, so when she returned to Hardwick in 1584 (after her last marriage had ended) she brought an experienced eye to remodelling and enlarging the old manor house. Hardwick Old Hall was where she began to experiment with many architectural devices – the transverse Entrance Hall positioned across the middle of the house, the Great Chambers, and the prominent staircase – all of which were also later developed for

Hardwick Hall (West, 2008). Although Hardwick Old Hall lacked a unified single design, it shows Bess's confidence to experiment with architecture and decoration within her social boundaries. Indeed, as a widowed countess, it is possible that she no longer needed to fit in with contemporary ideals of female decorum.

Figure 9 Dirck Coornhert (1522–1590) after Maarten van Heemskerck (1498–1574), Figure of Nephthali with a stag and broken figure of Mercury, etching from suite of prints *The Twelve Patriarchs*, 1550. Fitzwilliam Museum, University of Cambridge. Photo: © Fitzwilliam Museum/ Bridgeman Images.

The building fuses the forms of **Gothic** architecture with classical details, based on ideas from the **Northern Renaissance**. This taste is seen in the **printed sources** (see for example Figure 9) for the design of the plasterwork wall decorations, some of which still cling to the masonry four centuries after they were installed. Hardwick Old Hall accommodated key members of Bess's household, such as administrators and important servants, but also her aforementioned son William, a key figure in the running of her estates. It was her intention that William would continue her dynasty; one way this is reflected is in the choice of **plasterwork decoration** in his chamber, which we will look at in more detail in the following activity.

Figure 10 Attributed to Abraham Smith (working at Chatsworth in 1581), plaster overmantel with the Biblical figure of Nephtali riding a stag, late 1580s, Sir William Cavendish's chamber, Hardwick Old Hall. Photo: Anthony Wells-Cole.

Activity 3

(Allow around 5 minutes to complete this activity.)

In this activity we are going to examine the relationship between a printed source and plasterwork decoration. Please look at Figures 9 and 10 and read the captions accompanying them. (Note, an overmantel is the area of wall above a mantelpiece framing a chimney opening.)

Maarten van Heemskerck's *The Twelve Patriarchs* series depicted the sons of Jacob, who founded the 12 tribes of Israel described in the **Old Testament**, including the son shown here, Nephthali.

Jot down some brief notes about what elements from the biblical print (Figure 9) were adapted in the plasterwork panel (Figure 10), and what was different?

Discussion

In the plasterwork panel (Figure 10), the stag's crossed legs, beard and angle of the head all replicate the print shown in Figure 9. The torso and arms of the print's central figure, Nephthali, is also shown astride the stag, grasping an antler with one hand. His other hand rests on the plinth. However, the statue (of the classical god Mercury with a winged helmet and broken limbs) and the distant group of figures on the left-hand side of the print are omitted from the plasterwork in Figure 10, along with the verses that appeared below. The central scene in the plasterwork overmantel above the chimney opening is instead framed by trees and other vegetation.

The overmantel would have been viewed from floor level, which might explain the omissions of detail from the print in favour of a clearly visible, bold design more suitable for a large-scale plasterwork panel. The mythological relationship between Nephthali and Mercury, the messenger god, might also have been thought too obscure to translate easily onto the wall. The setting of trees suggests a forest, and the stag symbolises Nephthali's virtue of swiftness, referred to in the print's verses, which highlights his 'sweet words' (in Latin, *mitadas voces*). Given Bess's dynastic ambitions, there may be a deliberate visual connection to be drawn between William, the Cavendish coat of arms (which featured stags) and Nephthali's biblical status as the founder of one of the 12 tribes of Israel, despite not being the eldest son. As we shall see later in this chapter, motifs of deer, hunting and Old Testament figures also played a part in the dynastic and personal messages of Hardwick Hall's interiors.

4.2 Hardwick 'new' Hall: the exterior

If Hardwick Old Hall was a testing ground for new ideas, Hardwick Hall was a single unified design. It is an example of the Elizabethan style in architecture, associated with domestic building as well as a series of vast country houses constructed between *c*.1560 and *c*.1620 by a new group of patron-builders. Particularly during the Elizabethan period, these houses were built by courtiers to sustain households that might rival those of the royal court in scale and complexity as well as impress the queen. Often labelled 'prodigy houses', they were a means for newly ennobled lawyers, merchants and civil servants to enshrine their economic and social power through competitive building. In design they represented a break with the sprawling skylines of earlier houses, which were arranged horizontally around many courtyards. Burghley House in Lincolnshire (Figure 11; built for William Cecil, Lord Burghley, 1520–1598, Elizabeth's Secretary of State for much of her reign) is one example. Light and height are emphasised in its vertical orientation, use of large windows and many storeys and towers.

Bess would have been familiar with these models of architecture from her own travels as well as printed sources, but at Hardwick Hall she modified them to accommodate her own personal and dynastic ambitions. She did not require a vast house since, although her household was large, she and her granddaughter Arbella were the principal occupants, as other family members and key servants were accommodated at Hardwick Old Hall. The house's plan therefore did not need to occupy a big footprint. She did, however, adopt other Elizabethan architectural devices designed to signify power through the messages they carried. The first of these was height. Bess accentuated this through the choice of the castle form, and further raised the height of the towers during construction.

Figure 11 West front, Burghley House, Lincolnshire, built for William Cecil, Lord Burghley, *c.*1558–85. Photo: Tim Scrivener/Alamy.

Second, there was the use of large areas of glazing to flood rooms (such as the Entrance Hall and Long Gallery) with light. The vast windows were highlighted by William Cecil in what has become a well-known phrase: 'Hardwick Hall, more glass than wall'. This can be read literally as a comment on the building's appearance, but it also refers to the wealth required to obtain large quantities of glass, then a very costly material (as in ancient Rome where glazed panels were employed in the Domus Aurea). In order to secure a regular supply of window glass for the build, Bess set up her own glass furnaces at Wingfield near Hardwick. Cecil's assessment has further been read as a metaphor for how the huge windows visually transformed load-bearing walls into large areas of transparent glass, inverting the laws of building where walls are solid structures to bear weight. This device also reflected the Elizabethan enjoyment in thinking of architectural features as figures of speech. The effect of huge areas of glass has been described 'as if material substance [had] been translated into immaterial light', part of the pleasure that Elizabethan architecture sought to give by 'stirring' the mind (Gent, 2014, 91).

Figure 12 Jan Siberechts (1627–1703), *View of Longleat, Wiltshire*, 1678, oil on canvas, 122 × 169 cm. Victoria and Albert Museum, London (on loan). © Image; Crown Copyright: UK Government Art Collection.

Third, Hardwick Hall shows innovative planning in its design, incorporating up-to-date Renaissance theories, particularly those seen in the work of Robert Smythson (*c*.1535–1614). Smythson had trained as a stone mason, and by the 1560s he had become a master mason. Between 1572 and 1580, he assisted in the remodelling of the exterior of Longleat in Wiltshire (Figure 12) for the wealthy and well-connected Sir John Thynne (1515–1580), including carving external detail. At Longleat, Smythson became familiar with French printed sources for designing symmetrical façades. The elevations were made regular (four bays wide on the entrance façade, three on the others) with each storey of the shallow projecting bays decorated with **pilasters** using a different classical **order: Doric**, **Ionic** and **Corinthian** (Girouard, 2009, p. 181) (see Figure 13). It was this symmetry and regularity that reappeared at Hardwick.

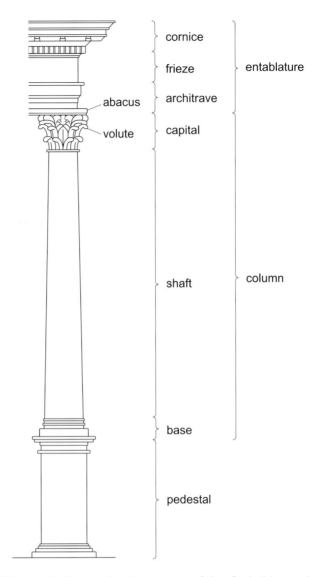

Figure 13 Classical orders: parts of the Corinthian order. © The Open University.

After Longleat, Robert Smythson moved north, where he was to spend the remainder of his career. By 1583 he was at Wollaton in Nottinghamshire, responsible for the house's design and building (Figure 14). Wollaton was built for Sir Francis Willoughby (1546–1596), whose wealth came not only from lands acquired since medieval times but also from more recent mining interests. Willoughby was a keen book collector, and once again this would have brought Smythson knowledge of continental designs. Smythson's contribution at Wollaton is singled out in his funerary monument, which further elevated his position from surveyor, calling him an 'Architecter and Surveyor unto the most worthy house of Wollaton and divers others of great account', suggesting he was valued for his skills in design as well as his knowledge of building (Girouard, 1983, p. 9).

Figure 14 West front, Wollaton, Nottinghamshire, built by Robert Smythson for Sir Francis Willoughby, 1580–88. Photo: Bailey-Cooper Photography/Alamy.

Activity 4

(Allow around 20 minutes to complete this activity.)

Examine Wollaton's exterior (Figure 14) and compare it to that of Hardwick Hall (see Figure 1), considering what you learned earlier about Hardwick's façade. Then apply the section on 'Architecture' in the visual analysis toolkit (Resource 2.1 in the Resources section at the end of this block) to compare and contrast what you can see. These images can be seen in more detail in the online gallery on the module website.

Discussion

Both houses were built on a huge scale. There are regular **mullioned** windows and projecting square towers in both buildings, but at Hardwick the towers appear taller. The most striking difference between the two buildings is the huge room with circular turrets at the corners that rises from the centre of Wollaton. You may have also noted that overall Wollaton appears less plain and is more detailed than Hardwick: the whole façade (not just the ground floor) is decorated with **columns** and **niches** and the entrance is clearly defined.

Entablatures divide up the storeys of both buildings, but at Wollaton these are more elaborate. At Hardwick there is a row of eight columns at ground floor level, which form an open-sided loggia. There are also differences in the way that the tops of the square towers are treated; at Wollaton these are turned into gables with strapwork and pointed **obelisks**, whereas at Hardwick there are no gables and the strapwork is open and supports Bess's monogram. Both buildings have balustrades at roof height, and at Wollaton these are on two levels.

Wollaton now lies within the city of Nottingham, its parkland has been vastly reduced in scale and forms part of a public open space. The house remains prominent on a hill, however, and (at the time of writing) a visitor can still walk on the roof and enjoy the views. Crucially, its hilltop site and castellated skyline (based on the model of a castle) provided a precedent for Hardwick. Why was this model chosen? One answer is that Hardwick Hall's site along a craggy outcrop, noted by Camden, invited a castle model, which accentuated the towers' height and the dramatic location. The castle also provided a ready association with landed power and a continuing family dynasty, expressing the social position of its occupant, similar to Cecil's Burghley (Figure 11) whose façade has been compared to that of a castle lodge (Figure 15). This continuity would have appealed to Bess, who as we know was seeking to establish a Cavendish dynasty on the site long associated with her family.

Figure 15 Anonymous, *Fancie of a Fowler*, a hunting scene based on a Flemish engraving of 1578 by Philips Galle after Johannes Stradanus, pre-1601, framed cushion cover applied needlework in silk and metal thread on velvet. Hardwick Hall. Photo: © National Trust/Robert Thrift. In the centre is a castellated hunting lodge, complete with battlements.

Although Robert Smythson is clearly documented as working at Wollaton, the evidence for his involvement at Hardwick is slim but it does exist. First, a plan drawn by him seems to show a version of the eventual Hardwick Hall design when the two are overlaid (Figure 16). From the outside, the front and rear (west and east elevations) of this house appear the same, with the minor additions of different steps and doors into the building. This uniform façade is, as we have seen, how Hardwick was eventually built. The key innovation that Bess had already experimented with at Hardwick Old Hall was the placing of the hall transversally across the centre of the building, stretching right through the space rather than facing lengthways along the front, and this is repeated in this plan and at the new hall. Smythson's plan also relates to the new hall at Hardwick in two other ways. It shows projecting towers and it is a double range deep: that is, it has two suites of rooms, one facing to the front and one to the rear. In fact, although it is vast in height, it is not vast in footprint in comparison to other Elizabethan great houses, since (as mentioned previously) it only accommodated the household of a woman in her sixties and her ward.

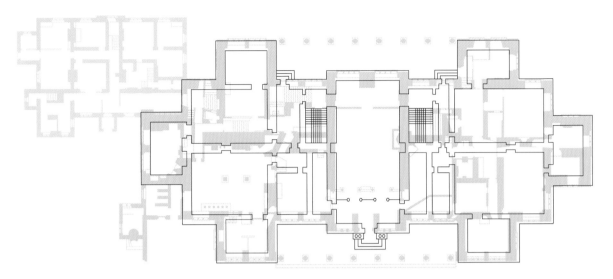

Figure 16 Robert Smythson (*c.*1535–1614), *Variant plan for Hardwick Hall, Derbyshire*, 1585, sepia pen drawing. RIBA Collections. Smythson's plan (in black) is annotated with the actual build (in orange). The service wing, built 1859–60, is shown to the north-east (in grey).

The final design also defines private and public areas in a very different way to the Athenian home that you studied in Block 1. There was a clear vertical progression from the more public areas on the ground floor to rooms for family, including Bess herself, on the first floor, while the entertaining and accommodating of important guests took place on the storey above. A final level, roof height, enabled promenading across the flat lead roof and access to the rooms in the turrets for banqueting. However, what the Smythson plan does not show is a further innovation in Hardwick Hall's design: the principal staircase. This was separate from the secondary stair that provided access to family areas on the first floor and then narrowed to the second floor and onto the roof. This secondary staircase provided access for servants and a more private route for Bess and her close associates. The principal stair was developed from the one Bess had experimented with in Hardwick Old Hall, reflecting taste for a separate processional route for important visitors. At Hardwick Hall the austere stone stair created an impressive route to the entrance to Bess's apartments, before winding on and up to reach the High Great Chamber and the Long Gallery beyond.

The uniformity of the plan and the hierarchy of rooms within it would have been evident to all who passed through the house; the increasing heights of the windows was another aspect of this. These features can be read as creating an image of order, and in turn give an impression of the woman who created and presided over the house. However, it's been pointed out that while authority is inherent in Hardwick Hall's design, its hierarchical plan is based on intimacy and closeness to Bess herself (Cooper, 2016, p. 38). This is a very different guiding principle to the one other patron-builders needed to adopt in order to accommodate vast households containing many different ranks of servants and officials.

5 Decorating Elizabethan Hardwick

Elizabethan prodigy houses such as Hardwick have also been seen as visual conceits, whose riddles and emblems needed to be unpicked to be understood. As previously mentioned, this was part of the understanding of buildings as linked to the enjoyment of thinking about architectural features as literary devices, such as a metaphor. In this respect, how buildings were seen is linked to language, and especially to the appreciation of poetry and the ancient art of rhetoric or persuasion. The exterior of Hardwick Hall shows this Elizabethan love of connecting words and buildings, not only in the use of large areas of glass to suggest buildings were not solid structures, as discussed earlier, but in the monogram 'ES' surmounted by a countess's coronet. This is repeated on each outer face of the six towers, an allusion to Bess's presence (Gent, 2014, p. 90). It is also reflected in the interiors, which displayed not only the Elizabethan elite's taste for combinations of different materials, textures and colours but also conveyed messages particular to Bess's dynastic ambitions, family history and personal identity.

Plasterwork, wood, stone and textiles all played a role in enabling Bess to knit her own identity into Hardwick Hall's interior spaces. The idea that ornament was a way of showing a building's use and character was central to Renaissance ideas about architecture. The Elizabethan period also coincided with the beginning of writings in English about architecture, and the emerging idea that the decoration of a building might express the character of the owner (Snodin and Howard, 1996, pp. 132–133). In 1624, Sir Henry Wotton (1568–1639) published *The Elements of Architecture*, in which he claimed that 'Every Mans [sic] proper Mansion House and Home' was 'the Theater of his Hospitality, the Seate of Self-fruition, the Comfortablest part of his owne Life, the Noblest of his Sonnes Inheritance, a kinde of private Princedome' (Wotton, 1624, p. 82). Home, then, is linked to privacy but also to the owner's relationship to the wider world, offering hospitality and comfort as well as indicating permanence and continuity on the public stage (ideas that you may recall from the discussion of public and private in the Athenian home and in relation to Nero's Domus Aurea).

Figure 17 Attributed to John Balechouse (fl.1570–d.c.1618), *The Conversion of Saul*, c.1600–01, painted cloth, Hardwick Hall. Photo: © National Trust/Robert Thrift. The first in a series of four painted hangings for the chapel at Hardwick. The figures are based on suites of prints by Maarten van Heemskerck.

However, as with portraiture, the rules of decor (decorum) still needed to be observed, since Wotton went on to point out that 'according to the degree of the master [sic]' the mansion should be 'decently and delightfully adorned', that is decorated with painting and sculpture (1624, p. 82). Too much ostentation must then be avoided, and decoration also needed to be in tune with the patron's place in the social order, otherwise it would be interpreted as a social faux pas. He also recommended that paintings were chosen in relation to a room's function: for example, galleries were suited to 'Graver Stories' and feasting and banqueting rooms to 'cheerful' paintings (1624, p. 99).

Figure 18 Attributed to John Balechouse (fl.1570–d.c.1618), *The Unannounced Return by Night of L. Tarquinius Collatinus and His Companions to Find His Wife Lucretia Weaving*, 1570, oil on canvas, 85 × 103 cm. Hardwick Hall. Photo: © National Trust Images.

It has been argued that John Balechouse (d.1618), Bess's painter and sometime clerk of works, may have been key to planning the overall programme of decoration at Hardwick. Bess certainly owned works by him, including the chapel hangings (Figure 17). She also owned a small painting by Balechouse (Figure 18), whose subject matter has been much disputed but which is now generally agreed to show an episode from the life of the Roman heroine Lucretia. She was a significant individual to Bess, who also owned an embroidered hanging depicting the same figure (which you will see later in the chapter in Figure 29). Additionally, the subject matter connects to Bess's own position as a virtuous wife working on embroideries during the Earl of Shrewsbury's long absences on duties at court and in connection with the custody of Mary, Queen of Scots.

5.1 Stone and plasterwork decorations: building a new dynasty

As at Hardwick Old Hall, aspects of the figurative decoration used in the new Hall were based on printed sources, linking the imagery to the cultural networks whereby prints circulated across Northern Europe during the Renaissance (Figures 21 and 23). It's been argued that Bess must have overseen their adaptation (perhaps from book illustrations known to her), because the messages seem very personal to herself and her family (Wells-Cole, 1997). Much of the decoration was based on biblical or classical prints; in the Renaissance, as in ancient Rome, classical (Greek) material could be used to signal cultural status.

It is uncertain how much individual craftsmen would have been responsible for the design of what they made. Thomas Accres, who had worked for Smythson at Wollaton, probably carved the polished alabaster and blackstone panelling in the Best Bedchamber (see Figure 19). There is no known printed source for the geometric design that makes use of the contrasts between the lighter English alabaster and blackstone, so perhaps this was Accres's own invention. Accres was evidently considered important to retain, since he was among the elite craftsmen who were given their own farms to work on between jobs and were paid wages, rather than by the measure of their work (i.e. the amount made) or by the job. Another retained stone carver (and plasterer), Abraham Smith, who may have had links to the plasterers at Longleat, carved the **terms** on the chimneypiece in Bess's own bedchamber (Figure 20), and he and Accres each carved one of Bess's coats of arms on the façade.

Figure 19 Thomas Accres, carved alabaster and blackstone panelling in the Best Bedchamber, 1599. Hardwick Hall. Photo: © National Trust.

Figure 20 The chimneypiece in Lady Shrewsbury's bedchamber carved with terms by Abraham Smith. Photo: © National Trust Images/John Hammond.

Stone was used for fireplaces and in certain high-status rooms such as the Entrance Hall and the suite of the High Great Chamber, the Long Gallery (which had two fireplaces) and the Best Bedchamber (Figure 19). It was also used for overmantels, but here (and for friezes) plasterwork was more usual. These designs often use strapwork (inspired by Antwerp pattern books) to create frames around a central **cartouche** or ornamental panel. The overmantel in Bess's own bedchamber (Figure 20) is the exception here in that it has a blank cartouche, perhaps because it was intended to be painted (Figure 21).

Figure 21 Pieter van der Heyden after Jakob Floris (1524–1581), engraved cartouche, 1566, height 17 cm. Hieronymus Cock, Antwerp. Victoria and Albert Museum, London. © Victoria and Albert Museum, London.

The decoration of Hardwick demonstrated the fashion of decorating with **heraldic devices**. This was especially important during a period when newly ennobled families wished to display the status they had earned (or believed they were entitled to), reflecting the value of heraldry as a sign of ownership. At Hardwick, this extended to the use of Bess's coat of arms of the Hardwick stag with an eglantine flower collar, suggesting her presence was everywhere, including covering over the hinds (female deer) in the coat of arms in the Gideon tapestries. These tapestries, discussed in the next section, were originally commissioned by another Elizabethan courtier, Sir Christopher Hatton (*c*.1540–1591), for his own Long Gallery at Holdenby House in Northamptonshire.

Figure 22 Detail of plasterwork frieze in the High Great Chamber showing a bear hunt, Hardwick Hall. Photo: © National Trust/Robert Thrift.

The key space where the possibilities of plasterwork were realised was as part of the unified scheme in the High Great Chamber (or Presence Chamber). This double height space (stretching across the centre of the west range on the hall's second storey) embodied the personal and dynastic associations of Hardwick's interiors in its tapestries, plasterwork and chimneypiece. It is possible that Abraham Smith designed the plasterwork **frieze** whose bold style and vast scale ensures legibility. It shows the Roman goddess Diana's court flanked by a hunting scene populated with exotic animals (Figures 22 and 24). The hunting scene includes a bear hunt, whose subject was based on another Antwerp print (Figure 23).

Sic capitur gladijs, et acutę cuſpidis haſtis,   Pręceps ſanguineâ dum ſe rotat ʋrſus arenâ.

Figure 23 Philips Galle after Johannes Stradanus, 'Bear Hunt with Nets', engraving from *Venationes Ferarum, Avium, Piscium*, Antwerp, 1578. British Museum, London © Trustees of the British Museum.

As you learned in your study of portraits in Chapter 1, the study of iconography (the interpretation of the visual images and symbols used in a work of art) can help us unpick symbolic references, which contemporaries would have recognised. Accordingly, the frieze can be read as an iconographic programme intended as a celebration of the Virgin Queen, Elizabeth I. Elizabeth's earthly court is compared to that of Diana, who is depicted with her mythical court above the High Great Chambers' embroidered canopy (Figure 24). Individual plaster figures of Cupid, Venus and Ceres in the window bays (symbolising spring and summer) may also allude to the prosperity and stability of Elizabeth's government, while the choice of the bear hunt may refer to the story of the nymph Callisto who escaped Diana by being transformed into a bear. At Hardwick, however, the dynastic message has a personal dimension too, since the frieze has been read as an elaborate compliment to the queen and her just and prosperous rule (Wells-Cole, 2016, p. 45). The hanging of tapestries representing the story of Ulysses (in Greek, Odysseus), the hero of Homer's *Odyssey*, and his wife Penelope (Figure 25) also had personal significance to Bess, in the same way as the painting of Lucretia (seen in Figure 18) symbolised her constancy.

Figure 24 Detail of the plasterwork frieze of Diana and her court above the Presence Canopy in the High Great Chamber, Hardwick Hall. Photo: © National Trust Images/Andreas von Einsiedel.

Figure 25 Niclaes Hellinck, Brussels, after a design attributed to Michiel I. Coxie, *The Homecoming of Ulysses*, *c.*1550–*c.*1565, tapestry: wool and silk. Photo: © National Trust/Robert Thrift. This is the final tapestry in the set that tells the story of Ulysses (in Greek, Odysseus), the hero of Homer's *Odyssey*, and his wife, Penelope. The set was recorded hung in the High Great Chamber in 1601 and remains there today.

In this Elizabethan country house, materials we would rarely use in decoration today – including elaborate stonework and plasterwork – had a function beyond purely covering the wall, since the shapes and scenes they portrayed were designed to be read by those with the appropriate cultural knowledge. Moreover, these hard surfaces were literally built into the fabric of Hardwick Hall. We will now turn to another more moveable aspect of the hall's decoration: the use of textiles.

5.2 Textiles: tapestry, needlework and embroidery

Textile wall hangings were the major item of expenditure for Hardwick Hall, and their use in programmes of decoration was carefully planned. Even within an elite context, Bess hung a greater number of tapestries than were employed in other Elizabethan country houses (as well as embroidered hangings and needlework panels). Why were these textiles central to the house's decoration? It has been argued that, given Bess's age and the pace of building, elaborate wood panelling would simply have taken too long to make (Wyld, 2012, p. 10). Textiles also gave warmth, colour and visual interest to austere interiors and could carry wider messages, based on contemporary, biblical or classical stories. However, for Bess they arguably also carried personal messages related to the value that she placed on textile work and her respect for the central role played by women in their production and cultural history.

Tapestries, the most expensive type of textile, often exceeded **plate** in valuations, and were costly status symbols that held their value (Levey and Thornton, 2001, p. 10). Bess tended to buy existing sets of tapestries rather than commission new designs from scratch. This was the case with the set of 13 tapestries in the Long Gallery depicting the biblical story of Gideon, which were bought during a buying trip to London in 1591–92. Nor were they all recently made, such as the fifteenth-century *Devonshire Hunting Tapestries*, which are in fact made up of different sets, perhaps from another Cavendish house, or they may have been a royal gift (Figure 26). It is thought that these tapestries were originally hung in the Entrance Hall, although in the 1601 inventory of Hardwick Hall , fragments were also recorded in Bess's Bedchamber (Levey and Thornton, 2001). They are now owned by the Victoria and Albert Museum, London.

Figure 26 Southern Netherlands, possibly Arras, 'The Boar and Bear Hunt', 1430s, tapestry: wool, height (centre) 380 cm. From the series known as the *Devonshire Hunting Tapestries*, hung in the Entrance Hall, Hardwick Hall, and still recorded there in 1813. Victoria and Albert Museum, London. © Victoria and Albert Museum, London.

Activity 5

(Allow around 10 minutes to complete this activity.)

Examine Figure 26, which shows one of the *Devonshire Hunting Tapestries*, and read its caption. This image can be seen in more detail in the online gallery on the module website.

Apply the 'Designed objects' section of the visual analysis toolkit (Resource 2.1 in the Resources section at the end of this block) to this other form of visual culture, noting down what indicators of wealth and status you can detect in the tapestry.

To help with this, also consider:

- the setting
- the activities shown
- the figures' costumes
- the season.

Discussion

The forested landscape is bordered by castellated buildings, representing castles or hunting lodges. This forms the setting for the aristocratic activity of hunting, here of boars and bears, literally divided on the top edge by the figure of a white hind. The figures are arranged into two groups: on the left, that accompanying the boar hunt; on the right, facing it, the bear hunt itself. Men carrying spears with horses and dogs are shown accompanied by a huntsman with his horn. Both men and women wear elaborate costumes, including fur-lined cloaks. For example, in the bear hunt (to the right), the woman feeding a hunting dog is dressed in pink with blue sleeves, her cloak lined with ermine, while the man on horseback (further to the right) wears a gold-trimmed blue cloak. The trees in leaf and the carpet of forest flowers along the lower border indicate that it is springtime.

Bear hunting (also seen in Figures 22 and 23) was an imaginary activity by the time this tapestry was woven, as the animals had already become extinct in England. The tapestry's springtime setting is also imaginary, as when bear hunting did take place it was done during the winter months. Nor is there any sign of the mud and grime of the hunt, rather the female figures are presented as a parade of leisured elegance, while the male figures are either on foot, gesturing to the hunt, or poised with spears on horseback (Wooley, 2002). A final point to make is the sheer sophistication of the handling of this huge composition and the multitude of figures and activities – tapestries are far from being lesser decorative arts, but rivalled paintings whose cost they exceeded. Indeed, they were woven from **cartoons** or designs, sometimes devised by well-known artists.

Like the Long Gallery (where the 13 tapestries depicting the biblical story of Gideon were hung), the Entrance Hall may even have been designed to accommodate the *Devonshire Hunting Tapestries*, since, when installed, they exactly matched the height of the overmantel's coat of arms (visible on the left-hand side of Figure 27). Their presence both in the public space of the Entrance Hall as well as probably in the private space of her own bedchamber (accessible to close family) is indicative of the tapestries' perceived value and personal significance to Bess. In this sense, the hanging of such a monumental and (by this date) antique set may be intended to suggest a long dynasty stretching back in time. The subject matter of the tapestries also linked the Entrance Hall to the surrounding landscape, a symbolic place of feasting supplied through the aristocratic pursuit of hunting.

Figure 27 John Buckler (1770–1851), *Interior view of the Hall at Hardwick*, 1813, watercolour and pen and black ink on cream wove paper, 50 × 36 cm. Yale Center for British Art, Paul Mellon Collection. Buckler was a topographical artist known for the accuracy of his depictions of buildings.

Bess also used embroidered and needlework hangings from other Cavendish houses as part of Hardwick Hall's decorative programme, and again these encoded particular messages that could be understood by viewers with knowledge of their cultural significance. In 1601, one of the two alternative sets of hangings recorded in the Withdrawing Chamber was a series of five embroidered **appliqué** wall hangings (see Figures 28 and 29). Entitled *Noble Women of the Ancient World*, they had originally been made in the 1570s for Chatsworth and may have been part of interiors designed by a **painter-stainer** with experience of working at court, so ambitious are the designs. Each features a female mythological or historical figure, flanked by **personifications** of their respective **virtues**.

Figure 28 'Penelope flanked by Perseverance and Patience', *c.*1573, embroidered appliqué panel. Hardwick Hall. Photo: © National Trust/Chris Timms. Part of a set recorded in the Withdrawing Chamber in 1601.

Activity 6

(Allow around 10 minutes to complete this activity.)

Study Figure 28, which is one of the four surviving *Noble Women of the Ancient World* panels, and read its caption. This image can be seen in more detail in the online gallery on the module website.

Apply the 'Designed objects' section of the visual analysis toolkit (Resource 2.1 in the Resources section at the end of this block) to consider what elements of this embroidered panel's composition might have been important to Bess.

Note down your thoughts about:

- the scale

- the architectural setting

- the treatment of the figures

- any symbols (don't worry if you don't know what they stand for).

Discussion

The panel is very large in scale, rivalling that of tapestry. The architectural setting includes a balustrade-like structure in the foreground, columns to each side, and an entablature running across the top. The central figure is more than life-sized, and the three figures are each contained within a Roman arch, creating the overall impression of a classical façade. The appearance of stonework is also imitated in costly gold thread.

The central figure of Penelope had (as we saw when looking at Figure 25) particular significance for Bess. Here, Penelope's left hand rests on a rolled-up piece of cloth (a reference to her weaving), again highlighted with gold thread. However, her pose is that of an upright, heroic figure, and the index finger of her right hand also gestures upwards. Heraldic symbols were important to Bess, and this panel is no exception, including as it does coats of arms and initials along the top.

Like the late portrait of Bess herself (see Figure 7), the central figures in each panel – mythological heroines such as Penelope and Lucretia, and the historical queens Zenobia, Artemisia and Cleopatra – are portrayed as authoritative and independent. Different theories have been put forward to explain the precise significance of the choice of these female figures. One concerns their role in relation to their position as exemplary wives or widows, roles that would have been recognised by educated Elizabethans familiar with the works of the poet Geoffrey Chaucer (1343–1400) (Slocombe, 2016, pp. 124–125). The hangings could also have been intended to encourage the viewer to adopt the values that Bess espoused and admired in others, especially patience and perseverance, the qualities exemplified in Penelope, the faithful wife of Ulysses (seen in Figure 28).

The *Noble Women of the Ancient World* hangings contain not only messages about behaviour but also dynastic messages too. This can be seen in their heraldry, which links Bess and Shrewsbury. Along the top of these hangings the reversed monogram 'GE' at either end refers to her marriage to George Talbot (Earl of Shrewsbury), as do their combined initials 'GES' above the central figure (a device that Bess was to use on a much larger scale in the monogram 'ES' on the Hardwick Hall towers more than two decades later).

It was not only classical heroines and queens who provided the subject matter for textile hangings. Bess's own knowledge of architecture comes through in the motif of a central figure appearing to emerge from beneath a receding triumphal arch (see Penelope in Figure 28 and Lucretia in Figure 29). Further evidence for this interest in architecture is seen in another series of panels of female allegorical figures representing the Liberal Arts, including figures of both Perspective and Architecture (Figure 30).

Figure 29 'Lucretia flanked by Chastity and Liberality', *c.*1573, embroidered appliqué panel. Hardwick Hall. Photo: © National Trust/Chris Timms.

Figure 30 *Architecture*, *c*.1580, embroidered appliqué panel. Hardwick Hall.
Photo: © National Trust Images/Brenda Norrish.

Bess's appreciation of textile work was also reflected in the materials and techniques employed for the panels. Some were repurposed from textiles seized from churches and monasteries during the Dissolution of the Monasteries (which may have become available to the embroiderers through Sir William Cavendish). It's been argued that this reflected Bess's ability to retain textiles for her own religious use as well as her links with Mary, Queen of Scots. A series of needlework panels intended as bed hangings, created by Bess and Mary with their gentlewomen (see Figure 31), invites further questions about their political, religious and dynastic symbolism (Katritzky, 2017).

Figure 31 Mary, Queen of Scots, *A Catte*, after a woodcut by Conrad Gesner, *c*.1569–84, embroidered canvas panel, 30 × 30 cm. Palace of Holyroodhouse, Edinburgh. Royal Collection Trust © Her Majesty Queen Elizabeth II, 2020, RCIN 28224. Photo: © Bridgeman Images.

Activity 7

(Allow around 1 hour to complete this activity.)

Turn to Readings 2.1 and 2.2, which relate to the *Noble Women of the Ancient World* hangings. As you read, make some notes relating to the hangings' format, setting and display.

When you have finished reading, use your notes to write a short summary (about 150 words) considering how the authors interpret the hangings' visual messages. This will give you practice in bringing together arguments from more than one secondary source by identifying the arguments made in two different extracts.

Discussion

These two extracts focus on the hangings' setting, display and links to classical and contemporary theatre. LaBouff argues that the architectural form and figures work together to form 'memory theaters', transforming literary content into visual prompts to encourage debate, arguing that they demonstrate Bess's knowledge of rhetoric. She also compares the architectural form of the hangings' scenes to Roman theatrical stages, reflecting the Renaissance rediscovery of classical architecture as well as Bess's own experience of theatrical performances.

On the other hand, Frye focuses on their display, arguing that Bess's Withdrawing Chamber became a 'theater of identity' of painted and embroidered portraits of notable female figures, one which also memorialised her earlier connection to Mary, Queen of Scots. Frye argues that this connection remained important to Bess, as it formed an important part of her claim to high social status along with her rank of countess.

As we have seen, textiles played an important part in the decoration of Hardwick. Not only did they have a practical role in providing warmth and pattern, enhanced by their portability, but they also had wider cultural significance through their choice of classical and biblical imagery and their signalling of Bess's dynastic and personal interests.

6 Furnishing Hardwick Hall

It was not only the materials used to decorate the walls that were part of the visual effects inside Hardwick Hall, furniture and other moveable objects played an important part too. The 1601 inventory is notable for how little moveable furniture is included: to our modern eyes, the interior often appears sparsely furnished! Inventories can be very useful to art historians, as they can provide insights into moments of time in the past. In this particular inventory, two groups of furniture can be identified: one intended for 'shew' (show) or display, and the other intended for more practical functions including seating, sleeping and storage. An understanding of these two groups will give us insights into the minds of those who commissioned, designed and made these pieces, and the place of furniture in the Elizabethan interior and at Hardwick Hall in particular.

6.1 Display furniture

The first group of furniture is often architectural in form and scale and combines innovative designs with costly materials, techniques and finishes. Designed more for display than for practical functions, if these pieces did have a function it might have been linked to entertainment and hospitality, such as a table inlaid with a board for chess, or fitted with leaves that could be 'drawn' (opened) for dining. However, display furniture also carried wider cultural messages. One example is the 'Sea dog' table, which was listed in the Withdrawing Chamber in the 1601 inventory (Figure 32). Here, it was described as 'a drawing table Carved and guilt [gilt] standing uppon sea doges inlayde with marble stones and wood, a Carpet for it of nedleworke' (Levey and Thornton, 2001, p. 47).

Figure 32 French, after Jacques Androuet du Cerceau, 'Sea dog' table, *c*.1570, walnut with gilding, marbling and inlay, height 85 cm. Hardwick Hall. © National Trust/Robert Thrift.

The makers' skills are shown in the deeply carved walnut, which represented the sea dogs' fur, feathers and scales, while different types of fruits are carved in the garlands around their necks. These are not the only exotic animals to feature in the table's design, since the base sits on carved tortoises or turtles and a lion's head decorates the frieze running around the top. Carving is not the only eye-catching skill in this piece, as the table top is inlaid with coloured marbles (albeit originally covered with a needlework carpet), a technique associated with late-sixteenth-century furniture made in France but which originated in ancient Rome. Parts of the table originally had gilding, so there would also have been vivid contrasts between the carved and inlaid woods, marbles and gilt.

Figure 33 Frontispiece to George Gascoigne (d.1577), *The Tale of Hemetes the Heremyte pronounced before the Queen at Woodstock*, 1576, pen and ink on paper. British Library, London. Photo: © British Library Board/ Bridgeman Images.

The 'Sea dog' table does not only display costly materials and skills, however. The leaves draw out to create a larger surface and it comes apart, perhaps so that it could be carried up to the banqueting house on the 'leads', or flat leaded roof, for occasional dining. As with the chimneypieces and plasterwork that we explored earlier in this chapter, the table's design can also be read in relation to contemporary print culture in the form of a design of sphinxes by the sixteenth-century architect Jacques Androuet du Cerceau (1515–1585), whose designs appear in other pieces of display furniture (Figure 35). Sphinxes form the table's base, albeit in the modified form of sea dogs. Why were they chosen by the designers of this table? They were undoubtedly part of du Cerceau's library of furniture designs, but the specific marine imagery may have had wider significance. Other printed sources can help us here; a similar imaginary animal, its paws clutching a circular object, appears as the side support to the throne in the frontispiece that illustrated a copy of a poem presented to Elizabeth I for New Year in 1576 (Figure 33).

This marine ornament may have had lasting significance, since it also appears in the form of gilt figures of mermaids in the chair of state depicted in 'The Armada portrait' of around 1588 (Figure 34). On this level, then, the 'Sea dog' table at Hardwick may have royal associations. However, its French associations (present in the choice of wood, the use of inlaid coloured marbles on the tabletop and the links to du Cerceau's designs) could indicate a provenance linked not to Elizabeth but to Mary, Queen of Scots, who was in fact involved in trying to acquire items of furniture for Shrewsbury from France in the 1570s (Jervis, 2016, p. 90). Whatever its origins, the table's presence at Hardwick Hall suggests that display furniture was another means adopted by Bess to signify her royal taste, similar to the way that she adopted the stance seen in portraits of royal women in her own late portrait (see Figure 7).

Figure 34 British School, *Elizabeth I ('The Armada Portrait')*, *c.*1588, oil on panel, 127 x 110.5 cm. Woburn Abbey, Bedfordshire. Photo: © Bridgeman Images.

6.2 Functional furniture

The second group of furniture we are going to consider was more practical in function. The 1601 inventory of Hardwick Hall included functional pieces such as formes (benches), which can still be seen in the Entrance Hall, showing how the household's practical needs for dining around long tables were accommodated. It is also littered with references to chests and trunks (such as Figure 36). These objects, along with coffers to contain personal belongings, were also needed for storage and for transferring possessions between Hardwick Old Hall and Hardwick Hall. Constructed of wood and often covered with leather and bound with iron, they were usually lined with paper to protect textiles and documents from dust and rust.

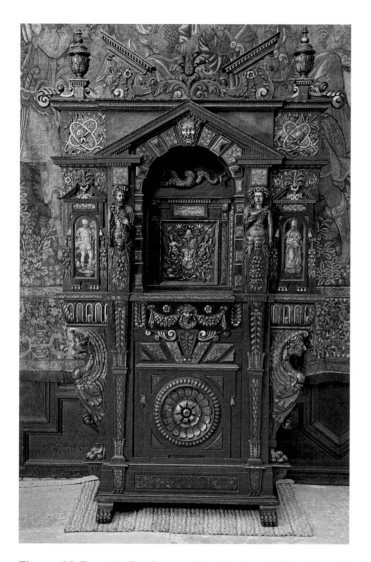

Figure 35 French, 'Du Cerceau' cabinet, *c.*1570, oak and walnut with gilding, marbling, compressed wood shavings, marbles and gilt and silver grisailles (painting executed in various tones of grey, often used decoratively to imitate stone sculpture) on leather, height 238 cm. Photo: © National Trust/Robert Thrift. The terms (seen in profile on either side of the base) relate to designs by du Cerceau.

The seating, such as a surviving, folding X-Frame armchair (whose frame still has traces of painted decoration), would have been used by Bess, her family and elite visitors on formal occasions. This piece of furniture might relate to the one listed as having been in the Best Bedchamber in the 1601 inventory, described as 'A great Chair trimmed with Crimson velvet embroidered with gold and gold fringe' [my modern translation] (Levey and Thornton, 2001). When upholstered, it would have resembled the example that survives at Knole in Kent, remodelled in the early 1600s, shown in Figure 37.

Figure 36 Probably South German, 'GT' chest, *c.*1575, oak with inlay of various woods and tinned iron hinges, 89 × 175 cm. Photo: © National Trust/Robert Thrift. The initials 'GT' may be those of Gilbert Talbot, 7th Earl of Shrewsbury (1552–1616), who married Bess's daughter, Mary.

As we have seen, furniture in the Elizabethan country house fulfilled practical needs – it often needed to be flexible, and able to be folded or opened up so that it could be moved around for different purposes. Furniture was used in the performance of sociable behaviour such as dining and entertaining guests. Like fixed decoration and textiles, certain key items of display furniture also carried messages about transcultural taste.

Figure 37 X-framed armchair ('Chair of state'), probably *c.*1600–25, beech frame covered in crimson velvet and crimson figured damask with silk and gold passementerie, height 134 cm. Knole, Kent. Photo: © National Trust/ Jane Mucklow.

7 Summary

This chapter has explored some of the ways in which an Elizabethan country house was the setting for a performance of power and status. Most obviously this is reflected in the sheer scale of the building projects at Hardwick as well as the innovations in height, planning and light that the two halls represent. Hardwick Hall's interiors displayed costly materials, but they also reflected the different functions of spaces within the house and the personal and dynastic interests of their female patron. As we have seen, Bess sought to establish dynastic power through her houses, using narratives of heraldic devices and classical and biblical stories to reinforce that message. This was a message intended for an elite audience with the necessary cultural knowledge to understand the hidden codes contained in the decoration and furnishings. However, hers was also a personal and moral message, rooted in the imagery of women who were significant to her, and in a house designed not for ranks of officials but for the household of a woman in her sixties and her favoured descendants.

You should now return to the module website to continue your study of this unit.

References

Camden, W. (1637) *Britain, or a chorographicall description of the most flourishing kingdomes, England, Scotland, and Ireland.* Translated from the Latin by P. Holland. London: Printed by F.K.R.Y. and I.L. for George Latham.

Cooper, N. (2016) 'The New Hall: realising intentions', in Adshead, D. and Taylor, D.A.H.B. (eds) *Hardwick Hall: a great old castle of romance.* New Haven, CT, and London: Yale University Press, pp. 18–38.

Cox, O. (2018) 'Downton Abbey and the country house: exploring new fictions', in Cannadine, D. and Musson, J. (eds) *The country house: past, present, future: great houses of the British Isles.* New York: Rizzoli, pp. 413–417.

Frye, S. (2013) *Pens and needles: women's textualities in early modern England.* Philadelphia: University of Pennsylvania Press, pp. 71–72.

Gent, L. (2014) 'Elizabethan architecture: a view from rhetoric', *Architectural History*, 57, pp. 73–108.

Girouard, M. (1980) *Life in the English country house: a social and architectural history.* London: Penguin Books.

Girouard, M. (1983) *Robert Smythson and the Elizabethan country house.* New Haven, CT, and London: Yale University Press.

Girouard, M. (1989) *Hardwick Hall.* London: National Trust.

Girouard, M. (2009) *Elizabethan architecture: its rise and fall, 1540–1640.* New Haven, CT, and London: Yale University Press.

Jervis, S.S. (2016) 'Furniture at Hardwick Hall-I', in Adshead, D. and Taylor, D.A.H.B. (eds) *Hardwick Hall: a great old castle of romance.* New Haven, CT, and London: Yale University Press, pp. 87–109.

Katritzky, M. (2017) 'Virtuous needleworkers, vicious apes: the embroideries of Mary Queen of Scots and Bess of Hardwick', in Münch, B.U., Tacke, A., Herzog, M. and Heudecker, S. (eds) *Künstlerinnen: neue perspektiven auf ein forschungsfeld der vormoderne.* Petersberg: Michael Imhof Verlag, pp. 48–61.

LaBouff, N. (2016) 'An Unlikely Christian Humanist: How Bess of Hardwick (ca. 1527–1608) Answered "The Woman Question"', *Sixteenth Century Journal*, 47(4), pp. 860–862.

Levey, S.M. and Thornton, P.K. (2001) *Of household stuff: the 1601 inventories of Bess of Hardwick.* London: National Trust.

Mandler, P. (1997) *The fall and rise of the stately home.* New Haven, CT, and London: Yale University Press.

National Trust (2017/18) *Annual report.* Swindon: National Trust. Available at: https://nt.global.ssl.fastly.net/documents/annual-report-201718.pdf. (Accessed: 27 February 2020).

Slocombe, E. (2016) 'The embroidery and needlework of Bess of Hardwick', in Adshead, D. and Taylor, D.A.H.B. (eds) *Hardwick Hall: a great old castle of romance*. New Haven, CT, and London: Yale University Press, pp. 110–132.

Snodin, M. and Howard, M. (1996) *Ornament: a social history since 1450*. New Haven, CT, and London: Yale University Press.

Taylor, D. (2016) 'A Derbyshire portrait gallery: Bess of Hardwick's picture collection', in Adshead, D. and Taylor, D.A.H.B. (eds) *Hardwick Hall: a great old castle of romance*. New Haven, CT, and London: Yale University Press, pp. 71–86.

Wells-Cole, A. (1997) *Art and decoration in Elizabethan and Jacobean England: the influence of continental prints, 1558–1625*. New Haven, CT, and London: Yale University Press.

Wells-Cole, A. (2016) 'Hardwick Hall: sources and iconography', in Adshead, D. and Taylor, D.A.H.B. (eds) *Hardwick Hall: a great old castle of romance*. New Haven, CT, and London: Yale University Press, pp. 39–52.

West, S. (2008) *Hardwick Old Hall*. London: English Heritage.

Wooley, L. (2002) *Medieval life and leisure in the Devonshire hunting tapestries*. London: V&A Publications.

Wotton, H. (1624) *The elements of architecture: collected by Henry Wotton, Knight, from the best authors and examples*. London: John Bill.

Wyld, H. (2012) 'The Gideon tapestries at Hardwick Hall', *West 86th: A Journal of Decorative Arts, Design History, and Material Culture*, 19(2), pp. 231–254.

Readings

Reading 2.1 Staging texts in memory theaters

Source: LaBouff, N. (2016) 'An Unlikely Christian Humanist: How Bess of Hardwick (ca. 1527–1608) Answered "The Woman Question"', *Sixteenth Century Journal*, 47(4), pp. 860–862.

Staging Text in Memory Theaters

Recent analysis of these textiles has focused on the identification of the female icons. Yet little attention has been paid to their setting and design layout. This section argues that the hangings do more than depict selections from *Famous Women*. The architectural motifs and human figures work together to organize textual information in a visual diagram, and were likely specifically designed to be memory theaters that supported recollection. If the textiles were used in such a way, they demonstrate Bess's knowledge of memorial practices, particularly those used within the discipline of rhetoric. These woven frameworks helped Bess convert literary content into memorable scenes that made her reading portable, easily retrievable for purposes of debate or conversation, and readily available for the kind of self-persuasion that was necessary for ethical training. In using her textile furnishings for such ends, Bess converted her chamber into a humanist studiolo.

Reading the visual content in the hangings as diagrammatic schemes requires careful consideration of the architectural elements. Each hanging includes a standardized stone edifice with ionic columns on either side and three rounded arches. These arches are rendered with depth and perspective shading (not always accurate) to convey that they are doorways leading into a dark background; the female figures all stand at the threshold of this background, just behind the doorways. Placed above these doorways are two roundels containing heraldic shields. In contrast, these are not rendered to convey depth but appear shallow, as if applied to the front of the masonry facade. The floor on which the structure rests appears to be a raised platform that extends out in front of the stone facade and is treated decoratively with tapered pilaster columns.

These embroidered structures bear striking similarities to ancient Roman theatrical stages. The masonry facade constitutes a scenery wall or *scaenae frons*, and the decorative niches within the wall are ornamented with heraldic shields rather than the statues that one might typically see in a classical theater. There are also three front-facing entrances to the stage, one central and two subsidiary, consistent with ancient custom, and the *proscaenium* is adorned with tapered pilasters. Grotesque masks above each entryway confirm the theatrical nature of the space. As viewers of the textiles, we are positioned close to their stages as if standing in the orchestra.

Bess probably never visited a Roman amphitheater, but firsthand observation of ancient theatrical structures would not have been necessary to account for her familiarity with their architectural elements. The Renaissance rediscovery of classical architecture, particularly Vitruvian styles, exerted a powerful influence on newly emerging spaces for entertainment in England. Though public playhouses bearing classical stamps (like the Swan or the Globe Theater in London) were not yet in existence, temporary sets for plays and masques in courtly and university settings were already staging ancient ideals. From their earliest English incarnations at the courts of King Henry VII and VIII, these settings mined elements from classical theater, particularly with respect to visual design. They often featured Greco-Roman settings, trompe l'oeil designs and perspective sceneries, and "antique" costumes. By the 1530s, these temporary settings alone promoted a new design vocabulary and the words *proscaenium*, *scaena*, and *theatrum* appear with greater frequency surrounding entertainments in the account books of Oxbridge colleges. As a member of courtly society, Bess would have had access to these elite entertainments and given her longstanding interest in architecture and her numerous building projects she would undoubtedly have been sensitive to the ancient architectural revival underway in the latter sixteenth century.

Reading 2.2 Women's textualities in early modern England

Source: Frye, S. (2013) *Pens and needles: women's textualities in early modern England*. Philadelphia: University of Pennsylvania Press, pp. 71–72.

[…] Bess's Withdrawing Chamber was a large but still intimate closet, opening from the Long Gallery on the third floor. In this chamber, she chose to place her hangings of Penelope, Zenobia, Arthemesia, Lucrecia, and Cleopatra produced twenty years earlier under her supervision at Chatsworth, when she and Mary were still often in one another's company. Bess had also gathered together a number of paintings and textile works related to Mary Queen of Scots in this room. The paintings adjacent to these textiles, which may have been mounted on the hangings themselves, are probably listed together in the 1601 inventory because they hung together. The listed paintings include portraits of Mary, Mary and Darnley as royal couple, and Mary's parents. Mary commissioned at least one of her portraits during her imprisonment in Derbyshire, and she probably had the portraits of herself and Darnley and of her parents sent to her along with the cartloads of possessions that followed her to England. All of the Stuart family portraits are still at New Hardwick. In the context of this Withdrawing Chamber—in part a shrine to Bess's connections with the Scottish queen—the female figure to the left of Lucrecia labeled "Chastity" would have been readily identified as still another portrait of Mary Stuart.

Why would Bess have dedicated a large portion of her Withdrawing Chamber to Mary in her New Hardwick Hall of 1597? Although Bess and Mary had fallen out about fifteen years before, Bess combined these images in her extraordinary room that was at once on display and for "withdrawing." The reason is that besides her marriage to the late earl, Bess's claim to an exalted social position lay in her former intimacy with Mary and the fact that Mary had become a member of Bess's family through the Lennox marriage, a kinswoman who connected Bess to both the Scottish and the English royal families. The same Bess who placed her granddaughter, Elizabeth Pierrepont, in Mary's retinue and who was one of Mary's principal mourners, assembled in this room a theater of identity populated with notable female figures that included other portraits both painted and embroidered. Bess might have taken comfort in memorializing the Queen of Scotland and Dowager Queen of France, albeit in a figure that is much smaller than the more commanding figures of Lucrecia and Penelope, who represent the countess's own virtuous, feminine authority.

This portrait of Mary in textile work may have been overlooked because the value of paint on canvas has to some extent blinded us to the widespread existence of portraits in textiles. Contemporary portraits in other textile media existed, like the portrait of Mary as Queen of Scotland praying on the ceiling of her state bed and the portrait of Catherine de Medici in black mourning that survives in a tapestry series of 1582–85. Seventeenth-century domestic needlework includes a number of examples of stitched portraits of Charles I, Charles II, and their queens, as well as one example of Mary Queen of Scots "entering Paradise" dated 1680. The tapestry-makers and professional embroiderers employed by Mary and Bess were artisans who may well have been portrait painters also. In *The Art of Limning*, Nicholas Hilliard attempts to distinguish between the "gentill painting" involved in "limning" and the "*Painting* or *drawing*" for "common men's use, whether for furnishing of Houses, or any patterns for tapestries," but in the sixteenth century, the lines between different kinds of design work and painting were still less distinct.

Chapter 3

Art against power:
satire and propaganda

Written by Warren Carter

Contents

1 Introduction

In the two preceding chapters, you focused on how power was constructed and displayed in relation to Renaissance portraiture and the Elizabethan country house. By contrast, in this chapter you will explore how art has been mobilised *against* power using either **satire** or **propaganda**. Satire is a **rhetorical device** that uses humour, irony, caricature or ridicule to expose the inadequacies of those in power, while propaganda is a more overtly political and systematic attack upon their vested interests. In practice though, there can be an overlap between the two as satire is often used for the purposes of propaganda. A key issue to be considered here is the type of media used for the forms of oppositional art that you will investigate in this chapter. Art produced to satirise the powerful for a popular audience, or designed as propaganda with a specific political issue in mind, is often made with a **mechanical means of production** such as **print** or photography, as distinct from the more traditional artistic forms of painting and sculpture. However, this is not a hard and fast rule, and artists invariably work in either mechanical or traditional media as and when they think the situation requires it.

It is worth bearing in mind that this chapter deals with art produced in the modern period onwards, which is generally characterised as beginning with the **French Revolution** of 1789. This was the moment when our contemporary understanding of politics as being divided on a spectrum between 'left' and 'right' first took shape. This division between competing political ideologies is something that characterises the kind of oppositional artworks that you will look at in this chapter. Although these works may be unfamiliar to you, many of them are by **canonical** artists, and I have chosen them as the subject of this chapter because they are the ones that, for me at least, speak most powerfully against injustice in the period in question. Some of them may seem shocking, but they were intended to function against powerful interests in the different contexts in which they were produced and, as such, they offer illuminating insights into how visual art can be deployed for a similar purpose today.

Figure 1 Francisco Goya, *Self Portrait in the Studio*, *c*.1790, oil on canvas, 42 × 28 cm. Real Academia de Bellas Artes de San Fernando, Madrid. Photo: © Bridgeman Images.

The first section of this chapter explores examples of art against war and begins with Francisco Goya (1746–1828; Figure 1) who produced oil paintings for the Spanish court as well as three satirical series of prints that challenged absolutist authority and reactionary superstition during the period in which he worked. The last of these print series, *The Disasters of War* (1810–20), will be our focus here. This work became the model for another print series by the German artist Otto Dix (1891–1969; Figure 2) entitled *The War* (1923–24) produced over 100 years later. Here, Dix used satire to document his experience of the horror of trench warfare in the First World War (1914–1918).

The next section explores the way in which art was deployed in the struggle against **fascism**. Here we will begin with the **anti-fascist** propaganda of another German artist, John Heartfield (1891–1968), produced in the period immediately preceding Adolf Hitler's (1889–1945) rise to power in Germany in 1933. Seeking to counter the powerful propaganda campaign that was being conducted by the **Nazis**, Heartfield used the new mechanical medium of **photomontage**, which, like the printmaking medium used by Goya and Dix, was designed for a wider dissemination than that of painting or sculpture. The status of Pablo Picasso (1881–1973; Figure 3) as one of the most celebrated modern artists of the twentieth century ensured that his own mural-sized, anti-fascist painting *Guernica* (1937), which we will look at later in this chapter, would quickly become a canonical work of art. Unlike the art considered beforehand, with its mechanical means of production, *Guernica* was painted in the more traditional medium of **oil on canvas**, and we will consider the effectiveness of such a work in relation to its use as propaganda against fascist military power in Spain.

Figure 2 Otto Dix, *Self-portrait as a Soldier*, 1914, oil on paper, 68 × 54 cm. Kunstmuseum Stuttgart. Photo: © akg-images. © DACS 2020.

Figure 3 Pablo Picasso alongside *Guernica*; photographed by David Seymour at the Spanish Pavilion of the International World Fair, Paris, 1937. Photo: © David Seymour/Magnum Photos. © Succession Picasso/DACS, London 2020.

Finally, we will turn from Europe to the United States to take a look at how the **poster** has been deployed in New York by radical artists from 1968 to the present day. We will first look at the propagandistic anti-Vietnam War poster produced by the Art Workers' Coalition, and then at the more recent posters of the Guerrilla Girls who challenge the inequities of gender relations within the art world, as well as in wider society, in an ironic and satirical fashion. Hence, we will finish by looking at how radical artists have sought to challenge the power of the art world itself in the here and now.

Study note

Please be aware that this chapter contains images of war that you may find disturbing.

2 Artists against war

Study note

This chapter ranges over the history of art from the early seventeenth century through to the present, focusing on oppositional practices that emerged through struggle against authoritarian forms of power, often in times of war. In the Resources section at the end of this block, you will find a very brief overview of these struggles in terms of who was fighting who, and why they were in conflict, which you can refer to while working through this chapter (see Resource 2.2).

Historically, most art depicting war has celebrated military victories with little, if any, reference to the violence or brutality involved. A famous example of this is *The Surrender of Breda* (1634–35; Figure 4) by the seventeenth-century Spanish painter Diego Velázquez (1599–1660). This painting depicts the Spanish victory over the Dutch in 1625 during the Thirty Years' War (1618–48) with the focus on the exchange of the key to the city of Breda in the foreground. However, both Goya's *The Disasters of War* and Dix's *The War* series took their cue from a series of prints by the printmaker Jacques Callot (1592–1635). The 18 small-scale works (collectively entitled *The Miseries and Misfortunes of War*) were produced in Nancy, the capital of the Duchy of Lorraine, in 1633 after it had been occupied by the French. The series offers a very different response to the Thirty Years' War than Velázquez's painting, as the prints depict atrocities carried out by enemy forces and the subsequent retribution by their peasant victims. The latter can be seen in the public hanging of captured French soldiers in Plate 11 of the series (Figure 5). What makes the print series by Goya and Dix different from that of Callot is that in these later works this anti-war sentiment is also mobilised against their own national regimes as well as that of the enemy.

Figure 4 Diego Velázquez, *The Surrender of Breda*, *c*.1635, oil on canvas, 307 × 372 cm. Museo Nacional del Prado, Madrid, Inv.: P01172. Image Copyright Museo Nacional del Prado © Photo: MNP/ Scala, Florence.

Figure 5 'The Hanging', etching from Jacques Callot, *The Miseries and Misfortunes of War* (Plate 11), Nancy, *c.*1633. National Gallery of Art, Washington, Rosenwald Collection 1943.3.2224. Courtesy of the National Gallery of Art, Washington.

2.1 Francisco Goya and *The Disasters of War*

Goya was born in Zaragoza in Aragon, Spain, just 75 miles from the French border. After arriving in Madrid in 1770, his artistic reputation grew steadily, and by 1789 he was court painter to King Charles IV of Spain (r.1788–1808; Figure 6). Goya moved in liberal circles and was committed to the **Enlightenment** ideals associated with France. During the reign of the previous king, Charles III (r.1759–88), there were serious attempts at modernising Spain in terms of these ideals, as its economic power had declined in relation to that of its European rivals in the north. This involved the development of free trade along lines being advocated by French Enlightenment thinkers, the modernisation of the agricultural sector and an attempt to curb the power of the Catholic Church, especially its Holy Office of the Inquisition (Eisenman, 1994, p. 86). However, as in France, the clergy and the nobility (upon whom the Spanish **Bourbon** court depended) opposed any reforms that challenged their power. It was the defeat of these forces north of the border during the French Revolution, which began in 1789, that brought the Spanish Enlightenment to an abrupt halt.

Figure 6 Francisco Goya, *Charles IV*, 1789, oil on canvas, 128 × 96 cm. Fundación Altadis, Madrid. Photo: © akg Images.

Relations between Spain and France collapsed as the Spanish king sought to stem the revolutionary tide that had seen the French monarchy replaced by a republican regime. By 1793 the two countries were at war, giving rise to a conservative reaction in Spain. Goya's loyalties were consequently torn between Spanish patriotism and an allegiance to the ideals of the French Enlightenment. The war was over by 1795, but hostilities resumed in 1808 when Napoleon Bonaparte, crowned emperor of France in 1804 (r.1804–14 and 1815), occupied the Iberian Peninsula and installed his brother Joseph Bonaparte (r. 1808–13) on the Spanish throne in place of King Ferdinand VII (r.1808 and 1813–33). The French revolutionary process had been transformed by Bonapartism, which sought to export the Enlightenment via imperial conquest. The Spanish people rose up against the Bonapartist regime on 2 and 3 May 1808 before being brutally repressed, leading to a protracted and violent Peninsular War (c.1807–14). This repression is the subject of Goya's anti-Napoleonic propaganda painting, *The Third of May 1808*, of 1814 (Figure 7).

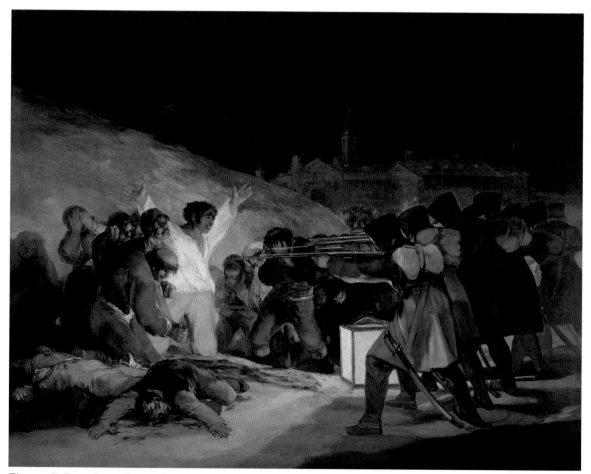

Figure 7 Francisco Goya, *The Third of May 1808*, 1814, oil on canvas, 268 × 347 cm. Museo Nacional del Prado, Madrid, Inv.: P00749. Image Copyright Museo Nacional del Prado © Photo: MNP/Scala, Florence.

Activity 1

(Allow around 10 minutes to complete this activity.)

1   Look at Goya's painting (Figure 7), which is loosely split into two
    halves. The captured Spanish patriots can be seen on the left and
    the invading Napoleonic forces are on the right. All the images in this
    chapter can be seen in more detail in the online gallery on the
    module website.

    Now apply the 'Paintings' section of the visual analysis toolkit
    (Resource 2.1 in the Resources section at the end of this block) and
    analyse Figure 7 in terms of its:

    ○   subject matter

    ○   composition

    ○   expression

    ○   pose

    ○   colour and lighting.

2   Then think about how these different components are combined to
    produce the propagandistic effect of the painting in its attack on
    Napoleonic power.

Discussion

1   The French are armed with rifles and have their backs to us so that
    we cannot see their faces. By contrast their Spanish captives
    opposite, who are about to be executed by firing squad, are clearly
    terrified. The patriot in the white shirt stands out by virtue of his
    height, his pose with his arms in the air and the brightness of his
    clothing.

2   The Napoleonic forces who have their backs to us seem impersonal
    and dehumanised, whereas the Spanish are shown as individuals,
    especially the man in the white shirt. The colour of his shirt
    symbolises innocence and his defencelessness is indicated by the
    fact that he has his arms in the air. The unnatural lighting of this
    figure does not seem to come from the giant lamp to his right, nor
    any moonlight above, but is instead used by Goya as a device to
    emphasise the bravery and martyrdom of the Spanish people in the
    face of Napoleonic power. In this way the combination of subject
    matter, composition, expression, pose, colour and lighting produces a
    painting that stands as a powerful piece of propaganda against
    French imperialism.

The effectiveness of a royally funded painting in oil on canvas such as *The Third of May 1808* as propaganda was limited by the fact that relatively few people would have been able to see it. By contrast, the medium of print offered Goya the opportunity to not only produce a series of works that depicted the brutal guerrilla tactics deployed during the Peninsular War, when Napoleonic forces laid siege to Spanish towns and cities, but also the possibility of a wider dissemination of his anti-war position as prints were cheaper and easier to reproduce and circulate.

Figure 8 Francisco Goya, 'I saw this', etching from *The Disasters of War* (Plate 44), *c.*1810–1814. The Metropolitan Museum of Art, New York, Harris Brisbane Dick Fund, 1932, Acc No.: 32.62.2.

The 82 prints in Goya's *The Disasters of* War series can be divided into three categories: scenes of the **war of attrition** begun in 1810; the 'year of famine' in Madrid in 1811–12; and other **allegorical** subjects, which were produced last. Goya saw the devastation in his home town of Zaragoza when he visited it a few months into the war, after Spanish forces had temporarily repelled the French soldiers who had besieged it. The subject matter of many of his prints consists of material based upon his eyewitness experience of events (Boime, 1990, p. 307). Returning to Madrid, he would have also witnessed the siege there as well as the consequent famine in which 20,000 people died of starvation.

Activity 2

(Allow around 10 minutes to complete this activity.)

Bearing in mind that I have mentioned that the Napoleonic forces laid siege to Spanish towns and cities, look at Plate 44 from Goya's series (Figure 8) and consider the following four questions:

1   What does Goya depict?

2   What does the plate's title ('I saw this') suggest?

3   Where do Goya's sympathies lie?

4   Who is presented as an object of satire?

Discussion

1   Goya depicts a train of Spanish refugees fleeing the town besieged by the French in the distance on the far right for the forest in the foreground on the left of the print. In the foreground, on the right, there is a peasant mother with two children; in the middle ground, on the far left, there is a parish priest marked out by his clerical outfit with a black hat.

2   The title implies that the print has a documentary quality that emphasises the artist's first-hand experience of the suffering of the Spanish people in a manner that prefigures the more modern practice of photojournalism.

3   Goya's sympathies lie principally with the isolated young peasant mother and her children depicted in the light of the right foreground, who thereby become a focus for our interest and sympathy too, especially because women and children are often the most vulnerable in wartime.

4   The rotund-looking parish priest (in the comparatively darker middle ground on the far left, at the very front of the exodus) is the object of satire, because he is clearly putting his own interests over and above others in his rush to get away. In this way, Goya indicates his distrust of the Catholic Church.

So, what exactly was Goya trying to achieve with his print series? Unlike his painting *The Third of May 1808* (Figure 7), *The Disasters of War* was not a direct commission. While the painting communicated Goya's sympathy for the Spanish people, it could also be understood as an attempt by the artist to again ingratiate himself with the royal court following the restoration of King Ferdinand VII of Spain in December 1813. Like the painting, the prints may initially have been conceived as a celebration of Spanish patriotism against a foreign intruder, as well as a means to garner some financial security in the absence of the royal commissions that had largely dried up by this point in Goya's career. However, the subject matter of these prints was much more politically and morally ambiguous in terms of its depiction of the Spanish people than *The Third of May 1808*.

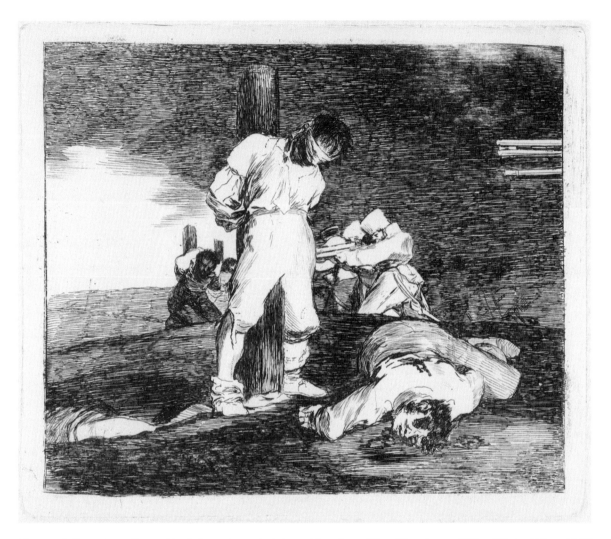

Figure 9 Francisco Goya, 'And there is no help', etching from *The Disasters of War* (Plate 15), *c.*1810–1814. The Metropolitan Museum of Art, New York, Harris Brisbane Dick Fund, 1932, Accession Number:32.62.17.

Goya's sympathy for his compatriots and his condemnation of the brutality of the occupying French forces is made clear by prints such as 'And there is no help' (*c.*1810–14; Figure 9). In this print, we see the same iconography used in Goya's painting (Figure 7), i.e. Spanish patriots being executed, if in a slightly different format that heightens the brutality of the French firing squads. However in other prints, Goya also depicts the violence dealt out to the occupying Napoleonic army. In 'They make use of them' (*c.*1810–14; Figure 10), for example, Spanish patriots strip the clothes off of slaughtered French troops as if their bodies are mere pieces of meat. In this way, the sympathy for the

Spanish people that he had evoked in the two former prints is subverted, as each side is shown to be culpable of war atrocities.

Figure 10 Francisco Goya, 'They make use of them', etching from *The Disasters of War* (Plate 16), *c.*1810–14. The Metropolitan Museum of Art, New York, Harris Brisbane Dick Fund, 1932, Accession Number:32.62.13.

Compared with his *The Third of May 1808* (Figure 7), Goya's *The Disasters of War* series presents a pessimistic view of human nature, particularly with regards to the Spanish people. Their relative conservatism was in large part due to the continuing authority of the Catholic Church. The patriotic peasantry, who had fought to fend off the Napoleonic forces by 1814, were generally anti-Enlightenment and not particularly interested in the land reforms associated with it. With the restoration of King Ferdinand VII in Spain, liberal reform was again put on hold and the power of the royal court and the Church restored. In this way, the grotesque violence in *The Disasters of War* works allegorically, as well as at the level of a purported reportage, to signify the desperate situation in which liberal Spanish Enlightenment supporters, like Goya, found themselves at this particular moment. As the art historian Stephen Eisenman has argued, *The Disasters of War* is therefore a despairing critique of 'the barbarism of Enlightenment itself in the person of Napoleon as well as the defeat of Enlightenment by Spain' (1994, p. 100). Due to this ambivalence, Goya's *The Disasters of War* prints were not actually reproduced until 1863, 35 years after his death.

2.2 Otto Dix and *The War*

As mentioned in the introduction to this chapter, Dix's *The War* series was produced over 100 years later in direct reference to Goya's *The Disasters of War* (Willett, 1998, p. 65). It is estimated that over 20 million people were killed during the industrialised slaughter of the First World War. Afterwards, those who survived returned to civilian life shattered by the experience, either psychologically in terms of shell shock or physically in terms of the tens of thousands who were disabled as a result of combat. While Goya may have witnessed some of the atrocities of the Peninsular War first-hand, Dix actually participated in the trenches as a machine gunner on the front for three years during the First World War. Most of Dix's prints depict landscapes and people in the aftermath of battle with mutilated bodies and decomposing corpses. Although he was certainly lucky to have returned to civilian life physically intact, the experience was still psychologically traumatic. He stated that, 'for years, for at least ten years', he 'constantly had these dreams in which I was forced to crawl through destroyed buildings, through corridors which I couldn't pass. The rubble was always there in my dreams' (quoted in Marno, 2017, p. 186). In this sense, the production of Dix's anti-war prints had a therapeutic function for the artist.

However, whatever personal significance the series may have had, for the purposes of this chapter, the most important point about Dix's prints is that they represented a critique of a German political, military and cultural establishment that he blamed for the barbarity of the war. Dix's comment made in one of his notebooks while at the front makes it quite clear on which side of the debate over the conflict he stood: 'Once people fought wars for the sake of religion; today it is for the sake of business and industry – a step backward' (quoted in Peters, 2010, p. 28). By contrast, conservative **nationalists** propagated a 'stab-in-the-back' myth, whereby the German army was not defeated on the battlefield so much as metaphorically stabbed in the back by anti-war radicals and **communists** at home. Military defeat was thus a deeply contentious and highly politicised issue.

Figure 11 Otto Dix, *War Cripples*, 1920. Photo: © Picture Alliance/Bridgeman Images. © DACS 2020.

Just as Goya's *The Disasters of War* can be compared with *The Third of May 1808*, so too it is useful to think about Dix's *The War* series in relation to the anti-war paintings that he produced in the post-war period. Dix's *War Cripples* of 1920 (Figure 11) was one of two works that he contributed to the **First International Dada Fair**, which opened in June the same year in Berlin, and most of it can be seen on the left-hand side in a photograph of the show (Figure 12). Dada was an **avant-garde** movement formed by a group of radical anti-war artists in Zurich in neutral Switzerland in 1916. It subsequently spread to other cities, most notably Berlin, Paris and New York. The Berlin group was the most politically radical and some of its members were friends of Dix, such as Heartfield who joined the German Communist Party as soon as it was founded in 1918, following the **Bolshevik Revolution** in Russia the previous year. That their attack upon the German political, military and cultural establishment hit a nerve can be inferred from the fact that, just a few months after the Dada show, Dix was prosecuted for defaming the German military.

Figure 12 Installation shot of the First International Dada Fair, Berlin, 1920. Photo: adoc-photos/Getty Images.

Activity 3

(Allow around 10 minutes to complete this activity.)

1   Look at Dix's *War Cripples* (Figure 11) and think about it in terms of its iconographic content, composition and pose with reference to the 'Paintings' section of the visual analysis toolkit (Resource 2.1 in the Resources section at the end of this block).

2   What do you think it is about this painting that disturbed German conservatives and nationalists?

3   And finally, would you say that the image is satire or propaganda?

Discussion

1 *War Cripples* depicts four disabled war veterans marching along a city street in full military regalia, including medals. Their dependence on mechanical surrogates such as prosthetics, canes and crutches wryly alludes to the mechanised nature of the actual war itself during which their bodies had been disfigured. They are flattened on the picture plane so that they resemble cut-outs, which gives the work a somewhat humorous quality.

2 Dix satirised war and nationalism by juxtaposing the military and national pride of these figures with the effect that the war has had on their bodies. In a post-war context, in which the reasons for the German defeat in the First World War were so politically contentious, the subject of soldiers returning to civilian life physically disfigured by the experience would have been a direct affront to conservative gallery visitors, especially given the fact that they look like cartoons.

3 The level of caricature in the painting gives it a satirical charge, but in its attack upon the post-war German political and military establishment (especially in the context of the Berlin Dada exhibition) it also operated as a work of propaganda against these interests.

I began the discussion of Dix with an outline of the various reasons that impelled him to channel his attack upon the German political and military establishment into a series of prints. While the motivation for his attack no doubt had personal and psychological aspects, the print series also had a strong public and propagandistic dimension since it was published to coincide with the year-long anti-war campaign in 1924, which was organised on the tenth anniversary of the start of the war by an alliance of war veterans for peace. It is also important to be aware that prints maximised the financial return on artistic labour, as their mechanical reproducibility allowed for multiple sales. The post-war years in Germany were marked by high inflation and artworks, especially ones at the cheaper end of the market such as prints, were a desirable commodity since they were more affordable and kept their price in times of financial uncertainty. Moreover, as already noted, Dix was undoubtedly aware of, and responding to, the precedent of Goya's *The Disasters of War*.

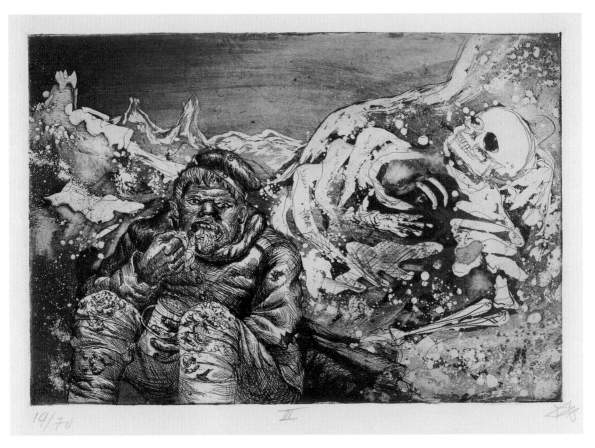

Figure 13 Otto Dix, 'Meal-time in the ditch (Loretto Heights)' from *The War* series, 1923–24, etching and aquatint on cream wove paper, 20 × 29 cm. Verlag Karl Nierendorf/Galerie Nierendorf, Berlin, 1924. Chicago, Art Institute, Inv. No. 1999.357.3. Photo: © akg Images. © DACS 2020.

Activity 4

(Allow around 10 minutes to complete this activity.)

Think about the similarities and differences between Dix's *The War* series and Goya's *The Disasters of War*. Then compare and contrast Dix's 'Meal-time in the ditch (Loretto Heights)' (Figure 13) with Goya's 'I saw this' (Figure 8) and consider how each artist dealt with the subject of war – Goya as an observer and Dix as a participant. Use the 'Prints' section of the visual analysis toolkit (Resource 2.1 in the Resources section at the end of this block) to help you.

Discussion

Dix's print depicts the horror of trench warfare with the skeleton of a dead German soldier on the right and a traumatised looking German soldier on the left looking blankly into the distance while eating his rations. Just as Goya highlights the almost documentary function of his prints with their titles – such as 'I saw this' – so too does Dix with the specificity of place (i.e. Loretto Heights).

In terms of differences, there is more light in Goya's print compared to the one by Dix, which is an effect that heightens the sombre aspect of the latter. Crucially though, it is important to reiterate the point that Goya was an observer of war, whereas Dix was an actual participant. The documentary aspect to many of Goya's prints register this observational mode of viewing, whilst the satirical power of many of Dix's prints register the experience of actually participating in the brutality of trench warfare in the First World War.

Figure 14 Otto Dix, 'Stormtroopers advance under gas' from *The War* series, 1923–24, etching and aquatint on cream wove paper, 20 × 29 cm. Verlag Karl Nierendorf/Galerie Nierendorf, Berlin, 1924. Chicago, Art Institute, Inv. No. 1999.357.2. Photo: © akg Images. © DACS 2020.

Figure 15 Otto Dix, *The Trench*, 1920–23, oil on canvas, 227 cm × 250 cm. Photo: © akg Images. © DACS 2020. Painting now lost and thought to have been destroyed in the Second World War.

It is also worth comparing another of Dix's *The War* prints entitled 'Stormtroopers advance under gas' (1923–24; Figure 14) with Goya's 'They make use of them' (Figure 10). Just as the latter is critical of the Spanish patriots' brutality towards the French enemy, so is Dix's depiction of his own fellow German soldiers far from complimentary. As they advance from the trenches through the battle-scarred landscape towards the viewer, with their gas masks and grenades, the German soldiers look more like mechanised monsters than human beings. Dix had already exposed the horrors of trench warfare in his monumental painting *The Trench* (1920–23; Figure 15) – in which painted flesh and bone were scattered across the canvas in a highly built up surface on which paint was layered over paint – and this critique of the war was continued in the prints. For these reasons, Dix's *The War* series, just like his paintings *War Cripples* and *The Trench*, was seen as unpatriotic by conservatives and nationalists in the interwar period, i.e. the time between the First and Second World Wars.

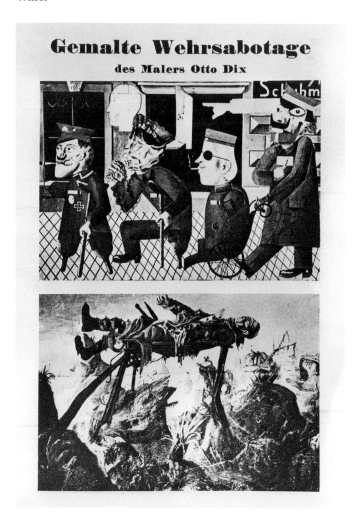

Figure 16 Otto Dix, *War Cripples*, 1920, and *The Trench* (detail), 1920–1923; Page 15 from the Catalogue for the Degenerate Art Exhibition, 1937. Photo: Scala, Florence/bpk, Bildagentur fuer Kunst, Kultur und Geschichte, Berlin. © DACS 2020.

Just how subversive Dix's work was can be seen from its inclusion in the **Degenerate Art Exhibition** organised by the Nazi Party in Munich in 1937. After taking power in 1933, the Nazis directly challenged what they described as 'Bolshevistic' tendencies in both the political and cultural spheres. On the one hand, they launched increasing attacks upon their political opponents (most significantly the communists), while on the other, they waged a similarly unrelenting campaign against modern art which culminated in this exhibition – still the most visited in German history. Dix featured prominently in the exhibition with nine paintings, including his *War Cripples* and *The Trench* (see Figure 16), and a full set of *The War* series. The catalogue stated that his art 'serves **Marxist** propaganda in support of refusal to perform compulsory military service' (quoted in Peters, 2010, p. 25).

By this point, Dix had already moved into 'internal exile' in the south-east corner of Germany where he had turned to landscape painting, a genre acceptable to the Nazis for it accorded with the nationalist ideology of '**blood and soil**' (Willett, 1998, p. 71). As I mentioned at the beginning of this section, what gave both Goya and Dix's anti-war print series their critical power was the way in which they used satire against their own national regimes as well as those of the countries with which they were at war. Goya decided to delay publishing his *The Disasters of War* series after the restoration of the Spanish Bourbon monarchy. Dix, on the other hand, paid the price for publishing his *The War* series in his lifetime, as after the Nazi seizure of power he was effectively marginalised as an artist (Willett, 1978, p. 188). Yet today, both series of prints are recognised as landmarks in the development of anti-war art.

3 Artists against fascism

As we have seen in their anti-war print series, Goya and Dix protested against what they perceived to be the moral iniquities and political backwardness of conservative power in Spain and Germany respectively. In this section of the chapter, we will examine the ways in which Heartfield and Picasso focused their attack more specifically upon fascism in the interwar period in the same two countries: the former in Germany with a new mechanical means of artistic production rooted in photography, and the latter in Spain with the more traditional medium of oil on canvas. Fascism originated in Italy during the First World War and was then adopted by Hitler in Germany and Francisco Franco (1892–1975) in Spain as the means to crush democratic and left-wing forces of opposition. What distinguishes fascism in Germany from its southern European manifestations is its intensive exploitation of a highly sophisticated propaganda machine, which deployed the modern mass media of radio, film, television, newspapers and magazines in an attempt to win over the hearts and minds of the German people.

3.1 John Heartfield and the anti-fascist photomontage

Heartfield's contribution to the First International Dada Fair in 1920 was the *The Petit-Bourgeois Philistine Heartfield Gone Wild Electro-Mechanical **Tatlin** Sculpture* (Figure 17, which can also be seen on the right-hand side of Figure 12) made specifically for the event with fellow Dadaist and Communist Party member George Grosz (1893–1959). Like Dix's contribution to the same exhibition, *War Cripples* (Figure 11), this shop mannequin, with its prosthetic lower right leg, was an indictment of the terrible injuries sustained by soldiers during the war and the inadequate treatment that often failed to disguise their appalling disfigurement. The medals that appeared on Dix's figures are replaced with the base metal of common cutlery on Heartfield and Grosz's sculpture, in order to satirise the purported glory of combat. In a similar way, and for the same reasons, Grosz, like Dix, was prosecuted for insulting the German military.

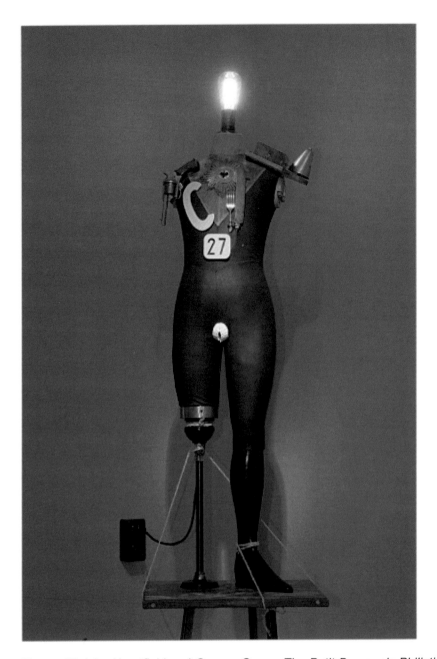

Figure 17 John Heartfield and George Grosz, *The Petit-Bourgeois Philistine Heartfield Gone Wild Electro-Mechanical Tatlin Sculpture*, 1920. The original is lost so this is a reconstruction by Michael Sellmann, 1988, height 130 cm. Berlinische Galerie, Berlin, inventory number: BG-O 7083/93. Photo: bpk/ Berlinische Galerie. © The Heartfield Community of Heirs/DACS 2020 and © Estate of George Grosz, Princeton, N.J./DACS 2020.

In an ambitious attempt to expand and develop the new medium of photomontage, Heartfield went on to work in the field of **applied arts** and produced book jackets for the left-wing publishing company Malik-Verlag, which he set up with his brother and Grosz in 1916. These were designed to appeal to as broad an audience as possible, with eye-catching covers that would encourage booksellers to display the books more prominently and thereby sell more copies.

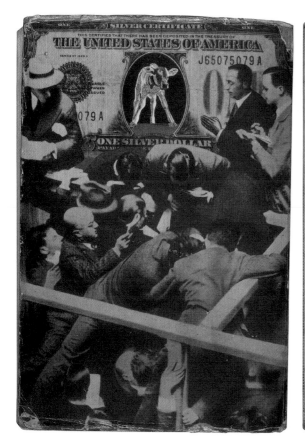

Figure 18 John Heartfield, cover design of the translation of Upton Sinclair, *So Macht Man Dollars (Mountain City)*, 1931. Toledo Museum of Art, Ohio, gift of Molly and Walter Bareiss, 1984.550. © The Heartfield Community of Heirs/DACS 2020.

For these cover designs, Heartfield used the photomontage technique that he had pioneered as a Berlin Dadaist with experimental typography and innovative composition (Figure 18). Photomontage was a relatively new process (later adopted by artists such as Peter Kennard in his *Haywain with Cruise Missiles*, 1980) whereby different photographic sources were cropped and then combined in a new photographic image in which the joins were thereby erased. It was these skills that Heartfield brought to the production of the satirical anti-fascist photomontages that he designed for *Arbeiter Illustrierte Zeitung (AIZ)* (*Workers' Pictorial Newspaper*) from September 1929 onwards. The *AIZ* was a Soviet-funded alternative to the illustrated magazines flooding the German market in the mid 1920s. It intentionally capitalised on the popularity of the medium to reach audiences that might not normally buy left-wing literature; at its peak in 1931 it had a weekly print run of half a million.

Heartfield was introduced to the readership just before the **Wall Street Crash** in October 1929 ushered in a global recession. The financial crash was particularly acute in Germany and it heightened the stand-off between the Nazis and their political opponents. This political polarisation had already spilled out into violence on the streets in late 1928, which gave the Berlin police chief Karl Zörgiebel the excuse that he needed to ban political demonstrations. He then extended this prohibition to include the marches that usually took place on 1 May for Labour Day. When in 1929 the demonstrations took place in defiance of the ban, Zörgiebel ordered them to be broken up, which resulted in over 30 civilians being killed and another 200 injured. This violence became the satirical subject of Heartfield's first photomontage with a self-portrait in *AIZ* that September (Figure 19), in which he is pictured looking out at the viewer while holding shears around the neck of the Berlin police chief. The text immediately above and below the image translates as 'use photo as a weapon!'.

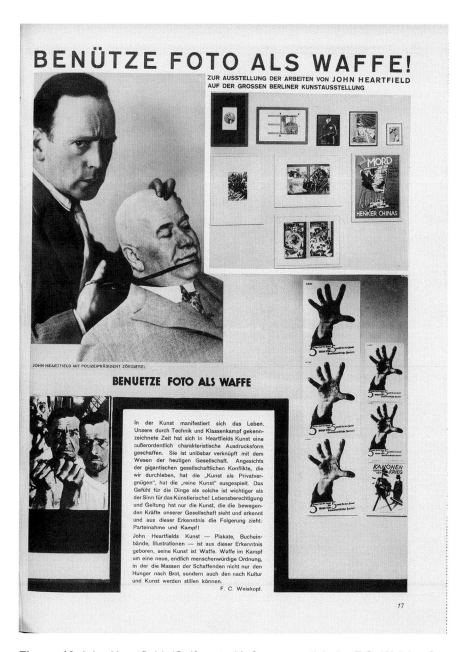

Figure 19 John Heartfield, 'Self-portrait', from an article by F.C. Weiskopf; *'Benütze Foto als Waffe!'* ('Use photo as a weapon!'). From *AIZ*, no. 37 (September 1929), p. 17. Staatsbibliothek zu Berlin. Abteilung Historische Drucke, Berlin. © 2020. Photo: Scala, Florence/bpk, Bildagentur fuer Kunst, Kultur und Geschichte, Berlin. © The Heartfield Community of Heirs/DACS 2020.

Activity 5

(Allow around 5 minutes to complete this activity.)

How does Heartfield use his first photomontage in *AIZ* (Figure 19) to demonstrate the radical political potential of the medium?

Discussion

By combining the photographs of himself with the shears (which he is using to literally slice the head off of the Berlin police chief, Zörgiebel, who had given the order to suppress the Labour Day demonstrations), Heartfield satirically alludes to the technical means by which he produced his photomontages, i.e. the cutting up of existing photographic sources to produce a new composite one. With the exhortation to 'use photo as a weapon!', there is an analogous relationship set up between the scissors that the artist would have used to prepare his source material and a set of shears capable of decapitating the police chief who those on the left of the political spectrum blamed for the violence against those trying to demonstrate for what they believed in.

Subsequent photomontages by Heartfield offered an even more strident political message. In 1932, as the political polarisation between the left and the right became more acute, he produced his *Adolf the Superman: Swallows Gold and Spouts Junk* (Figure 20). This image started life as a photomontage in the issue of *AIZ* published on 17 July that year. It served as the visual accompaniment to an article inside that exposed the financial resources of the 'Hitler Army' by detailing the millions 'swallowed' up by the Nazi Party. Its effectiveness as a piece of propaganda was so appreciated by the cosmopolitan Count Harry Kessler (a long-time supporter of Heartfield) that he paid for its reproduction as a poster, which was then plastered all over Berlin in the lead up to the July Reichstag (parliament) elections. The image thereby became a focal point of the street violence in Berlin, as young communists stood guard to protect the posters from being ripped down by their Nazi opponents.

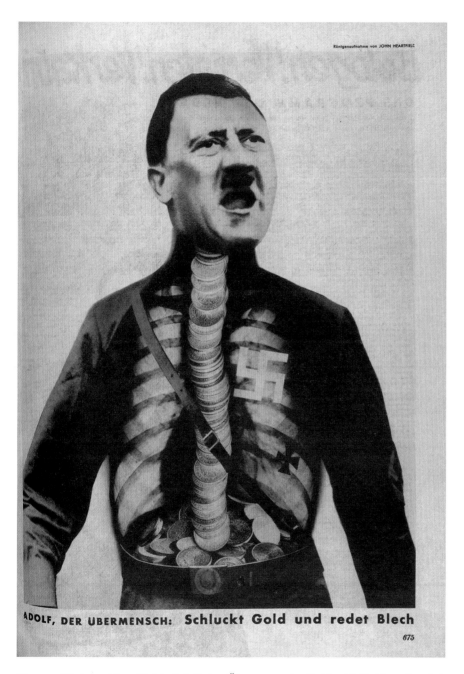

Figure 20 John Heartfield, *Adolf der Übermensch: Schluckt Gold und redet Blech* (*Adolf the Superman: Swallows Gold and Spouts Junk*). From *AIZ*, no. 29 (17 July 1932), p. 675. Staatsbibliothek zu Berlin. Preußischer Kulturbesitz, Berlin. Photo: bpk/Staatsbibliothek zu Berlin. © The Heartfield Community of Heirs/DACS 2020.

Activity 6

(Allow around 10 minutes to complete this activity.)

Look at the photomontage shown in Figure 20 and try to answer these four questions:

1   What does the photomontage actually depict?
2   How does the iconography of this image echo the claims made by the accompanying article in the magazine?
3   How does Heartfield's use of photomontage here compare to his introductory self-portrait in *AIZ* (Figure 19)?
4   What is it about the image that you think could have led to it becoming the focus of fighting between communists and Nazis in the streets of Berlin?

Discussion

1   The photomontage depicts a fictitious X-ray of Hitler's ribcage with a swastika (the emblem used by the Nazi Party) where his heart should be and his gastrointestinal tract which is full of coins that collect at his waist.

2   The iconography echoes the article by depicting Hitler literally 'swallowing' the money so that the Nazi leader becomes the visual personification of the party itself, as befitting the emphasis upon a strong and demagogic leader so typical of fascism.

3   Heartfield's introductory photomontage is relatively primitive in that it combines just two photographs; the self-portrait holding shears with another portrait of the Berlin police chief. The one here combines, at the very least, an image of Hitler, an X-ray of a ribcage and another of the money that is ingested within it in a seamless unity that belies the fact that this is an accumulation of different photographic sources.

4   The communist youth that stood guard over the poster may not have necessarily been sympathetic to avant-garde art, but they appreciated the power of the image as propaganda, hence their efforts at protecting the posters from being ripped down by their Nazi opponents.

Figure 21 John Heartfield, *Der Sinn Des Hitlergrusses: Kleiner Mann bittet um grosse Gaben. Motto: Millionen Stehen Hinter Mir!* (*The Meaning of Hitler's Salute: a Little Man asks for a big Sum. Motto: Millions Are Behind Me!*). Front cover of *AIZ*, no. 42 (16 October 1932). Photo: Bridgeman Images. © The Heartfield Community of Heirs/DACS 2020.

This skilful combination of multiple photographic sources into one composite image was also equally demonstrated on the cover of the 16 October edition of *AIZ* with Heartfield's *The Meaning of Hitler's Salute* (Figure 21), in the lead up to yet another election. In the image, the text between the corpulent capitalist handing over the money and Hitler translates as 'millions are behind me'. The visual pun here is the slippage from 'millions' meaning voters to 'millions' meaning money, in reference to the business interests bankrolling the Nazi election campaigns. The difference in scale between the two figures is part of the joke by which Hitler is represented as a mere puppet in hock to corporate power. As befitting a work of visual satire, the message is quick and easy to understand and, as such, highly effective as propaganda.

Heartfield was not included in the Degenerate Art Exhibition in 1937. It is possible he was excluded because the anti-fascist photomontages that he produced were constructed from photographic sources and not considered to be a work of art like an oil painting or a print. However, the Heartfield scholar Sabine Kriebel argues that the Nazis considered it too dangerous to include his photomontages in the exhibition precisely because they were so effective as propaganda (2014, p. 218). This effectiveness also ensured that a later generation of radical activists would use Heartfield's precedent as a model for their own political propaganda in the period after 1968, as we will explore in the next section on the radical poster.

3.2 Pablo Picasso and *Guernica*

Before we move on to look at the radical poster in more detail, let us consider the very different anti-fascist work produced by Picasso, whose oppositional art was inspired by the Spanish Civil War (1936–39). Although Spanish, Picasso had long been based in France and had not previously produced any directly political art, so his case is very different from that of the Dadaists, especially those based in Berlin such as Heartfield and Grosz. The Spanish Civil War began after the military leader General Franco led a coup against the democratically elected government in Spain in 1936 to uphold the conservative values of the Church and monarchy against the Popular Front coalition of the Spanish left (including communists, socialists and anarchists) that briefly held power. Despite an international non-intervention treaty, the conflict quickly assumed the political polarities of the day so that, in the ensuing war, the fascist regimes in Germany and Italy supported Franco while the Soviet Union backed the republican government, which had now gone into exile in France.

After the bombing of the ancient Basque capital of Guernica (Gernika in Basque) by the German Condor Legion in April 1937, the government in exile commissioned Picasso to produce anti-fascist propaganda work for the Spanish pavilion at the **International Exhibition of Art and Technology in Modern Life** in Paris. His *Guernica* (Figure 22), named after the destroyed Basque city, stands out from most of the other works that we have looked at in this chapter. Not only was it produced in the traditional medium of oil on canvas – as opposed to the more mechanical media of print or photography – but it does not directly represent the bombing. Instead, it reuses allegorical motifs that had already featured in previous works by the artist. *Guernica* is also distinct in terms of scale and its large size allows it to function almost like a portable mural. Picasso surely had Goya's *The Third of May 1808* (Figure 7) in mind when he undertook this commission, because the earlier work set a powerful precedent in terms of representing the violence formerly dealt out to the Spanish people by another foreign aggressor.

Figure 22 Pablo Picasso, *Guernica*, 1937, oil on canvas, 350 × 782 cm. Museo Nacional Centro de Arte Reina Sofia, Madrid. Photo: Art Resource/Scala, Florence/John Bigelow Taylor. © Succession Picasso/DACS, London 2020.

Activity 7

(Allow around 15 minutes to complete this activity.)

Now have a go at deciphering what is actually shown in Picasso's painting (Figure 22). Remember, this image can be seen in more detail in the online gallery on the module website.

Consider the following questions in order to make sense of how the various iconographical elements come together to form an overall meaning:

1   What figures and motifs can you identify in the painting and how might these symbolise the bombing of Guernica?

2   How does the colour of the painting contribute to its meaning?

3   How might this work relate to Goya's *The Third of May 1808* (Figure 7)?

Discussion

1   This is probably the most difficult work that you will look at in this chapter, so please do not worry if you did not manage to pick out all of the salient details. From left to right, the iconographic elements consist of:

   o   a woman holding a dead child

   o   above her a bull

   o   below them a fallen warrior clasping a broken sword

   o   above him a gored horse

   o   to the right a couple of grieving women

   o   another woman on the far right of the painting in a burning building with her hands in the air.

   It is the final detail in the list that most directly references the horrific razing of Guernica by aerial bombardment. Otherwise, the bombing is evoked allegorically in the general sense of horror, suffering and confusion depicted in the painting.

2   In terms of colour, the mainly monochromatic palette of black, grey and white adds to the sombre appearance of the work.

3   The detail of the woman with her hands aloft is also the one that most closely recalls Goya's painting in that it references the patriot in the white shirt who has his arms raised in a similar manner. While the allegorical and abstract nature of *Guernica* may seem categorically different from Goya's *The Third of May of 1808*, both dramatise the brutality of foreign military power; the earlier painting through Spanish patriots being executed by a phalanx of Napoleonic soldiers, and the later one in the horrific aerial bombing of Basque civilians by German planes.

The exact meaning of the symbolism in *Guernica* has been much debated, but the artist claimed later that the horse (as a victim) represents the people, and the bull (in its brutality) represents fascism. That the work had a propagandistic function was made clear in 1945 when Picasso himself stated: 'There is no deliberate sense of propaganda in my painting [...] except in the *Guernica*. In that there is a deliberate appeal to a people, a deliberate sense of propaganda' (quoted in Frascina, 1996, p. 134). This assertion by Picasso certainly challenges the idea that propaganda cannot make for good art, as *Guernica* is generally considered to be a canonical painting.

Figure 23 Dora Marr, photograph of early stage of Pablo Picasso's *Guernica*, at his studio, Rue des Grands-Augustins, Paris, 1937. Photo: © Archives Charmet/Bridgeman Images. © Succession Picasso/ DACS, London 2020. © ADAGP, Paris and DACS, London 2020.

Yet, the precise way in which *Guernica* worked as propaganda changed within the short time in which it was conceived and produced, reflecting the power dynamics of the Spanish Civil War itself. The Popular Front, made up of different left-wing groups, disintegrated as the communists disarmed and then disbanded the socialist and anarchist forces at the behest of Joseph Stalin (1878–1953). He sought to close down the possibility of any actual social revolution happening outside the orbit of Soviet control. In preparatory sketches for the painting, the fallen soldier representing republican forces had a clenched fist, as depicted in an earlier stage of the mural (Figure 23), and in yet another one he was also holding a hammer and sickle – obvious references to communist iconography. Yet under the weight of communist repression on the ground, and the military superiority of the fascists from above, this symbolism was simply no longer tenable, and it did not make it into the final iconographic scheme (Frascina, 1996, p. 135). In this way, the meaning of *Guernica* shifted from a militant call to arms to an anguished rebuke against the first large-scale aerial bombardment of a civilian population.

Figure 24 Postcard of the International Exhibition in Paris, 1937. Photo: © Archives Charmet/ Bridgeman Images.

As previously mentioned, *Guernica* was commissioned for the 1937 International Exhibition, which was principally concerned with trade and popular entertainment. At the exhibition in Paris, the opposition between the forces of communism and fascism was played out symbolically with the German pavilion (on the left in the postcard commemorating the event (Figure 24)) set squarely opposite the Soviet one (on the right), both towering over the horizon either side of the Eiffel Tower. In contrast to these monumental buildings, the Spanish pavilion was built along the latest modern **functionalist** lines (Figure 25). Today, Picasso's painting may be considered the most celebrated artwork that was displayed in the pavilion, yet it was part of an ensemble that included many other works by contemporary anti-fascist Spanish artists.

Figure 25 Spanish pavilion at the International Exhibition in Paris, 1937. Photographed by François Kollar. Photo © Ministère de la Culture – Médiathèque de l'architecture et du patrimoine, Dist. RMN-Grand Palais/ François Kollar. © RMN – Gestion droit d'auteur François Kollar.

These works jostled alongside various large photomontages on a whole range of progressive themes, including the emancipation of women, made under the supervision of Josep Renau (1907–1982). In his *The New Woman* (1937; Figure 26) the passive and conservative looking woman on the left (dressed in traditional Spanish regional clothing) is contrasted with the militiawoman on the right (who is striding heroically forward, ready for battle) to signify the role that women played in terms of active combat in the defence of the republic. Renau was Spain's most prominent photomontage artist and had learned the practice through close study of Heartfield's work in *AIZ*. Just like the photomontages produced by Renau under the influence of Heartfield, *Guernica* was monumental and monochromatic; both its size and muted palette gave it a clear relationship to these other propagandistic works that surrounded it in the Spanish pavilion.

Figure 26 Josep Renau, *The New Woman*, 1937, photo montage. Photographed by François Kollar. Photo © Ministère de la Culture – Médiathèque de l'architecture et du patrimoine, Dist. RMN-Grand Palais/ François Kollar. © RMN – Gestion droit d'auteur François Kollar.

Heartfield also produced a work commemorating the aerial bombing of Spanish civilians entitled *This is the salvation that they bring!* (1938; Figure 27). However, unlike Heartfield's photomontages which fell into relative obscurity until the late 1960s, after the Spanish pavilion closed, *Guernica* was exhibited around the world to raise proceeds for the republican cause. It then ended up at the **Museum of Modern Art** (MoMA) in New York because Picasso insisted, after General Franco's victory in 1939, that it should not return to Spain until the fascist regime was over. It duly did so six years after Franco's death and the return to democracy in 1975. As the art historian Romy Golan has argued, it is precisely due to the fact that the painting went on its travels alone, without any of the other works that constituted its original context, that it came to be viewed as an isolated masterpiece (2009, p. 176). In this sense, the meaning of the painting shifted once again from an anguished rebuke against the fascist bombing of a civilian population to a pacifist statement against war in general. It is only by situating *Guernica* within the actual context in which it was commissioned, produced and exhibited that its original meaning can properly be understood.

With this in mind, it is useful to compare Picasso's *Guernica* with his two-part print, *The Dream and the Lie of Franco* (1937; Figure 28). Picasso agreed to produce these prints at the same time as he accepted the commission for *Guernica* to raise funds to help republican refugees from Spain. They were reproduced in a postcard format and put on sale in the pavilion during the exhibition. In the 18 different images, Franco is satirised as a ridiculous and malevolent grinning polyp (a tissue growth) to symbolise the threat that the monarchy, the Church, and particularly the army, posed to a modern republican Spain.

„In der Zeitschrift »Archiv für Bio-
logie und Rassenforschung, Berlin,
ist ein Artikel unter dem Titel
»Nutzen, welchen das Luftbombar-
dement vom Standpunkt der rassi-
schen Selektion und der Sozial-
hygiene bringt« erschienen. In dem
Artikel heißt es u. a.: »Am meisten
leiden unter Luftbombardements die
stark bewohnten Teile der Städte.
Da diese Gegenden zumeist vom
Lumpenproletariat bewohnt sind,
wird die Gesellschaft dadurch von
diesen Elementen befreit. Schwere
Bomben mit einem Gewicht von
einer Tonne bringen nicht nur den
Tod, sondern rufen auch sehr oft
Irrsinn hervor. Menschen mit schwa-
chen Nerven können derartige Er-
schütterungen nicht aushalten. Das
gibt uns die Möglichkeit, Neurasthe-
niker zu konstatieren. Dann bleibt
nur noch übrig, solche Menschen zu
sterilisieren. Dadurch wird die Rein-
heit der Rasse gesichert.«"
(Prager Abendzeitung, Nr. 118)

Tokio. (United Press.) Ein Sprecher
der japanischen Marine, Vizeadmi-
ral Noda, erklärte, daß die Marine
mit den bisherigen Erfolgen des
Bombardements auf Kanton sehr
zufrieden sei. Die Bombardements
würden fortgesetzt werden.

Das ist das Heil, das sie bringen!

Fotomontage: John Heartfield

Figure 27 John Heartfield, *Das ist das Heil, das sie bringen!* (*This is the salvation that they bring!*), from *AIZ*, no. 28 (29 June 1938). Photo: Scala, Florence/bpk, Bildagentur fuer Kunst, Kultur und Geschichte, Berlin. © The Heartfield Community of Heirs/DACS 2020.

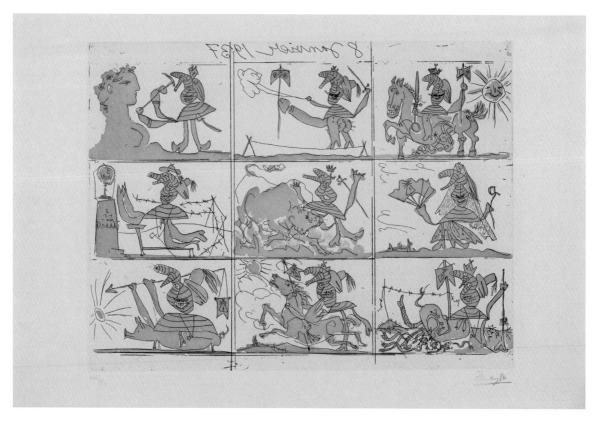

Figure 28 Pablo Picasso, *The Dream and the Lie of Franco I*, 1937, etching and aquatint. Fitzwilliam Museum, University of Cambridge. Photo: © Bridgeman Images. © Succession Picasso/DACS, London 2020.

Just as Picasso had Goya's *The Third of May 1808* in mind when he produced *Guernica*, so here he was referencing *The Disasters of War*. As with *Guernica*, the iconographic scheme in these prints is allegorical and repeats certain themes that had been the subject of Picasso's work in the period beforehand. It is, however, the focus upon Franco that clearly relates them to the photomontages by Heartfield that depict Hitler (Figures 20 and 21), both of which were, of course, produced mechanically. If the personal symbolism in *Guernica* allowed its purported meaning to shift according to the changing contexts in which it was exhibited, then the satirical focus on Franco in the prints ensured that the oppositional meaning of these works would remain relatively fixed and constant by comparison. As such, these works by Picasso and Heartfield constituted powerful propagandistic statements against fascism in both Spain and Germany respectively.

4 The radical poster

It is no small irony that the Nazi attack on modern art for its 'Bolshevistic' tendencies in the Degenerate Art Exhibition opened a week after the unveiling of *Guernica* in the Spanish pavilion. This attack contributed to the status of Picasso's painting and the moral revalidation of modern art more generally in the period after the Second World War, so that it was enshrined as the de facto art of Western **liberal democracy** against **totalitarianism** (Werckmeister, 1999, p. 93).

After the Second World War (1939–1945), the centre of the art world shifted from a war-ravaged Europe to New York, and powerful cultural institutions in the city, such as MoMA, played a crucial role in promoting a particular type of **abstract art** as the most significant within its already extensive collection of modern painting and sculpture. In short, curators and museum officials at MoMA were highly influential in determining what actually constituted the canon in modern art, and this is the context in which to understand the post-Second World War omission of avant-garde artists such as Heartfield from that canon. Heartfield's radical propagandistic works did not fit with the sanitised interpretation of modern abstract art propagated by institutions such as MoMA in New York. This is also the context in which *Guernica* was depoliticised and turned from a strident attack on fascism into an abstract symbol against war per se. It was not until the late 1960s, when there was a wave of generalised unrest and revolt across the globe, that young radicals rediscovered early twentieth-century avant-garde groups such as the Dadaists that had been previously excised from dominant accounts of twentieth-century art.

So far, the types of oppositional art that we have looked at have been made by individuals – white men at that. Now we will turn to **artist collectives** such as the Art Workers' Coalition (AWC) and the Guerrilla Girls, formed in New York in 1969 and 1985 respectively. Although separated by 16 years, these groups shared, firstly, an emphasis upon collective activity over the more traditional focus upon the individual artist; secondly, a corresponding commitment to broaden the range of artists shown in art galleries to include more women and people of colour; and thirdly, the use of mechanical media that combined photography and text to produce propagandistic posters to apply pressure on cultural institutions to make such changes to their acquisition policies. The precedent set by Heartfield's photomontages was exemplary in this respect.

4.1 Art Workers' Coalition

The major driving force of the civil unrest in the United States in the late 1960s was opposition to racism at home and the Vietnam War (1955–75) abroad. Over 30,000 American troops had died in this war by the end of 1968; half of them in the previous 12 months. By this point the government was spending 30 billion dollars per year with over half a million troops deployed to fight a war that had escalated massively since initial United States involvement in 1962. At the same time, one in seven United States citizens officially lived in poverty, a figure that included a disproportionate number of African Americans. African Americans also represented a disproportionate number of those drafted to fight in Vietnam. Resentment turned into anger and widespread rioting after the assassination of the black civil rights leader Martin Luther King, Jr. (b.1929) in April 1968. This rioting was mirrored in the violent disorder on the streets of Chicago after the defeat of the anti-war faction at the Democratic National Convention in August. The election of the conservative Republican Party candidate Richard Nixon in the presidential elections in November escalated matters and swelled the ranks of left-wing groups such as Students for a Democratic Society, who organised anti-war demonstrations on campuses in cities across the United States.

This is the political context in which radical artist groups such as the AWC formed, and they quickly began to ask questions about the role that MoMA played as cultural tastemaker in the visual arts. These questions included the possible links between the economic, political and cultural interests of the board of trustees at the gallery, many of whom were also on the boards of multinational companies with links to the war in Vietnam. Hence, as one leading AWC member explained: 'To fight for control of the museums is also to be against the war' (quoted in Bryan-Wilson, 2009, p. 18). The relationship between the two became concrete with the poster, *Q: And Babies? A: And Babies* (Figure 29), which was produced and published anonymously by the Artists Poster Committee of the AWC in 1970 with the promise from MoMA that they would help with distribution. The poster was a direct response to the My Lai massacre in which 583 women, children and elderly Vietnamese civilians had been indiscriminately killed by United States infantrymen on 16 March 1968.

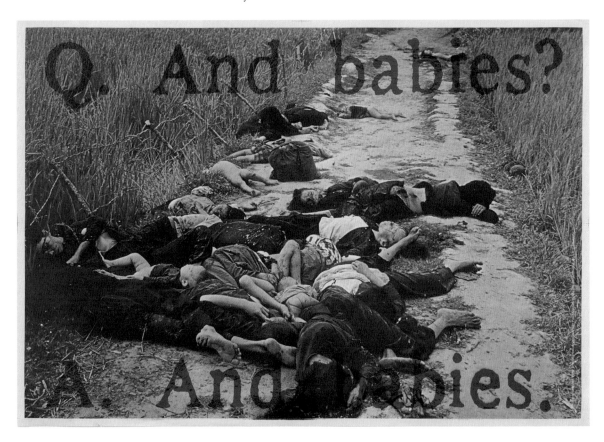

Figure 29 Art Workers' Coalition, *Q. And Babies? A. And Babies*. Photograph by Ronald L. Haeberle, poster published by The Art Workers' Coalition (AWC), 1970, offset lithograph, printed in colour, 64 × 97 cm. Gift of the Benefit for Attica Defense Fund. Acc.n.: 498.1978. © 2020. Digital image, The Museum of Modern Art, New York/Scala, Florence.

The full horror of the massacre became public knowledge in May 1970 when the details of what had taken place were published in *Harper's Magazine*. Subsequently, the AWC used the famous photograph of the aftermath of the event (taken by Ronald Haeberle) that had been reproduced in *Life* magazine in December 1969. The image was overprinted with the text taken from an interview between a journalist and one of the officers involved in the massacre in a font that resembles that of a contemporary typewriter, thereby enhancing the documentary status of the poster. It was produced in colour using offset lithography, which was the most sophisticated mechanical means of production available at that time. The same technology was used to produce high-quality mass images, including those that appeared on billboards, so the poster looked every bit as glossy as the contemporary adverts that were part and parcel of United States visual culture at the time. Although it was originally intended to be distributed in association with MoMA, once the trustees learned about the proposed collaboration they decided to veto it. In response, 50,000 copies of the poster were printed by the lithographers' union and distributed worldwide to sympathetic artists and activists who used it on placards in protest marches, during which it was televised and reproduced in newspapers.

Activity 8

(Allow around 10 minutes to complete this activity.)

Compare and contrast Heartfield's *This is the salvation that they bring!* (Figure 27) with the poster by the AWC (Figure 29). In what way does the later image relate to the anti-fascist photomontage?

Discussion

In terms of iconography, both works depict innocent civilians killed in warfare, their dead bodies strewn across the landscape. Text is used in both to heighten the power of the photographic imagery. The AWC poster is in colour as opposed to black and white, which was unusual for war photography, and this heightens its impact. Although both are made with the most sophisticated mechanical media available at the time in which they were produced, Heartfield's image is a composite one produced by combining different photographic sources; the one by the AWC is unmanipulated except for the addition of text. The photograph was considered to be sufficiently powerful enough in its own right as propaganda against United States militarism.

The AWC's initial response to the publication of the details of the My Lai massacre had been to organise an open letter to Picasso, urging him to tell the directors and trustees of MoMA that his *Guernica* could not remain on public view 'as long as American troops are committing genocide in Vietnam' (quoted in Frascina, 1999, p. 161). Although the petition never actually reached Picasso, the implied comparison between the bombing of Guernica and United States military intervention in South East Asia was made manifest at two demonstrations organised by the AWC in 1970, in which they held up copies of their poster in front of the painting at MoMA (Figure 30). What is significant here is that not only did these demonstrations dramatise the scale of the violence meted out by the United States military in South East Asia but they also reactivated the original meaning of Picasso's painting. In this way, the AWC drew attention to what they described in their letter to Picasso as 'the hundreds of Guernicas […] which are taking place in Vietnam' (quoted in Frascina, 1999, p. 166) as well as highlighting the fact that his painting was first and foremost a powerful piece of propaganda against the barbarity of fascism as well as being a cornerstone of the collection of modern art at MoMA.

Figure 30 Art Workers' Coalition demonstration in front of Pablo Picasso's *Guernica* at the Museum of Modern Art, New York, 1970. Photographed by Jan van Raay.

4.2 Guerrilla Girls

One of the most significant outcomes of the political dissent of the late 1960s was the emergence of **second-wave feminism**. Women who were radicalised by the war in Vietnam began to challenge the subordinate role that they played both within the anti-war movement as well as in wider society. This development is one of the reasons that the AWC folded in late 1971; many of its female members left to pursue more feminist-orientated political campaigns. Although second-wave feminism led to tangible gains for women in the United States, the election of the Republican Party president Ronald Reagan in 1980 did much to turn back these achievements. His administration was premised on a return to conservative family values and corresponding traditional gender roles. This conservatism was mirrored within the art world as the 1980s witnessed a resurgence of blockbuster shows by male painters, which marginalised the more politicised art of the 1970s in which women had played a central role. In this sense, the Guerrilla Girls picked up where the AWC left off in their focus on the United States' gallery system and the push for greater representation of women and people of colour.

Just like the AWC, the Guerrilla Girls decided that the radical poster reproduced mechanically in multiple copies, and fly-posted in the art districts of Lower Manhattan, New York, was the best way to get their message across. What marks their strategy out from a lot of second-wave feminist political campaigns, which were all too often unfairly caricatured as puritanical and humourless, is the emphasis upon satire and irony (Chave, 2011, p. 104). This aspect of their work is exemplified by their donning of gorilla masks, which not only plays on the semantic slippage from 'guerrilla' to 'gorilla' but also accentuates the shock value of their art world interventions in a deliberately playful and ironic way. Importantly, it also served to ensure that the artist activists involved in the group could maintain their anonymity, a strategy that had also previously been deployed by those responsible for the AWC poster. The maintenance of anonymity was borne out of a desire to keep the focus upon issues as opposed to personalities. However, their appropriation of the names of earlier women artists – such as Käthe Kollwitz (1867–1945) and Frida Kahlo (1907–1954) – as their pseudonyms also had the further strategic advantage of pulling attention to important figures often marginalised in the male-defined artistic canon promoted by cultural institutions such as MoMA at the time.

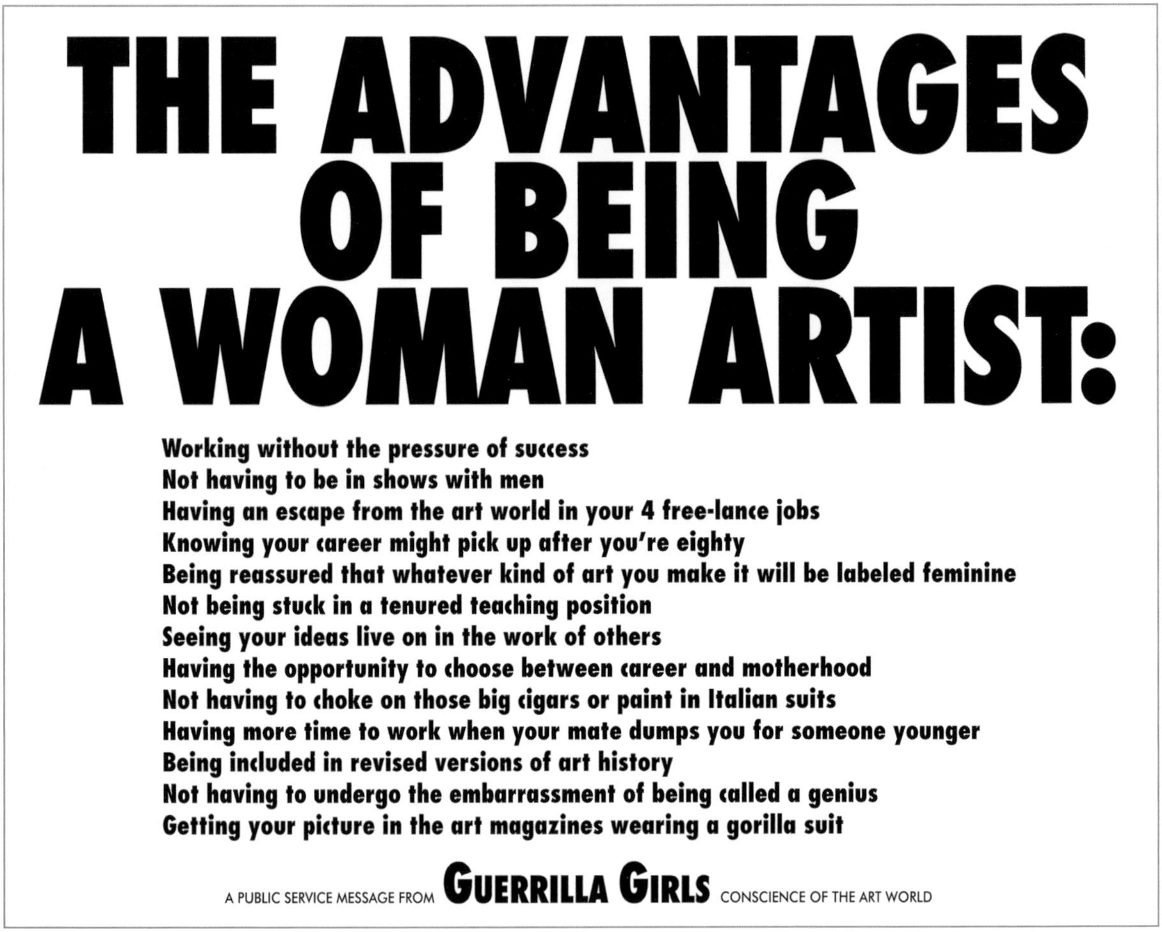

THE ADVANTAGES OF BEING A WOMAN ARTIST:

Working without the pressure of success
Not having to be in shows with men
Having an escape from the art world in your 4 free-lance jobs
Knowing your career might pick up after you're eighty
Being reassured that whatever kind of art you make it will be labeled feminine
Not being stuck in a tenured teaching position
Seeing your ideas live on in the work of others
Having the opportunity to choose between career and motherhood
Not having to choke on those big cigars or paint in Italian suits
Having more time to work when your mate dumps you for someone younger
Being included in revised versions of art history
Not having to undergo the embarrassment of being called a genius
Getting your picture in the art magazines wearing a gorilla suit

A PUBLIC SERVICE MESSAGE FROM **GUERRILLA GIRLS** CONSCIENCE OF THE ART WORLD

Figure 31 Guerrilla Girls, *The Advantages of Being a Woman Artist*, 1988. Copyright © Guerrilla Girls, courtesy guerrillagirls.com.

The group's humour can be seen in what the Guerrilla Girls themselves call their 'all-time favorite' poster (Chave, 2011, p. 104): *The Advantages of Being a Woman Artist*, produced in 1988 with its ironic 13-point list (Figure 31). The satire here is derived from the fact that all the disadvantages of being a woman artist are comically inverted to instead be presented as advantages. Another example that combines imagery and text in a method that is very similar to Dada photomontage (if updated with the latest typography drawn from the world of advertising) is *Do Women Have to be Naked to Get into the Met. Museum?* (Figure 32). 'Met.' is an abbreviation of the Metropolitan Museum, which is another extremely prestigious cultural institution in New York that has a collection ranging from classical antiquity through to the present.

Figure 32 Guerrilla Girls, *Do Women Have to be Naked to Get into the Met. Museum?*, 1989. Copyright © Guerrilla Girls, courtesy guerrillagirls.com.

Activity 9

(Allow around 30 minutes to complete this activity.)

Now turn to Reading 3.1, which contains information about *Do Women Have to be Naked to Get into the Met. Museum?* (Figure 32) taken from the Tate Modern's website.

Once you have read the text in relation to the poster, attempt to answer these questions:

1   Having read Reading 3.1 what exactly is the satirical message of Figure 32?

2   How was the poster circulated to maximise its effects as a work of propaganda?

Study note

It is important to point out that Reading 3.1 is a printed version of text that originally appeared online. You may find it useful to take a closer look at the original text by searching for it on the Tate's website after you have finished reading this chapter.

Discussion

1   Reading 3.1 reiterates the poster's statistic that while less than five per cent of the artists in the modern art section are by women, 85 per cent of the nudes are female. The body of the reclining figure in the poster is appropriated from the famous female nude entitled *La Grande Odalisque* (1814; Figure 33) by the French artist Jean-Auguste-Dominique Ingres (1780–1867), which hangs in the Louvre in Paris (another prestigious cultural institution). The head of Ingres's model has ironically been substituted by a gorilla mask that directly relates the figure to the Guerrilla Girls and turns a passive female nude into an active woman artist.

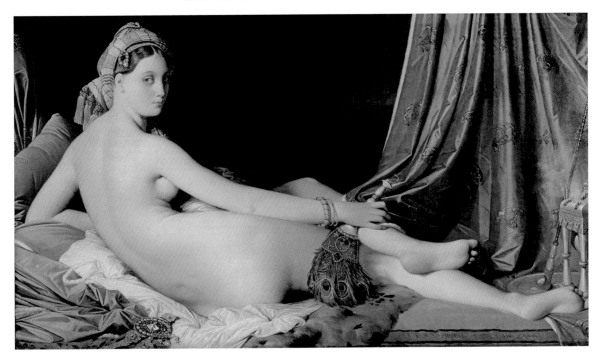

Figure 33 Jean-Auguste-Dominique Ingres, *La Grande Odalisque*, 1814, oil on canvas, 91 × 162 cm. Musée du Louvre, Paris. Photo: © Bridgeman Images.

2   The image was originally designed to be a billboard, which would have been even more effective as propaganda than their usual medium of the poster. Once this idea was rejected, the Guerrilla Girls then rented advertising space on buses (Figure 34) to get their message across, until this was cancelled by the bus companies as well.

Figure 34 *Est-ce que les femmes doivent être nues pour entrer au Metropolitan Museum?* (*Do women have to be naked to get into the Met. Museum?*), Montauban, France, 2009. Copyright © Guerrilla Girls, courtesy guerrillagirls.com.

Activity 10

(Allow around 30 minutes to complete this activity.)

Now turn to Reading 3.2, which is a 2018 article by the feminist art historian Helen Gørrill. In the article, Gørrill weighs up the Tate's claims of inclusivity against its acquisition policy in relation to women artists.

How does Gørrill challenge these claims, and what ulterior motive does she ascribe to the Tate's patronage of the Guerrilla Girls?

Discussion

In a manner akin to the strategy used by the Guerrilla Girls, Gørrill uses statistics to demonstrate that the Tate's claims of inclusivity are not borne out by the actual figures. Despite the fact that 74 per cent of fine art graduates are women, the Tate has a 30 per cent cap in its annual budget for the acquisition of works by female artists, of which only 13 per cent has been used in recent years. Given these statistics, she argues that Tate's 'support of the activist art collective Guerrilla Girls is a clever tactic that gives the illusion of equality'.

As Gørrill demonstrates then, there is still much work to be done in making the art world truly inclusive in terms of gender; and this extends to BAME people too, as they are also underrepresented in public collections. However, in the 1990s, and just like the AWC before them, the Guerrilla Girls subsequently expanded the target of their attack from one focused on the museum and gallery system to other examples of inequality and oppression within wider society. Their poster *Guerrilla Girls Demand a Return to Traditional Values on Abortion* (Figure 35) is an urgent reminder that women's control over their reproductive rights – a fundamental issue in second-wave feminism – was, and still is, a contentious issue in the United States.

GUERRILLA GIRLS DEMAND A RETURN TO TRADITIONAL VALUES ON ABORTION.

Before the mid-19th century, abortion in the first few months of pregnancy was legal. Even the Catholic Church did not forbid it until 1869.*

*Carl. N. Flanders, Abortion, Library in a Book, 1991

A PUBLIC SERVICE MESSAGE FROM **GUERRILLA GIRLS** CONSCIENCE OF THE ART WORLD

Figure 35 Guerrilla Girls, *Guerrilla Girls Demand a Return to Traditional Values on Abortion*, 1992. Copyright © Guerrilla Girls, courtesy guerrillagirls. com.

However, as the feminist art historian Anna C. Chave has argued, even if the Guerrilla Girls' insistent critique of the art world for its glaring omission of women and artists of colour has unfairly earned them the label of 'quota queens', it is nevertheless due to their tireless art activism that:

> no one could plan an exhibition [...] in the contemporary art world any longer without considering the gender and complexion of the participants, and having a compelling defense ready if those elements were homogenous.
>
> (Chave, 2011, p. 110)

Indeed, it was after the Guerrilla Girls' appearance at the Tate Modern in 2006 that the gallery introduced its policy on acquiring more works by women artists.

5 Summary

This chapter has explored how art has been deployed against power, using either satire, propaganda or, more often than not, a combination of both when satire has been deployed for propagandistic purposes. Using a range of examples from the paintings and prints of Goya in early-nineteenth-century Spain, through to the contemporary posters by the Guerrilla Girls in New York, we have seen how artists have strategically used different media to challenge the inequities of power within the different contexts in which their works were produced. In each case, it has been demonstrated that these politicised practices were part of a broader culture of opposition from which the artists drew their strength and inspiration. Throughout this chapter we have judged the relative success or failure of these oppositional strategies in terms of their challenge against power, on the basis of these broader contextual factors.

We have also considered how post-1968 artist collectives have targeted internationally renowned cultural institutions for their restrictive exhibition policies; and also how some of these institutions have sought to appropriate oppositional works for their own ideological ends, whether this be MoMA with Picasso's *Guernica*, or the Tate with prints by the Guerrilla Girls. Just as traditional histories of art presented in leading cultural institutions emphasise the formal relationship between artists and their works across generations, so do oppositional practices often make reference to earlier models in terms of technique or media. This process can even happen when such practices have been excluded from the traditional canon that is promoted by prestigious museums and galleries; as is the case with the radical anti-fascist photomontages of Heartfield in the early 1930s, which were discovered by a later generation of radical artists seeking to challenge powerful vested interests in the late 1960s and after, from the Art Workers' Coalition through to the Guerrilla Girls.

You should now return to the module website to continue your study of this unit.

References

Boime, A. (1990) *Art in the age of Bonapartism: 1800–1815*. Chicago, IL, and London: University of Chicago Press.

Bryan-Wilson, J. (2009) *Art workers: radical practice in the Vietnam War era*. Berkeley, CA, and London: University of California Press.

Chave, A.C. (2011) 'The Guerrilla Girls' Reckoning', *Art Journal*, 70(2), pp. 102–111.

Eisenman, S. (1994) 'The tensions of Enlightenment: Goya', in Eisenman, S. (ed.) *Nineteenth century art: a critical history*. London: Thames & Hudson, pp. 82–101.

Frascina, F. (1996) 'Picasso, surrealism and politics in 1937', in Levy, S. (ed.) *Surrealism: surrealist visuality*. Edinburgh: Keele University Press, pp. 125–147.

Frascina, F. (1999) *Art, politics and dissent: aspects of the art left in sixties America*. Manchester and New York, NY: Manchester University Press.

Golan, R. (2009) *Muralnomad: the paradox of wall painting, Europe 1927–1957*. New Haven, CT, and London: Yale University Press.

Gørrill, H. (2018) 'Are female artists worth collecting? Tate doesn't seem to think so', *The Guardian*, 13 August. Available at: https://www.theguardian.com/commentisfree/2018/aug/13/tate-female-artists-museum-diversity-acquisitions-art-collect?page=with%3Aimg-2 (Accessed: 3 March 2020).

Kriebel, S.T. (2014) *Revolutionary beauty: the radical photomontages of John Heartfield*. Berkeley, CA, and London: University of California Press.

Manchester, E. (2004/2005) 'Guerrilla Girls: do women have to be naked to get into the Met. Museum?'. *Tate*. Available at: https://www.tate.org.uk/art/artworks/guerrilla-girls-do-women-have-to-be-naked-to-get-into-the-met-museum-p78793 (Accessed: 3 March 2020).

Marno, A. (2017) 'The etching series *Der Krieg* (*The War*, 1924). Otto Dix's main graphic work in his Düsseldorf years', in Meyer-Büser, S., Manacorda, F. and Barnes, L. (eds) *Otto Dix – The Evil Eye*. Munich, London and New York, NY: Prestel, pp. 182–189.

Peters, O. (2010) 'Intransigent realism: Otto Dix between the world wars', in Peters, O. (ed.) *Otto Dix*, pp. 13–31. Exhibition held at Neue Galerie, NYC 2010 [Exhibition Catalogue].

Werckmeister, O.K. (1999) *Icons of the left: Benjamin and Eisenstein, Picasso and Kafka after the fall of communism*. Chicago, IL, and London: University of Chicago Press.

Willett, J. (1978) *The new sobriety 1917–1933: art and politics in the Weimar period*. London: Thames & Hudson.

Willet, J. (1998) 'Dix: war', in Griffiths, A., Willett, J. and Wilson-Bareau, J. (eds) *Disasters of war: Callot, Goya and Dix*, pp. 59–89. Exhibition held at South Bank Centre, London 1998 [Exhibition Catalogue].

Readings

Reading 3.1 The Guerrilla Girls

Source: Manchester, E. (2004/2005) 'Guerrilla Girls: do women have to be naked to get into the Met. Museum?'. *Tate*. Available at: https://www.tate.org.uk/art/artworks/guerrilla-girls-do-women-have-to-be-naked-to-get-into-the-met-museum-p78793 (Accessed: 3 March 2020).

This is one of thirty posters published in a portfolio entitled *Guerrilla Girls Talk Back* by the group of anonymous American female artists who call themselves the Guerrilla Girls. Tate's copy is number twelve in the edition of fifty.

Since their inception in 1984 the Guerrilla Girls have been working to expose sexual and racial discrimination in the art world, particularly in New York, and in the wider cultural arena. The group's members protect their identities by wearing gorilla masks in public and by assuming pseudonyms taken from such deceased famous female figures as the writer Gertrude Stein (1874–1946) and the artist Frida Kahlo (1907–54). They formed in response to the *International Survey of Painting and Sculpture* held in 1984 at the Museum of Modern Art, New York. The exhibition included the work of 169 artists, less than 10% of whom were women. Although female artists had played a central role in experimental American art of the 1970s, with the economic boom of the early 1980s in which artwork prices rose steeply, their presence in museum and gallery exhibitions diminished dramatically. Dubbing themselves the 'conscience of the art world', in 1985 the Guerrilla Girls began a poster campaign that targeted museums, dealers, curators, critics and artists who they felt were actively responsible for, or complicit in, the exclusion of women and non-white artists from mainstream exhibitions and publications.

Like American artists Barbara Kruger (born 1945) and Jenny Holzer (born 1950), the Guerrilla Girls appropriated the visual language of advertising, specifically fly-posting, to convey their messages in a quick and accessible manner. They pasted up their first posters on SoHo streets in the middle of the night. Combining bold block text with lists and statistics that were compiled by the Girls themselves or reinterpreted from existing sources such as art magazines and museum reports, the posters named New York galleries that showed no more than 10% women artists (Tate) and listed successful male artists who allowed their work to be shown in galleries showing little or no work by women (Tate). Other posters, such as 'We Sell White Bread' (1987, Tate), first appeared as peel-off stickers on gallery windows and doors. With such posters as 'The Advantages of Being a Woman Artist' (1988, Tate) and 'Relax Senator Helms, the Art World is your kind of place (1989, Tate) the Girls used wit and irony to point a critical finger at double standards prevalent in the art world and elsewhere.

The group gradually widened their focus, tackling issues of racial discrimination in the art world and also made more direct, politicised interventions. They organized forums at the Cooper Union where critics, curators and dealers could tell their side of the story (1986, Tate), inserted flyers inside the covers of all the books in the Guggenheim Museum's bookstore, and, concurrently with the 1987 Whitney Biennial, made an exhibition of information exposing the museum's poor record on exhibiting women and artists of colour (Tate). In 1992, at the opening of the Guggenheim Museum SoHo, after instigating a postcard-writing campaign attacking the museum for proposing to show only white male artists, they organized a demonstration, handing out bags with gorilla heads printed on them for protesters to wear over their heads. To date they have produced more than ninety posters, three books, numerous stickers and other printed projects and have undertaken actions about discrimination in art, film and politics. They make presentations and run workshops at schools, museums and various organisations. Their individual identities are always concealed behind the signature gorilla masks.

This print is based on the 1989 poster that asks 'Do women have to be naked to get into the Met. Museum?' above a reclining naked woman who wears a gorilla mask. The image is based on the famous painting by Jean-Auguste-Dominique Ingres (1780–1867) entitled *La Grande Odalisque* 1814 (Musée du Louvre, Paris) and accompanied by the facts: 'less than 5% of the artists in the Modern Art Sections are women, but 85% of the nudes are female'. The poster was originally designed to be a billboard commissioned by the Public Art Fund in New York, but it was rejected on grounds of not being clear enough. The Guerilla Girls recount: 'we then rented advertising space on NYC buses and ran it ourselves, until the bus company cancelled our lease, saying that the image ... was too suggestive and that the figure appeared to have more than a fan in her hand.' (Quoted in Chadwick, p.61.)

Reading 3.2 Are female artists worth collecting?

Source: Gørrill, H. (2018) 'Are female artists worth collecting? Tate doesn't seem to think so', *The Guardian*, 13 August. Available at: https://www.theguardian.com/commentisfree/2018/aug/13/tate-female-artists-museum-diversity-acquisitions-art-collect?page=with%3Aimg-2 (Accessed: 3 March 2020).

The dire situation for equality in the British visual arts has been laid bare. We've reversed back into the Victorian age, where women can't paint and women can't write. My research suggests that female creatives are less likely to succeed now than they were in the 1990s. Today, when men's artwork is signed, it goes up in value; conversely when work by women is signed, it goes down in value, and the addition of a woman's signature can devalue artwork to the extent that female artists are more likely to leave their work unsigned. Hysteria, the female-specific Victorian malady, has returned to the UK, with women accused of being mad and out of control if they don't conform to gallerists' often unreasonable demands.

Pulling greedily from the public purse, our great institutions are largely to blame. This summer, Tate has offered a lively programme of events to entice young people to delve into its collections and ensure the Department for Digital, Culture, Media and Sport continues to be the bedrock of its funding. Museums are responsible for our future histories, which look spectacularly masculine as far as Tate is concerned.

We cringe at the voices of famous male artists and critics declaring their disdain for artists who happen to have been born female: women can't paint! There's no such thing as a great woman artist!

And Tate appears to align with these views by collecting only a token proportion of work by women, who form the 74% majority of our fine art graduates. The young people who visit the museum this summer will learn that art's future is mainly masculine.

While Tate appears to have a 30% cap on the collection of female artists, its allocation of annual budget is even worse, with as little as 13% spent on works by female artists in recent years. This perpetuates the dominance of male artists in the collections and suppresses the

the dominance of male artists in the collections and suppresses the value of women's work. It has been proved that Tate's collections affect the art market – its former director Alan Bowness even wrote a book on the subject.

The great inequality machine continues to churn and force women out of practice, while the institution's publicly funded PR department works tirelessly to demonstrate its apparent support for female artists. Last year, Tate announced the progressive appointment of its first female director, Maria Balshaw, but it wasn't a great start when she offered a trivial response to sexual harassment, perpetuating a blame-the-victim mindset.

Tate's support of the activist art collective Guerrilla Girls is a clever tactic that gives the illusion of equality, yet politically correct press releases from the likes of Tate championing female artists could actually be doing more harm than good. It could be argued that museums raise the question of whether female artists are worthy of collection at all, because no similar promotional material or articles discuss the worthiness of male artists. With gender income gaps for artists reaching up to 80% in the UK – among the worst in the world – this issue needs to be urgently addressed.

Tate fails to mention gender or equality in its collection policy, seeking only to collect works of art of outstanding quality as well as works of distinctive aesthetic character or importance. Taking this policy and Tate's acquisition data into account, it can be reasonably assumed the museum perceives that great works of art are mostly created by men. Its diversity policy inadequately addresses gender, yet the board of privileged directors are clearly aware that it is a key issue – and are happy to congratulate themselves for paltry efforts to equalise collections.

Meanwhile, annual acquisitions continue to have a stark gender disparity. The imbalance at Tate is particularly important given the role museums have played in defining and subverting gender roles and identities throughout art history. According to the Museums Association, public galleries such as Tate are also responsible for reducing inequalities between the rich and poor. Public service equality duty should therefore apply, yet the Equality and Human Rights Commission remains ambivalent.

Our great universities are also failing to address equality issues in their research. One research funder told me their master would never allow the use of his tools to dismantle the master's house. As the self-proclaimed master of our nation's art collection, Tate should make urgent efforts to reflect the diversity of the population in its collections and allow female graduates the same life chances as men. Do not waste any more of our money on persuasive PR. We know the collections are unfair and unequal. We need to encourage our daughters as well as our sons, and we need to provide role models for everyone.

Come on Tate. Put our money where your mouth is.

Block 2 Resources

Resource 2.1
Visual analysis toolkit

Introduction to the toolkit

Visual analysis is a key skill for Art History, but it is also applicable to other disciplines, as learning how to describe what you see is also useful for Classical Studies, English Literature and Creative Writing. This visual analysis toolkit is provided to help you develop this useful skill. It's intended as a handy guide that you can use throughout the module, including when you come to prepare for your assessment.

There's no need to read it all in one go (although, of course, you can if you would like to) as time to explore the toolkit has been built into your studies when we meet different paintings, prints, sculpture, designed objects and architecture over the course of the module.

This toolkit is made up of the following sections:

1. Approaching artworks
2. Paintings
3. Prints
4. Sculpture
5. Designed objects
6. Architecture

In the following sections, you will find an explanation of each artworks' various components and all the tools you will need to conduct a formal analysis. There are also examples of how you might apply these tools to artworks as you go along.

Study note

For a list of helpful weblinks supporting the toolkit, please visit the online version of this resource on the module website.

1 Approaching artworks

Written by Leah R. Clark

There are three main areas to consider when looking at an artwork: form, subject matter and function. Let's go through them one by one.

1.1 Form

Form encompasses a range of related factors that together determine how and why an artwork looks the way that it does (composition, scale, pose, gesture, expression, colour, light and viewpoint). Analysing form demands skills of close scrutiny, yet it is different from simply describing what you can see in an artwork. The formal elements vary depending on the medium of the work (such as a painting, print, sculpture, designed object or architecture). For example, in looking at objects and buildings the overall design and its features will be key, whereas when looking at prints line may also be important.

The most common approach to describing representational artworks is to refer to the recognisable objects depicted, e.g. the fallen tree in the foreground or the kneeling figure to the side. Art historians refer to these observable properties, which resemble features in the world, as the picture's subject or 'content'. It is crucial when studying works of art to understand that content is always mediated by form; that is to say, content is always presented in a particular way from a range of possibilities. Whatever an artist depicts is conveyed using compositional techniques and approaches. Art historians have developed various ways to account for the formal dimensions of artworks, and coming to terms with the ways that form shapes subject or content is an important part of what art historians do.

Study note

While the following definitions will provide a helpful reference guide, seeing these components actually applied to a work of art and trying visual analysis out for yourself is probably the best way to develop your skill. You will therefore find examples that should help make things clearer in this toolkit and across the module.

Definitions of form:

- **Scale:** the illusion of size relationships between objects and figures in a painting. Or, simply the size of an artwork itself.

- **Composition:** how the various elements of an artwork are organised into a whole. You might identify particular shapes (squares, rectangles, pyramids), or if there's a central axis or a particular symmetrical or asymmetrical arrangement. Do these contribute to movement in the work?

- **Pose and gesture:** how people or animals are represented in an artwork. How they gesture might be historically or culturally specific. For instance, a hand raised in the air by a preacher in a Renaissance painting could be a sign of benediction, but used in a different context, it could be a 'stop' sign. Pose and gesture can also create an impression of power or weakness in the figures.

- **Expression:** expression can refer to the expression of the people depicted in a work. Like hand gestures, expression on faces can be culturally or historically specific. Expression can also be related to the formal qualities of the work itself. Certain bright colours in a painting, for instance, can be interpreted as expressive.

- **Colour:** colour is not simply about the different colours applied in a work of art, but it can also be related to the temperature – cool or warm colours that might affect meaning or how a viewer interacts with a work.

- **Light:** like colour, this can be related to temperature. But it can also determine what our eye is drawn to: we usually notice something in light before we notice something in shadow. Light and colour can also create diagonal lines that draw our eyes to a focal point. The material of an artwork might also affect how light plays on its surfaces.

- **Viewpoint:** allows us to consider where the viewer is positioned in relation to the work of art. If there are people depicted in a painting, are they looking at the viewer? Viewpoint, when analysing a work of sculpture can often help us to determine where a statue may have been placed. Is it made to be looked at from above, below or at eye level?

1.2 Subject matter

Subject matter involves *what* the work depicts, for example, who the people in the image are and whether it depicts a narrative. Related to subject matter is the term iconography. Iconography refers to the identification, description and interpretation of the content of images. It pays attention to the subjects depicted, the particular compositions and details used to depict them, and the symbols employed. Identifying iconographic elements of a work of art helps us to interpret that work within its historical and/or cultural setting. For instance, the symbol of the cross is recognised as a sign for Jesus Christ or Christianity. Iconographic elements are not always so easily interpreted, particularly when we are studying a culture that is historically distant from our own, such as ermines (small mammals with highly prized white fur) used in Renaissance paintings to signal purity.

1.3 Function

An artwork's function relates to how it was used and considers the requirements that shaped it, such as original location, patron, purpose and audience. Functional issues are related to context, and can also require visual analysis, for example, deciding how a work of art was designed to suit a particular location or patron. The content of an artwork – its subject matter – may also relate to function. The function of a work might change over time, or might change if it is moved from one location or setting to another.

Study note

We are now going to look at these visual analysis components in more detail in order to apply them to each medium and type of artwork that you will encounter on A112, including paintings, prints, sculpture, designed objects and architecture.

You'll see that these components are applied in slightly different ways, or in a different order, according to the artwork you are looking at.

2 Paintings

Written by Leah R. Clark

Let's look at paintings first. Before we begin an analysis, it's helpful to understand some of the terminology that art historians use when talking about paintings. For example, the literal surface simply refers to the physical surface of the canvas that we can touch. On this level, we understand that a painting is just a flat object.

Pictorial space means something different for artworks that are on flat surfaces. It usually alludes to the way in which the artist creates the illusion of a three-dimensional space on what is in fact a flat plane or surface. This can be linked to viewpoint (which we will explore together when analysing Figures 1 and 2), as well as style and the use of perspective. Some artists intentionally render an image to appear 'flat' by using odd perspective, for example. Art historians usually refer to pictorial space as having a foreground, a middle ground, or background.

How does the painter create (by using various techniques – perspective, colour, tone, texture) a sense of 'depth' into which the eye 'enters' and can 'wander'? The 'front' of the picture space is imagined as 'nearest' to us (the foreground of the picture) and it is referred to as the picture plane.

Helpful definitions:

- **Foreground:** what appears closest to the viewer
- **Middle ground:** between the foreground and the background
- **Background:** what appears farthest from the viewer.

Here are the key aspects to consider when analysing a painting:

1 **Scale:** what is the size of the painting? Is it monumental? Are the things depicted in the painting represented in life-size, or miniscule?

2 **Material/medium:** is it painted in oil, tempera, watercolour? What are the material supports (the material that has been painted)? Is it on canvas, wood, paper, cardboard? Is the paint applied in thick dabs (a technique known as 'impasto') or is it hard to even see the paint?

3 **General condition:** is it damaged? Has it been cracked? Broken? Is the paper or canvas ripped? Have the pigments been bleached or are they discoloured? Is it clean or dirty? Has the paint abraded?

4 **Subject matter:** who or what is being represented? Is there a story or narrative? How successful is it in telling that story? Are all scenes of the story represented? Or is it only one moment in the story? There are different genres of paintings that also determine subject matter such as portraiture, landscape, still life, history painting, etc.

5 **Space, composition and picture plane:** is there an illusion of space within the painting? How does this relate to the use of perspective? Is it an idealised space? Is there a repetition of certain elements in the painting? Is there a balance in the composition? Is it simple or complex?

6 **Pose, gesture and expression:** this aspect will be relevant if people or animals are represented. Are the poses seated, standing or in another position? Is gesture used to highlight a particular element? Can you see the faces of figures, or are their expressions hidden?

7 **Line:** is it crisp, neat brushwork? Are brushstrokes only visible under close examination? Are there angular elements? Or sinuous, 's-curves'? Are contours defined or obscured?

8 **Colour:** are bright colours used? Are there dark colours? Is there a contrast between colours? Are they warm or cold?

9 **Light:** where is the source of light? Are there shadows? Is there an extreme contrast between light and dark (a technique known as 'chiaroscuro')?

10 **Viewpoint:** where is the viewer positioned? If figures are depicted in the painting, are any looking towards the viewer?

11 **Display/function:** where was it meant to be viewed? Private or public space? A secular or religious space?

So let's take a look at a painting and see how we can analyse it using our toolkit. I've chosen an artwork by the eighteenth-century French artist Jacques-Louis David, called *The Oath of the Horatii.*

Figure 1 (left) Jacques-Louis David, *The Oath of the Horatii*, 1784, oil on canvas, 330 × 425 cm. Museé du Louvre, Paris. Photo: © Bridgeman Images. **Figure 2 (right)** Viewers in front of the painting. Photo: Steven Zucker. Used under this licence: https://creativecommons.org/licenses/by-nc-sa/2.0/.

> **Study note**
>
> If you would like to record your initial thoughts on this piece of art, please do so now.

Here are my thoughts on the painting:

1 **Scale:** the architecture is grand – the painting shows a basic classical structure that dominates and frames the action. By placing the action close to the picture plane, the men are depicted large, particularly in their stances, while the women appear diminutive. It is also a large painting, as you can see by the image of the male viewer standing in front of it in Figure 2.

2 **Material/medium:** painted in oils on canvas.

3   **General condition:** the painting appears in good condition.

4   **Subject matter:** the painting is inspired by an event in early Roman history, which appears in a number of classical texts. In the seventh century BCE, Rome was in conflict with the neighbouring kingdom of Alba. Rather than engage in a large battle, both cities designated champions to fight each other to settle the dispute: Rome chose three brothers (known as the Horatii) and Alba also chose three siblings (known as the Curiatii). To make it more complicated, the two families were linked by marriage. One of the wives in the painting, Sabina, is a sister of the Curiatii and the other, Camilla, is engaged to one of the Curiatii brothers. Jacques-Louis David depicts the Horatii swearing to defeat their enemies or die for their country. The importance of this painting is its ability to render a complex story into a single moment that maximises drama.

5   **Space, composition and picture plane:** you'll notice how the scene is divided by three arches in the background, which also divides the scene into three. The central action is framed by the central arch; this draws the viewer into the focal point of the painting. In addition, we have diagonals that are both vertical and horizontal: the three men's arms on the left direct our focus to the vertical lines of the swords. The Horatii also form the shape of an X, which is mimicked by the father, who holds the swords in an X stance. On the contrary, the women on the right of the composition are rendered in soft curves and flowing poses. There are clear and outlined forms that work to create drama in the painting.

6   **Pose, gesture and expression:** the gestures by the men are heroic: they raise their arms, ready to take their swords; their bodies are erect and vigorous, their muscles tensed. They are three, but they are so close together that they also appear as one. The women on the other hand appear weak and soft, lethargic even, not able to take action. Camilla rests her head on the shoulder of her sister-in-law, Sabina.

7   **Line:** the brushwork is very smooth.

8   **Colour:** the men wear bright colours (red, white and blue), whereas the women, although wearing similar colours, appear more muted, even earthy. The simple grey of the background architecture works to highlight a contrast with the central action.

9   **Light:** the light draws our attention to the central action. The artist has paid particular attention in rendering the light to highlight the

men's muscles as well as the swords, and it also falls on the right side of the painting, on the women in mourning. The light source is invisible, but the shadows suggest that it is coming from the left side of the painting, from a window above. The way the paint is rendered with the light makes it appear almost photographic in its precision.

10 **Viewpoint:** the viewer is very close to the action, but the light and drama make it feel as though we're watching a theatrical display.

11 **Display/function:** the painting was commissioned in 1784 by the King of France and was exhibited at the Salon of 1785 in Paris – so it originally had a public viewership. The painting's reception is complex and it won't be dealt with here, but the formal elements of the painting certainly work to convey particular messages about the subject, and articulate war and sacrifice on gendered terms.

3 Prints

Written by Warren Carter

Another type of artwork is the print (an artwork printed onto paper or another support), which you encounter in Blocks 2 and 3.

Here are the key aspects to consider when analysing a print:

1 **Scale:** consider the size of the print (if the caption has dimensions, use those to help you judge this).

2 **Material/medium:** has the paper or other support been tinted or coloured? Which printing method has been used, e.g. etching, engraving, lithograph, screen print, woodcut?

3 **General condition:** is it damaged? Is the paper ripped? Have the pigments been bleached or are they discoloured? Is it clean or dirty? Has the surface become worn (abraded)? Has it been cut down?

4 **Subject matter:** who or what is being represented? Is there a story or narrative? How successful is it in telling that story? Are all scenes of the story represented, or is it only one moment in the story? Is it part of a series?

5 **Space, composition and picture plane:** is there an illusion of space within the artwork? How does this relate to the use of perspective? Is it an idealised space? Is there a repetition of certain elements in the print? Is there a balance in the composition? Is it simple or complex?

6 **Pose, gesture and expression:** this aspect will be relevant if people or animals are represented. Are poses seated, standing or in another position? Is gesture used to highlight a particular element? Can you see the faces of figures, or are their expressions hidden?

7 **Line:** how do the methods used produce contrast, e.g. cross-hatching in engraving to suggest light/shade?

8 **Colour:** is the print monocrome (black and white)? If colours are used, are these bright or muted? Are there dark colours? Is there a contrast between colours?

9 **Light:** where is the source of light? Are there shadows? Is there an extreme contrast between light and dark (a technique known as 'chiaroscuro')?

10 **Viewpoint:** where is the viewer positioned? If figures are depicted in the painting, are any looking towards the viewer?

11 **Display/function:** where was it meant to be viewed? By many people, by one person or a small group? Is it a 'finished' work of art or a preparatory work, to be used for reference by the artist (often inscribed 'artist's proof')? Is there a figure recorded along the lower edge, for example '4/12' (which would be the fourth print made out of a total of 12)?

So let's take a look at a print by the early twentieth-century Mexican artist, José Guadalupe Posada, and see how we can analyse it using our toolkit.

Figure 3 José Guadalupe Posada, *A firing squad executing two men, a priest and other figures in the background*, c.1880–1910, etching on zinc, 12 × 17 cm. Metropolitan Museum of Art, New York, Gift of Jean Charlot, 1930.

Study note

If you would like to record your initial thoughts on this piece of art, please do so now.

Here are my thoughts on the print:

1 **Scale:** 4 5/8 × 6 3/4 in. (12 × 17 cm). From the dimensions, you can see that it is not a large print: about the size of a small book.

2 **Material/medium:** prints can be made in a number of different ways, which have a bearing on *how* the final product looks. Printmaking follows the basic principle that the final image is a result of transferring an image from a matrix onto another surface. The matrix is essentially a template and the choice of its material results in the type of print it is: woodcut, engraving, etching, lithograph or screen print. The photomechanical process that the Mexican artist Posada used to make this print involved him drawing on white card covered with compressed china-clay coated with Indian ink, after which white lines were scraped out. The image was then photographed onto a sheet of metal coated with a light-sensitive acid resist and turned, by etching the resultant acid-resistant photographic plate, into a relief-printing line-block. This technique imitates the older technique of woodblock printing, which usually results in thicker lines.

3 **General condition:** it is in relatively good condition, bearing in mind that the paper on which this image was printed was of low quality to deliberately emphasise the rough-and-ready nature of the type of broadsheet in which it was illustrated.

4 **Subject matter:** the subject of the print is the brutal execution of two men by a firing squad of five soldiers using rifles, directed by a sixth soldier with his sword. Three male figures standing behind and to our left, facing the viewer, are apparently onlookers. The sensationalised themes of crime, violence, murder and catastrophe were staple subjects in the broadsheets that Posada illustrated, as they often still are today in parts of the media.

5 **Space, composition and picture plane:** as befitting its purpose, it is a deliberately simple looking design in which the firing squad in military uniform on the right execute two figures on the left, one of whom is already dead, the other falling to the ground as he is being shot.

6 **Pose, gesture and expression:** the fixed stance, gesture and expression of the soldiers contrasts with those of their victims. Of the standing figures behind, the one on the right can be identified by his clothing and holding of an object (a crucifix) as a priest in the Catholic Church (in fact, the print is to meant be read as the Church sanctioning the killings). These three figures frame the

composition to the left, while the right is framed by the firing squad who are depicted so similarly that their individual identity is obscured by their collective identity as soldiers.

7 **Line:** line is particularly important in prints. This is a rather tight composition with the three groups filling the picture plane with little illusion of space. The foreground and background are left relatively clear compared to the vigorous lines etched on to the figures in the print. Despite the relatively sophisticated photomechanical nature of its production, the print appears to be crudely drawn and naively carved with little reference to the conventions of Renaissance picture making. There is very little detail beyond the people depicted: for example, there is no landscape, instead Posado uses lines to suggest shadows and recession of space at the background of the image, between the soldiers and the three men to the left. A few undulating lines in the sky suggest clouds but also work to frame the composition.

8 **Colour:** as with many prints this one is monochrome, but light and shade are used to evoke emotion. On the right-hand side the phalanx of soldiers are shooting a victim wearing a white shirt who falls to the ground. This links the print to an earlier painting by Goya (see Block 2, Chapter 3, Figure 7). The whiteness of the victim's shirt, in contrast to the dark tones of the clothing of the other figures in the composition, signifies his innocence and purity. This relationship between light and shade in the design gives the print its balance as well. There are also different shades of black with finer, faint lines contrasting with the thicker, broad lines used to depict the soldiers.

9 **Light:** there is little use of shadow in this print, which gives the etching a simplicity that resembles the imagery that its intended audience would have seen in the popular broadsheets of the time. Posada utilises his lines to explore how light can denote material and motion. For example, the faint lines that come out of the guns suggest fast moving bullets in the air. Posada was a highly trained and skilled artist who altered and adapted his earlier, more detailed and sophisticated, style to produce a cruder looking imagery for the popular audience for whom it was designed.

10 **Viewpoint:** the standing figures at the back look out towards the viewer, who appears to be looking up from the ground level.

11 **Display/function:** Posada's prints were designed for a wide distribution in the penny press of the period (cheap, mass-produced

newspapers) such as those owned by Mexican publisher Antonio Vanegas Arroyo. Arroyo employed Posada to illustrate topical ballads and sensational events in his broadsheets, which were then hawked around the streets and at public gatherings. Their place was therefore in the street where they were consumed by a popular audience who would often have been illiterate. The style of these prints was therefore intentionally easy to understand, conveying a direct visual message.

4 Sculpture

Written by Leah R. Clark

Now let's think about a medium that has been important to artists since antiquity: sculpture. You encounter examples of sculpture in both Blocks 1 and 2.

Here are the key aspects to consider when analysing a sculpture:

1 **Size:** what is the size of the sculpture? Is it monumental? Life-size? Small? Miniscule (such as a coin)?

2 **Material and execution:** is it made from bronze, marble, terracotta, stone, wood or another material? The material determines how a work is made – is it carved or cast? Metals are generally cast; while marble, ceramics and wood are usually carved. Is the surface smooth or rough?

3 **General condition:** is it damaged? Are pieces missing, such as an arm?

4 **Display:** where was it meant to be viewed? A private or public space? A garden setting or a church?

5 **Subject matter:** what or who is being represented? Is there a story or narrative? How successful is it in telling that story? Are all scenes of the story represented, or is it only one moment in the story?

6 **Space:** how does it occupy space? Is there an illusion of space within the sculpture? Does it interact with the space it inhabits? Does it make use of negative space?

7 **Volume:** are there particular three-dimensional forms that make up the sculpture: cubes, pyramids, cylinders? Is it bas-relief or 'in the round'? Bas-relief (also known as low relief) refers to sculpture that is still attached to a solid background. 'In the round' means the sculpture can be viewed from all sides, in complete three-dimensional form.

8 **Line:** what are the lines of the sculpture? Are they sinuous or in the form of s-curves? Are they angular or jagged?

9 **Light:** has the artist considered the effects of light on the work? Does the light vary depending on your position as the viewer? Might it shift if you were to hold the sculpture in your hand?

So let's take a look at an equestrian statuette of Philip IV, King of Spain, which can be found in the Metropolitan Museum of Art in New York, and see how we can analyse it using our toolkit.

Figure 4 Possibly after a model by Pietro Tacca, Equestrian statuette of Philip IV, King of Spain, seventeenth century, cast possibly nineteenth century, bronze. Metropolitan Museum of Art, New York, bequest of Mary Cushing Fosburgh, 1978.

Here are my thoughts on the sculpture:

1 **Size:** From the Metropolitan Museum website, we are told the size is:

Horse and rider: 16 1/8 × 7 × 12 5/8 in. (41 × 17.8 × 32.1 cm)

Rider: 12 3/8 × 7 × 5 1/8 in. (31.4 × 17.8 × 13 cm)

Horse: 12 × 5 5/8 × 12 5/8 in. (30.5 × 14.3 × 32.1 cm)

Base: 9 × 7 3/4 × 15 in. (22.9 × 19.7 × 38.1 cm)

The title 'statuette' already indicates that this is a small sculpture and certainly not life-size.

2 **Material and execution:** it is made from bronze and was therefore cast. There are some particularly fine details in the execution of some of the smaller parts of the horse, such as the delicate ears. Attention has been paid to rendering the different tactile surfaces of the statue. For example, the horse's body is smooth, while the veins in the legs are clearly visible. The horse's tail and mane replicate hair with individual tendrils and would be less smooth to touch. The king's armour is also carefully executed with details of its decoration. It is not always easy to get very fine details in bronze, and this is evident in the king's face. While his features are clear (there is evidence of a moustache and goatee as well as details such as eyelids) these are not as delicate or refined as some examples we see in bronze by Renaissance masters who excelled at this medium, such as Giambologna (1529–1608).

3 **General condition:** It looks like it is in good condition and intact. Considering that there are only two legs of the horse fixed on the ground, the balance of this statue might be rather delicate. This is probably why a plinth is so important, to ensure that it stays upright. From the pictures, it doesn't look like it has been damaged, but it is hard to tell without closer examination.

4 **Display:** it is hard to know without any further information, but such a small statue was likely intended for private display, perhaps to show allegiance to the king. From portraits and paintings of the

time, we know that these small statuettes would often be placed on desks or shelves in a study.

5   **Subject matter:** the subject is Philip IV, King of Spain on horseback. It might be depicting him in a particular battle, but with an unconfirmed date of execution it is hard to know. The horse is in motion but is not rearing, which suggests that it might even be in a stately procession rather than in a battle. The king's facial expression is rather neutral; he doesn't look like he's exerting too much energy or is scared about going into a battle.

6   **Space:** the statue alludes to movement with two of the horse's hooves in the air, utilising the space around it. The horse's mane also falls to one side as its head turns the other way, also using space to allude to the horse's movement.

7   **Volume:** the sculpture is in the round. The horse's four legs descend from the central body of the horse, but they are not static with two in the air. The bulk of the statue is at the centre, concentrated around the horse's body. You could say that there is a verticality to the statue, but not as vertical as it would be had the horse been rearing. The central body of the horse acts like a rectangle, with four lines that support it (the legs) while the body of the king creates a vertical line, upwards.

8   **Line:** the body of the horse follows an s-curve while the king's body is erect. The horse's legs are also curved.

9   **Light:** the medium of bronze also gives a shiny quality to the statue, where the different materials alluded to, react to light in different ways. If the sculpture was viewed in the round in real life, as the viewer moved around it, light would play on different surfaces, adding to the sense of movement, as if giving life to the statue. As it is small, it could also be lifted up by the viewer and as it was turned in the hand, light would play on the different textures of the statue.

5 Designed objects

Written by Clare Taylor

In Blocks 1 and 2 you encounter examples of designed objects, such as textiles, ceramics and furniture. We are now going to take a look at how these artworks might be analysed. Here, form and subject matter are still important, but function can often be more prominent, too.

Here are the key aspects to consider when analysing a designed object:

1 **Scale:** what is the size of the piece? Is it monumental, miniscule or somewhere in between? Can you pick it up and place it on a table or is it intended to be placed in a larger space?

2 **Overall design:** what forms or shapes does the work employ? Are any conventions or symbols used (floral, geometric, vegetal, figurative)? If figures are used, are they human, animal or imaginary? Are they part of the design? How are they treated in terms of pose, gesture and expression? Is there an illusion of setting?

3 **Colour and materials:** for textiles, one material may be used or several in combination, perhaps by applying other textiles (appliqué) or embroidered cut-outs (slips) or lining with contrasting materials. Does the piece incorporate any 'found' materials, either contemporary ones or collected from the past?

   For furniture, are different woods and/or stones used? If so, how are they employed to suggest contrast, for example, are they coloured or gilded or used to show different grains of wood?

   For ceramics, is there a contrast between the colour scheme used in the vessel's decoration, or is it all one colour?

4 **Making and decoration:** were these processes carried out by one person, or by many, over several stages? For textiles, do they involve weaving (such as tapestry), needlework (for example, embroidery, appliqué) or other techniques? Does the piece use coloured thread alone, or other materials too, such as gold or silver wire wrapped around the thread?

   For furniture, have elements been carved or inlaid? Do textiles form part of the piece, as upholstery?

For ceramics, is the vessel decorated with painted or printed images? Or has the surface been decorated with applied decoration, that is by clay being adhered (stuck) to it, or patterns or shapes incised into it using a tool or the artist's hands?

5 **General condition:** can be especially important for designed objects: is it complete or are pieces or parts of an item or a set missing? Has it been remounted (i.e. for textiles cut out and sewn onto another material)? If a ceramic, have metal mounts been added?

6 **Subject matter:** what or who is being represented? Is there a story or narrative? How successful is it in telling that story? Are all scenes of the story represented? Or is it only one moment in the story? If there is no apparent story, are symbols important?

7 **Function:** is it part of a set, or not? Where was it meant to be viewed? In what kind of space? Is it intended to be viewed as an artwork, or rather does it have a practical function too, e.g. as a chair to provide seating, a ceramic vessel to contain liquid, or a table for the serving of food?

So let's take a look at Grayson Perry's *Posh Art* (1992) and see how we can analyse it using our toolkit.

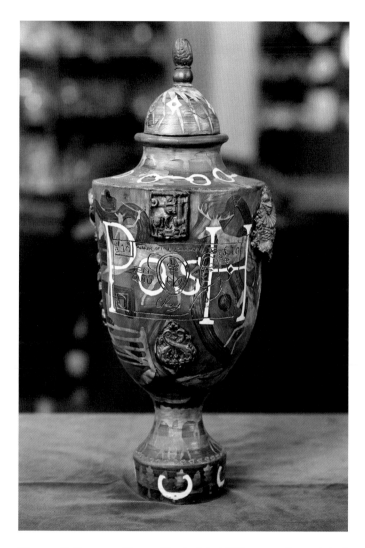

Figure 5 Grayson Perry, *Posh Art*, 1992, ceramic, painted and glazed, impressed with stamps, 43 × 18 × 18 cm. Victoria Art Gallery, Bath. © Grayson Perry the artist and Victoria Miro Gallery, London.

Study note

If you would like to record your initial thoughts on this piece of art, please do so now.

Here are my thoughts on the designed object:

1 **Scale:** 43 × 18 × 18 cm.

2 **Overall design:** the vase is an elongated urn shape with ring handles. It sits on a circular foot and has a raised lid. It may have reminded you of the red-figure vases that you studied in Block 1.

3 **Colour and materials:** it is all made of clay. The underlying colour (produced by coating the pot in liquid glaze) is turquoise, but this appears duller as the surface is also painted with words and images in creams and greys. Some parts of the vase (the knob on the lid, and the different shaped plaques) have been deliberately left unglazed and they haven't been painted either.

4 **Making and decoration:** according to the caption, the vase has been glazed and then overpainted by the artist in different colours before incised and impressed details have been added. The words 'PosH' (on one side), 'ART' (on the other) and some semi-circular motifs (painted in creams) stand out more. A design of men on horseback who appear to be jockeys in a race (they are wearing caps and carry whips), apparently chasing deer, runs around the vase. The artist has also scratched into the surface of the clay using a tool, seen for example in the outline of the £10 banknote. He has also created mini 'tablets' by impressing designs into clay and then fixing them onto the surface of the vase; these are the unglazed plaques. One of these (partly visible on the right-hand edge in the frontal view) shows the portrait head of Elizabeth I.

5 **General condition:** it appears complete and there is no sign of damage.

6 **Subject matter:** the vase's title relates to the connection between art, class and wealth, reflected in the form (adopting a classical shape) and the decoration.

7 **Function:** the piece is not intended to hold wine or oil. Rather, it is a 'one-off' or unique artwork to be admired for its visual qualities. It was purchased by the Victoria Art Gallery in Bath not only to represent the artist's ceramic work, but because its shape linked it to motifs of the city's classical architecture. Its decoration is also designed to be read and understood by those with the appropriate cultural knowledge. In particular, it employs wit to comment on the relationship between art, taste and wealth.

6 Architecture

Written by Susie West

In Blocks 1 and 2 you encounter examples of architecture, both in the ancient world and in Britain. We are now going to take a look at how buildings might be analysed. Buildings are giant objects, and like sculpture they can usually be viewed from more than one angle. The way to start your analysis is to identify the front of a building, as this is usually the most important view in design terms. So we will be focusing on how to analyse an exterior face of a building, called the façade.

Here are the key aspects to consider when analysing architecture:

1   **Site:** where is the building located? Is it on its own, or part of a sequence on a street or market place? Is it adjacent to other buildings or natural features?

2   **Scale:** is it monumental and vast or smaller (we often use the phrase 'domestic') in scale? Can you use details such as figures, cars, trees or other buildings to help you judge this? Are some parts taller than others?

3   **Overall design:** for a building, we need to think about what shape it makes, and how that big shape might be composed of a number of smaller shapes. A typical child's drawing of a house uses a square for the body of the house and a triangle for the roof: this shape is regular, symmetrical and based on a square. Hardwick Hall in Derbyshire (see Block 2, Chapter 2) is a very large house and is based on rectangles. A skyscraper is an elongated vertical rectangle. Very modern buildings designed using complex computer-generated forms may break away from regular geometry and symmetry, and use organic shapes with curves.

4   **Features:** for a building, we can think about the clues that the exterior gives about spaces inside. Can you tell how many internal levels there are (three storeys, a basement, an attic)? If there is more than one entrance visible, which is the most important one and why? Do the windows show you if some rooms are bigger than others, or have a better view? In a very regular front, it may be impossible to tell what is going on behind it: from the outside, a skyscraper clad in glass is intended not to show which is the

chairman's floor and which is the staff canteen. On the other hand, a medieval building (and some contemporary buildings) is designed exactly to match what is going on inside with external features, like small windows for small rooms, and towers for stairs.

5   **Design:** the design should indicate the heritage that the architect has drawn on. An established design tradition has a pattern for how buildings should look. For the Western classical tradition, these are conventions for using pillars, arches and domes; the same features are treated differently within the Islamic tradition of architecture. To identify the design tradition, try to isolate distinctive features like the shape of an arch or the style of a column, the use of visible construction features (like buttresses on a Gothic cathedral), and a repertoire of decoration and colour.

6   **Structure:** buildings have to stay up, and they all use construction materials and techniques, but these may be disguised or revealed, depending on the design tradition being used. The glass skyscraper is clad in glass, but it stays up because of its steel beam construction, hidden by the glass skin. Hardwick Hall reveals its stone construction in every wall, but the enormous windows defy the weight of the stone through the hidden arches above them. A Gothic cathedral shows its load-bearing skeleton in the form of pillars, roof vaults and buttresses. Try to identify the materials visible in a façade: very often, historic buildings cover their construction materials in a coat of plaster (render), especially if good building stone is not available. What effects do the choice of materials create?

7   **General condition:** is the building in the state in which it was first built? Have there been losses? Can you tell if any additions have been made, for example by a different roof line, newer materials or irregularity to one side of the building, or simply a different appearance?

8   **Function:** was the building designed for a religious, political, economic or social function, or a combination of these? Has its usage changed over time, for example, was it once a domestic home and is now a heritage attraction?

So let's take a look at the façade of a building that is familiar globally, that of London's Buckingham Palace, and see how we can analyse it using our toolkit.

Figure 6 Buckingham Palace, The Mall, London, east front by Edward Blore 1847–50, refaced 1913 by Aston Webb. Photo: MICHAEL DUNLEA / Alamy.

Study note

If you would like to record your initial thoughts on this piece of art, please do so now.

Here are my thoughts on the architecture:

1   **Site:** the palace is free-standing and separated from the public road by a forecourt behind elaborate railings and a gateway.

2   **Scale:** there are no people in Figure 6, but the building demonstrates a monumental sense of scale (there are five levels with windows, of different sizes). The measurements are 108m long and 24m high. For comparison, a typical suburban house in the UK is about 10m high.

3   **Overall design:** the body of the palace is a very long rectangle, with no visible roof line. You can break this big rectangle down into two symmetrical halves, either side of the central rectangular feature. Each half has one rectangular block at the end that projects forward slightly. The architectural language for these components calls the end projections 'pavilions' (as if they are little buildings);

the central feature is called a centrepiece, and it is a wider version of the pavilions.

4 **Features:** what has the architect needed to show on the exterior that gives us a clue about what is behind the walls? Looking horizontally from left to right, there are many windows, and each represents a single storey. The windows are evenly spaced and it is impossible to judge whether the rooms behind them vary in size. It is more revealing to look at the building from bottom to top. Here it becomes clearer that of the five storeys revealed by the number of windows, some are more important than others.

The ground floor has high windows and a number of arched and flat openings. In fact, the arched openings offer routes under the building, as there is a courtyard behind it. The flat openings (that is, those without arches) lead to doorways into the building, but they are not emphasised as of importance. Above this level, there is a storey of very short windows, suggesting a floor of less importance with a lower ceiling height. Both of these storeys are identifiable by distinctive channels cut horizontally into the stone: this is called 'rustication' and in the classical tradition it is used to indicate the idea of a basement or working zone, below the high-status floors. Notice how this basement is firmly separated from the rest of the building by the continuous horizontal line of a balustrade with a balcony behind. The tall windows at balcony level sit between massive fluted pilasters (a flattened column attached to the wall surface), and each has its own little pediment over the top (there is some variation on this in the pavilions), which gives them extra visual emphasis.

The band of windows above these, effectively the fourth storey, are still tall but lack the pediments. Above these, still between the giant pilasters, are short windows like those we noticed in the rusticated second storey, much less visible as they are tucked in between the capitals that finish off the pilasters. This is another floor of lower-height rooms, of lesser status. Because the building uses features found in a classical temple, the roof line is hidden and we are unable to see if there are windows in a pitched roof.

5 **Design:** having worked through the distinctive features, it is now clear that this building is within the Western classical tradition, using a classical order called Corinthian (see Block 2, Chapter 2, Figure 13), and this determines the proportions of the pilasters, the type of capitals that they have, and the detailing of the massive

entablature (the decorated horizontal beam that finishes a classical wall) that crowns the buildings. The centrepiece and the pavilions are designed as if they are Corinthian temple fronts, with richer detailing from the use of pairs of engaged (attached, not free-standing) columns as well as pilasters, and pediments above. Designed in 1913, an ancient Roman from 13 CE would be able to identify these features. Importantly, the ancient Roman would also agree that this is the appropriate form and design for a palace, using monumental scale and a richly detailed order to present a very high-status front to the world.

6 **Structure:** this is a stone-faced building. As we know that it was originally constructed in 1847, we can predict that it follows building practices of the time, using load-bearing walls that both keep the building upright and keep the weather out. By the time it was refaced in 1913, steel and reinforced concrete were available but in this classical design would be hidden behind facing stone, if they were used at all. All window frames would be made of wood.

7 **General condition:** as the official residence of the British monarch when in London, and as a building listed by Historic England as Grade I, Buckingham Palace is in active use and well maintained. As a historic property with the highest level of legal protection against adverse change, its visual qualities are unlikely to change.

8 **Function:** it has been an official royal residence of the monarch since 1837. Prior to that, the much smaller house on this site, first built in 1703 for the Duke of Buckingham, was purchased in 1761 by George III. He and his wife Charlotte used it as a comfortable house near to their official residence in St James's Palace. Buckingham Palace is now the administrative headquarters for the monarch. Its function has therefore changed from aristocratic house, to unofficial royal residence, to official status as a palace. It has a symbolic function as a highly recognisable building, for London and for the heritage of the British monarchy.

Resource 2.2
History of conflicts from 1618 to 1975

Written by Warren Carter

Thirty Years' War (1618–1648)

This was a series of wars fought by various nations due to religious, dynastic, territorial or commercial rivalries. Overall, the struggle was between the Habsburg Holy Roman Empire, which was Catholic, and a network of Protestant towns and principalities that relied on the chief anti-Catholic powers of Sweden and the United Netherlands. A parallel conflict took place between France and the Habsburg Empire allied with Habsburg Spain, which had been attempting to construct an alliance of anti-French forces. When the contending powers finally met in the German province of Westphalia in 1648 to end the bloodshed, the balance of power in Europe had been radically changed. Spain had not only lost the Netherlands, which was now recognised as an independent republic, but had been superseded as the dominant power in Western Europe by France. Sweden now had control of the Baltic and the member states of the Holy Roman Empire were granted full sovereignty. Hence the ancient notion of a Roman Catholic empire of Europe, headed spiritually by a pope and temporally by an emperor, was permanently abandoned, and the essential structure of modern Europe as a community of sovereign states was established.

Peninsular War (1807–1814)

This was a military conflict between the Napoleonic Empire and Bourbon Spain for control of the Iberian Peninsula during the Napoleonic Wars (1803–1815). The war began when the French and Spanish armies invaded and occupied Portugal in 1807 and it escalated in 1808 when France turned on Spain, previously its ally, after which Britain entered the war in support of the now allied Iberian powers against the French. The war on the peninsula lasted until the defeat of Napoleon in 1814 and it is regarded as one of the first wars of national liberation involving the emergence of large-scale guerrilla warfare on the part of the civilian population.

First World War (1914–1918)

The First World War was an international conflict that embroiled most of the nations of Europe along with Russia, the United States, the Middle East and other regions. The war pitted Germany, Austria-Hungary and Turkey against France, Great Britain, Russia, Italy, Japan and the United States from 1917. After unprecedented slaughter, carnage and destruction,Germany, Austria-Hungary and Turkey were defeated in 1918. The First World War was one of the great watersheds of twentieth-century geopolitical history. It led to the fall of four great imperial dynasties in Germany, Russia, Austria-Hungary and Turkey, and helped produce the conditions for the Bolshevik Revolution in Russia in 1917 and, in its destabilisation of the balance of power in Europe, it laid the groundwork for the Second World War.

Spanish Civil War (1936–1939)

When a military coup against the Republican government failed to win control of Spain, a bloody civil war ensued. The nationalists received aid from fascist Italy and Nazi Germany; the Republicans received aid from the Soviet Union, as well as from the International Brigades that were composed of volunteers from Europe and the United States. The nationalists were mostly Roman Catholics and consisted of important elements of the military, most landowners and many businessmen; the Republicans were urban workers, most agricultural labourers and many of the educated middle class. A succession of governmental crises culminated in the elections of 16 February 1936, which brought to power a Popular Front government supported by most of the parties of the left and opposed by the parties of the right. Internecine conflict compromised the Republican effort from the outset. On one side were the anarchists and militant socialists, who viewed the war as a revolutionary struggle and inaugurated widespread collectivisation of agriculture, industry and services; on the other were the more moderate socialists and republicans, whose objective was the preservation of the Republic.

Second World War (1939–1945)

The Second World War involved almost every part of the world although the principal belligerents were the Axis powers – Germany, Italy and Japan – and the Allies – France, Great Britain, the United States, the Soviet Union and, to a lesser extent, China. The war was in many respects a continuation of the disputes left unsettled by the First World War. The 40–50 million deaths incurred in the Second World War make it the bloodiest conflict, as well as the largest war, in history. Along with the First World War, the Second World War was one of the great watersheds of twentieth-century geopolitical history. It resulted in the extension of the Soviet Union's power to nations of Eastern Europe, enabled a communist movement to eventually achieve power in China, and marked the decisive shift of power in the world away from the states of Western Europe and toward the United States and the Soviet Union.

Vietnam War (1955–1975)

This was a protracted conflict that pitted the communist government of North Vietnam and its allies in South Vietnam, known as the Viet Cong, against the government of South Vietnam and its principal ally, the United States. The war was also part of a larger regional conflict in Indochina and was a manifestation of the Cold War between the United States and the Soviet Union and their respective allies. At the heart of the conflict was the desire of the North Vietnamese, who had defeated the French colonial administration of Vietnam in 1954, to unify the entire country under a single communist regime modelled after those of the Soviet Union and China. The South Vietnamese government, on the other hand, fought to preserve a Vietnam more closely aligned with the West. The costs and casualties of the growing war proved too much for the United States to bear and its combat units were eventually withdrawn by 1973. In 1975 South Vietnam fell to a full-scale invasion by the North.

Acknowledgements

Grateful acknowledgement is made to the following sources:

Block 1

Chapter 1
Aristotle, Athenian Constitution, *Eudemian Ethics, Virtues and Vices*, translated by H. Rackham, Loeb Classical Library 285, Harvard University Press, 1935. Copyright © 2020 President and Fellows of Harvard College.

S. I. Rotroff, 'Commerce and Crafts around the Athenian Agora', in *The Athenian Aagora: New Perspectives on an Ancient Site*, ed. J. McK. Camp II and C. A. Mauzy (Zaberns Bildbände zur Archäologie), Mainz am Rhein 2009, p. 40.

Rihll, T.E. (2011), 'Classical Athens' in Bradley, K. and Cartledge, P. (eds.) *The Cambridge World History of Slavery: Volume I*, Cambridge University Press. Copyright © Cambridge University Press 2011. Reproduced with permission of the Licensor through PLSclear.

Demosthenes, *Speeches 39–49*, translated by Adele C. Scafuro. Copyright © 2011. By permission of the University of Texas Press.

Chapter 2
Pliny, *Natural History*, Volume IX: Books 33–35, translated by H. Rackham, Loeb Classical Library 394, Harvard University Press, 1952. Copyright © 2020 President and Fellows of Harvard College.

Pliny, *Natural History*, Volume X: Books 36–37, translated by D.E. Eichholz, Loeb Classical Library 419, Harvard University Press, 1952. Copyright © 2020 President and Fellows of Harvard College.

Pausanias, *Description of Greece*, Volume IV: Books 8.22–10 (Arcadia, Boeotia, Phocis and Ozolian Locri), translated by W.H.S. Jones, Loeb Classical Library 297, Harvard University Press, 1935. Copyright © 2020 President and Fellows of Harvard College.

Pliny, *Natural History*, Volume IX: Books 33–35, translated by H. Rackham, Loeb Classical Library 394, Harvard University Press, 1952. Copyright © 2020 President and Fellows of Harvard College.

Suetonius, *Lives of the Caesars*, in Edwards, C. (trans.) Oxford World's Classics, Oxford University Press. Copyright © Catherine

Edwards 2000. Reproduced with permission of the Licensor through PLSclear.

Hopkins, K. and Beard, M. (2005), *The Colosseum*, Profile Books. Copyright © Keith Hopkins and Mary Beard, 2005.

Chapter 3
Pausanias, *Description of Greece*, Volume IV: Books 8.22–10 (Arcadia, Boeotia, Phocis and Ozolian Locri), translated by W.H.S. Jones, Loeb Classical Library 297, Harvard University Press, 1935. Copyright © 2020 President and Fellows of Harvard College.

Thucydides, *The War of the Peloponnesians and the Athenians*, in Mynott, J. (ed. and trans.), Cambridge University Press. Copyright © In the translation, introduction and editorial matter Cambridge University Press 2013. Reproduced with permission of the Licensor through PLSclear.

Block 2

Chapter 2
Frye, S. (2010), *Pens and Needles*, pp. 71–72, University of Pennsylvania Press. Reprinted with permission of the University of Pennsylvania Press.

Chapter 3
Manchester, E., 'Do Women Have To Be Naked To Get Into the Met. Museum?', December 2004/February 2005, Tate. https://www.tate.org.uk/art/artworks/guerrilla-girls-do-women-have-to-be-naked-to-get-into-the-met-museum-p78793

Gørrill, H. (2018), 'Are female artists worth collecting? Tate doesn't seem to think so', 13th August 2018, The Guardian. Copyright © Guardian News & Media Ltd 2020.

Glossary

abstract art rather than seeking to represent external reality, abstract artists instead attempt to achieve an effect on the viewer through formal techniques, such as the use of shape and colour, etc.

allegorical works of art that have a secondary meaning that refers to things outside of the image or text in question to make some broader comment on events in the real world.

amphictyony a religious association of the peoples of northern and central Greece, which was in charge of the sanctuaries of Apollo at Delphi and Demeter at Anthela, near Thermopylae. The term comes from *amphi* and *ktiones*; 'those dwelling around'.

amphitheatre a large circular or oval-shaped open-air building, with seating arranged around a central space in which spectacles or contests (such as gladiatorial combat) could be staged.

anti-fascism opposition to fascist ideology, groups and individuals.

antiquarian a term describing a collector of antiquities.

applied arts art that is associated with functional objects as opposed to the more traditional media of painting and sculpture, etc.

appliqué in textiles, the technique of embroidering pieces of textile and other materials onto a textile base.

archon sometimes translated as 'magistrate', a civic official with a one-year term and specific duties, particularly regarding lawmaking.

Archon Basileus of the ten archons ('magistrates') elected every year by the Athenians to deal with administrative matters in the city, the Archon Basileus had particular jurisdiction over religious matters and the adjudication of homicide.

artist collective a group of artists working together towards shared objectives.

avant-garde originally a French term applied to the advanced guard in military combat in the nineteenth century and subsequently used to designate art that was supposedly at the forefront of artistic developments.

blood and soil translated from *blut und boden*, the term accentuates the mythical connection between a nation and the land that it occupies or cultivates.

Bolshevik Revolution another name for the 1917 October Revolution in Russia, which was led by the Bolshevik wing of the Russian Social-Democratic Party under Vladimir Lenin.

Bourbon the family dynasty that held the thrones of France from 1589–1792 and Spain from 1700–1931.

bust when used in relation to portraiture, a representation of the upper part of a person, including head and neck and variable portion of chest and shoulders.

canon the body of artistic works that are generally accepted to be of high aesthetic value and universal quality so that they are bought and displayed in internationally prestigious museums and galleries.

cartoon full-scale preliminary design, e.g. for a tapestry or painting.

cartouche ornamental panel with curling edges, usually with an inscription.

centaur (pl. **centaurs**) a creature from classical mythology with the upper body of a human and the lower body and legs of a horse.

Circus Maximus a large stadium in the city of Rome, located next to the Palatine Hill and used primarily for chariot racing.

city-state in the Renaissance, the Italian peninsula was composed of independent city-states – either courts or republics – that took their names from the main city they were governed from.

column vertical free-standing structural support of circular section. In classical architecture, columns were detailed according to one of the **orders** (**Doric**, **Ionic**, **Corinthian**, Composite) and incorporated a base, shaft and capital.

communism a political theory derived from revolutionary Marxism that sought to overthrow capitalism to create a classless society through the social ownership of the means of production.

condottieri (sing. *condottiere*) military commanders of mercenary troops, often associated with Renaissance Italy. They held a military contract (*condotta*) to raise and command mercenary troops, often serving other states.

Corinthian in classical architecture, one of the **orders**.

corpus the entire collection of works produced by a writer.

court overseen by a royal person (king, queen, duke, duchess, etc.), this refers not only to the physical building (usually a palace) where the court resides but also the household and the political entity. Rulers generally inherit the throne and are not elected.

courtier a person who attends a royal court, often as a companion or adviser to the ruler.

cultural translation in the process of transfer and the migration from one cultural situation to another, an object or symbol is introduced into a new context and takes on a new meaning.

darbar giving audience, part of Mughal courtly ceremony.

dedication (pl. **dedications**) an item set up or left in a temple as a gift to a god, either in thanks or supplication; these included cult statues, votive offerings, and other objects such as shields and dramatic masks.

Degenerate Art Exhibition the Nazi exhibition *Die Ausstellung 'Entartete Kunst'* ran from 19 July to 30 November 1937 in Munich and consisted of 650 works of art confiscated from German museums; it was staged to highlight the dangers of 'cultural degeneracy' in line with Nazi ideas on racial degeneracy.

democracy (pl. **democracies**) a form of government where the whole eligible population is represented. From the Greek words *demos* ('people') and *kratos* ('power').

diachronic happening over a period of time.

direct democracy a democratic system where the citizens vote directly on the running of the state, rather than through representatives.

Dissolution of the Monasteries the break-up of religious houses under King Henry VIII (r.1509–47).

Doric in classical architecture, one of the **orders**.

double portrait a genre of portraiture that often depicts husband and wife together, sometimes in a hinged format with two parts (known as a diptych).

early modern widely used to replace the term 'Renaissance', it roughly correlates to 1400–1750.

Enlightenment the Enlightenment was founded on a commitment to the importance of reason in opposition to the established power of the Church and the absolutist state; the major philosophical works date from the mid to late eighteenth century and share the belief that critical thought itself could be the means to defeat both religious and secular despotism.

entablature in the classical system, the upper part of an **order**, made up of architrave, frieze and cornice.

epigram a wide-ranging genre in Latin poetry, which began in the form of funerary epitaphs but developed to include a wide range of other topics, including erotic poetry and satire.

epithet a word used to describe the specific attributes of a god or goddess and to distinguish one specific form of the god from another.

equestrian portrait a particular genre of portraiture that depicts a sitter (usually male) on horseback.

exemplar someone who serves as a model worthy of emulation.

fascism an authoritarian form of government centred on a strong and demagogic leader who propagates the superiority of one national or ethnic group over others.

First International Dada Fair the *Dada-Messe* ran from 30 June to 25 August 1920 in a well-situated private gallery in Berlin, and the 200 or so works exhibited were deliberately selected to cause an affront to public taste.

Flavian the term of description for the dynasty of Roman emperors belonging to the Flavia clan that succeeded the Julio-Claudians with the accession of Vespasian in 69 CE and ruled until the assassination of Domitian in 96 CE.

forensic oratory the genre of speeches delivered as part of trial proceedings.

French Revolution the overthrow of the monarchy and the establishment of a republican government in France during the period 1789–1795.

frieze (pl. **friezes**) an area of sculpted or painted decoration, usually on a wall near the ceiling. In architectural history, a term for the middle part of the **entablature**, but also applied more broadly to horizontal bands of ornament on furniture and below ceiling level on walls.

functionalism a movement in architecture advocating that the design of buildings should be determined by their function rather than by aesthetic considerations.

gesso a mixture of finely ground plaster and glue.

gilding the application of gold leaf (gold beaten into paper-thin squares) onto an object for decoration (can be applied to picture frames, furniture, the surface of a painting, metalwork, ceramics and silver).

globe a map of the world in the form of a sphere.

Gothic an architectural style that spread through Europe from England and France from the second half of the twelfth century.

Habsburg a Royal German family and one of the principal sovereign dynasties of Europe from the fifteenth to twentieth centuries. In the Renaissance, the Habsburg dominion expanded dramatically over continental Europe, not only through military conquest but also through carefully chosen marriage alliances.

heraldic devices coat-of-arms or personal badge often used in architecture and decoration to convey status.

heroes humans who featured in Greek epic or myth, where they behaved or died in extreme ways, and who received religious attention after their deaths. Heroes might also be founders of cities or other historical figures.

Homer composer of the epic poems the *Iliad* and the *Odyssey*, sometime between the late eighth and mid sixth centuries BCE.

inscription letters marked onto a surface of an object (e.g. a marble or bronze sculpture, a stone statue base or ceramic vessel) often by scratching, chiselling or painting.

International Exhibition of Art and Technology in Modern Life the *Exposition internationale des Arts et Techniques dans la Vie moderne* that ran from 25 May to 25 November 1937 in Paris was a massive spectacle designed to celebrate human achievement and world peace; an aspiration that would be shattered less than two years later with the outbreak of the Second World War.

Ionic in classical architecture, one of the **orders**.

Jesus Christ son of God and the Virgin Mary. For Christians, he is central to the story of the New Testament of the Bible, where he was crucified to redeem the sins of the world.

jharoka a balcony in Indian architecture, often used as an audience throne as part of Mughal courtly ceremony.

knightly Order (or chivalric order) a confraternity or society of knights often overseen by a ruler. These were bestowed with accompanying accessories, such as a cloak and the Order's symbol. For example, knights in the Order of the Ermine received a gold ermine on a collar (chain) that they wore to show allegiance to the Order. Famous examples include the Order of the Garter (England) and the Order of the Golden Fleece (Burgundian court).

kouroi (sing. **kouros**) the ancient Greek word for 'youth' used to describe nude, free-standing sculptures of young men, usually made from marble. Note that the female equivalent is a kore (plural korai), meaning 'maiden' or 'young girl'.

liberal democracy a democratic system of representative government in which individual rights and civil liberties are officially recognised and protected, and the exercise of political power is limited by the rule of law.

Line of Demarcation a line drawn along a meridian in the Atlantic Ocean to distinguish new lands claimed by Portugal from those of Spain as part of the Treaty of Tordesillas in 1494.

Lydia a wealthy and powerful (non-Greek) kingdom located in the west of Asia Minor (part of modern-day Turkey).

lyric poetry a type of ancient Greek poetry that was intended to be sung rather than recited or spoken, often to the accompaniment of stringed instruments or pipes.

Marxism the ideas, theories and methods of Karl Marx, developed together with Friedrich Engels and later built upon by their followers to form the basis for the theory and practice of communism.

mechanical means of production a range of media used in cultural production that involves mechanical processes from print through to photography and importantly including **photomontage**.

metic (pl. **metics**) a resident foreigner in Athens.

miniature a small brightly coloured and highly detailed painting mostly used to illustrate manuscripts.

mullioned windows where vertical bars (usually of stone) separate the glazing within the window frame.

Museum of Modern Art MoMA opened on 7 November 1929 in Midtown Manhattan and has from this time been pivotal in the collecting, categorising and display of modern art to the extent that it is generally considered to be the most influential museum of modern art in the world.

nationalism the assertion of the interests of one nation over and above the interests of others or the common interests of all nations.

Nawruz New Year festival

Nazism the fascist doctrine of the National Socialist German Workers' Party implemented by Adolf Hitler and his followers from the early 1920s that promoted totalitarianism, asserted Aryan racial superiority, and was committed to the expansion of the German state.

niche a recess set in a wall, sometimes with a shelf (for a statue or vase).

Northern Renaissance a distinctive cultural period, *c.*1400–1600, in Europe beyond Italy, fusing Gothic traditions with new interests in classical sources. See also **Renaissance**.

obelisk a tapering, four-sided stone pillar (or **column**) with a pyramidal apex.

obverse the side of a coin or medal bearing the head or principal design (the front). It can also be used to refer to the front of any double-sided work of art.

oculus from the Latin for 'eye', it is a circular opening in the centre of a dome found in classical architecture and revived during the Renaissance.

oikos (pl. *oikoi*) an Athenian home, or collectively the members of the household.

oil on canvas the principle medium for producing artworks from the fifteenth century onwards.

Old Testament a collection of 39 books which, together with the New Testament, form the Christian bible.

omphalos meaning 'navel', a carved stone at Delphi that was understood to mark the centre of the Greek world.

oral traditions the ways in which the history and customs of a community are passed down the generations via word of mouth or the regular verbal recounting of (often instructive) stories or songs.

orders term used to describe the ways in which **columns**, bases, pedestals and **entablatures** were combined in classical architecture. The principal orders were **Doric**, **Ionic**, **Corinthian** and Composite.

painter-stainer artist who designs and paints ('stains') a range of hangings and decorations.

Panhellenic a modern term used to describe a sanctuary that was open to all Greeks and not limited to those of the controlling *polis*. The locations of the great Panhellenic festivals and games at Olympia, Delphi, Nemea and Isthmia are usually considered Panhellenic. This modern term is also sometimes used in a more general sense to mean relating to 'all Greeks'.

patron in art history, an individual or group responsible for commissioning an artwork such as a painting, sculpture or building.

pendant one of two paintings hung as a pair.

performance as it is often employed more broadly in the humanities, this refers not to a theatrical performance but the way in which our identities are performed or 'staged'.

personification the depiction of human figures carrying attributes or wearing clothes that identify them as standing for particular qualities or concepts, for example, the **virtues**.

photomontage a collage constructed from photographic sources.

phratry (pl. **phratries**) a social group within an Athenian tribe, of which every citizen had to be a member and to which a newly born male child would be introduced to confirm his legitimacy as a citizen.

pilaster a flattened **column** attached to the wall surface.

plasterwork decoration decoration sculpted in plaster to create figurative and ornamental subjects.

plate in inventories, a term used to describe silver and gold wares.

polis (pl. *poleis*) an ancient Greek city-state: i.e. a city that operated as an independent political entity.

poster a mass-produced print designed for public consumption for a whole range of purposes from advertising through to political propaganda.

princeps (pl. *principes*) the Latin title, roughly meaning 'first man', by which Roman emperors often chose to be known.

print the process for reproducing text and imagery using a master template from the invention of the woodblock onwards.

printed sources by end of the sixteenth century, printing was being used for book illustrations, including antique texts and the Bible. Many of these, together with designs for architecture and decoration, were produced in Antwerp, a city with close trading links to England during the Elizabethan period. (These prints influenced the decoration and furnishings at Hardwick.)

propaganda the systematic dissemination of information to promote a political cause or point of view.

prytanis (pl. **prytaneis**) each of the members of the Athenian Boule (or council) serving in a specific **prytany**.

prytany (pl. **prytanies**) each of the ten periods into which the Athenian council's term of office was split, when it was overseen by each of the ten tribes in turn.

putti (sing. **putto**) small male babies, often winged, depicted in Renaissance art, drawn from classical tradition.

Renaissance a period in time (*c.*1400–1600) traditionally used to refer to the revival of classical antiquity in arts and culture in Europe, but the term can also be applied to any culture that has a period of flourishing of arts and culture.

Republic, the the period in Roman history between 509 BCE and *c*.27 BCE when Rome was governed by two consuls, alongside a Senate and various other assemblies and magistrates.

republic a political entity made up of elected officials (as opposed to a court), e.g. the Republic of Venice.

reverse the side of a coin or medal bearing the secondary design (the back). It can also be used to refer to the back of any double-sided work of art.

rhetorical device a technique whereby the author seeks to persuade an audience of their own particular perspective or understanding of something.

satire the use of humour, irony, exaggeration or ridicule to expose and criticise public stupidity, particularly in the context of contemporary politics and other topical issues.

second-wave feminism a renewed period of feminist activity from the 1960s through to the 1980s that went beyond the earlier struggles over female suffrage to emphasise solidarity among women in their fight for social and economic equality and wider access to birth control.

sphinx (pl. **sphinxes**) a creature from classical mythology with the head of a human, the wings of a bird of prey and the body of a lion.

stucco a technique in interior decoration in which fine plaster is moulded and applied to surfaces to create decorative and ornamental patterns.

studiolo a study or collecting space, which emerged in fifteenth-century Italy.

Tatlin Vladimir Tatlin (1885–1953) was a prominent Russian artist, architect and stage designer in the Soviet avant-garde in the early twentieth century and is most famous for designing the *Monument to the Third International* (1919–20), more commonly known as the Tatlin Tower.

term a pedestal supporting a sculpted human, animal or mythical figure.

tholos a type of circular building, usually with a ring of columns outside the walls supporting the roof.

totalitarianism a system of government that is centralised and dictatorial and requires complete subservience to the state.

treasury (*thesauros* in Greek) a solidly built storehouse for precious offerings made to the gods.

tripod a three-legged item of furniture used in ancient sacrifice, often made from metal.

tyrant (*tyrannos* in Greek) the name used for a wealthy and powerful ruler of some Greek city states, derived from its connection with a form of government known as a tyranny. Tyranny was a form of monarchy set up by usurpers, but did not always involve a reign of terror. Tyrants were members of the aristocracy who came to power either through a violent coup with the support of a discontented populace or in order to resolve a crisis, and their rule could be benevolent or malevolent. By the fourth century BCE, tyranny had acquired the negative reputation that is still associated with the word today.

uomini famosi in the Renaissance, cycles of portraits of famous men (in paintings or sculpture) decorated homes and public spaces acting as **exemplars**, models worthy of imitation.

vault an arched architectural form that covers and usually encloses a space as a ceiling or a roof.

villa (pl. **villas**) in the ancient world, this generally denotes a domestic building, often quite extensive. Their functions could range from luxurious pleasure palaces to working farms, and they could be located close to cities as well as deep in the countryside.

virtues divided into the Theological (Faith, Hope and Charity) and the Cardinal virtues (Prudence, Justice, Fortitude and Temperance).

votive offering an object dedicated or vowed to a deity as a gesture of thanks for their divine support or intervention.

Wall Street Crash the major stock market crash that began on Wall Street in New York in September 1929 and precipitated a massive worldwide economic depression.

war of attrition a military strategy whereby each side seeks to wear down the other to the point of collapse by focusing on taking out enemy personnel and supply lines.

Index